Scotland

The Quest for the World Cup

A Complete Record

Clive Leatherdale

TWO HEADS
PUBLISHING

Published in association with
Desert Island Books

This edition first published in 1994 by

Two Heads Publishing
in association with Desert Island Books
12A Franklyn Suite
The Priory
Haywards Heath
West Sussex
RH16 3LB

ISBN   1-897850-50-6

Photograph credits.
Front cover, pages 101, 104, 127, 129, 151, 180, 181, 203, 205,
208, 209 - Colorsport.
Pages 105, 123, 149, 153, 177, 183 - Popperfoto.
Pages 19, 29, 42, 43, 73, 82, 83, 87, 107, 113, 223 - Glasgow Herald.

Cover design by Doug Cheeseman

Printed & bound by Caldra House Ltd., Hove, Sussex

Scotland

The Quest for the World Cup

A Complete Record

About the author
Clive Leatherdale was born in 1949. He is a writer, journalist, lecturer, and publisher, and a person with wide interests. Born with sport in his blood, he has been writing histories and trenchant articles on football for many years. He has backpacked around much of the globe, has lived in Saudi Arabia, China, and Korea, and written histories or travel books on all three countries. He has a Ph.D. in Arabian history and is an international authority on Dracula.

Author's Note
An earlier version of this book appeared in 1986 under the title *Scotland's Quest for the World Cup*. Recent matches are the easiest to recall, with the help of memory, video, and saturation coverage in the press. These aids were not available half a century ago, when the researcher is restricted to newspaper coverage of no great objectivity, some parochialism, and much wishful thinking. In the absence of alternative sources, historians must tread warily.

I had the pleasure to live in Scotland, in Aberdeen, from 1977 and to serve as a sports columnist for the *Aberdeen Press and Journal*. In 1989 I left Scotland to live and travel in the Far East.

My thanks in particular to Tony Griffin, David Barber and Julia Johnson for their assistance in getting this book shipshape.

Clive Leatherdale, April 1994

CONTENTS

Foreword

It is a great pleasure to be asked to write a Foreword for a book which embraces the magic and achievements of Scotland's World Cup history. It is a success story which must not be devalued. For a small country of five million people we have managed to compete in seven World Cup finals going back to Switzerland in 1954, Sweden in 1958, West Germany in 1974, Argentina in 1978, Spain in 1982, Mexico in 1986 and Italy in 1990. These achievements make this book a collector's gem.

As a small boy with heroes of these earlier sojourns, I well remember the humiliation by Uruguay by 7-0 in Switzerland when the players of that era were household names: Tommy Docherty, Willie Fernie, Jimmy Davidson, and Johnny McKenzie, and when they were beaten 7-0 I just couldn't believe it. It is interesting to note that Scotland took only thirteen players to the World Cup finals in 1954, and only a trainer (no manager) in 1958, and when you think of the number of players we take now, plus technical and medical staff, it shows how much the game has advanced from those early days. In 1958 we did not reach beyond the first stage in a group which consisted of Paraguay, France and Yugoslavia. A small insight into the planning of those days was that Archie Robertson, then a player, was actually doing the spying on the opponents in the World Cup and no doubt this contributed later to his success as a manager.

We then had a big lapse and it wasn't until 1974 in West Germany that we managed to reach the finals again; here we set something of a record by not losing a game in the World Cup finals yet still being knocked out. Of that team, Kenny Dalglish was an emerging international and the great Denis Law was reaching the twilight of his career; it was to be his last appearance in a Scotland jersey. So as one great player came, another went. The manager at that time, Willie Ormond, proved that the gift of balancing and picking players was as important as any aspect of management.

1978 was again a World Cup year and we were rather downcast. I felt that the manager, Ally MacLeod, did a great job in giving hope to the people. Unfortunately, that hope did not materialise and Ally was left to face the disappointment. However, sometimes progress is made through failure and if Argentina was to be a lesson then it was surely a watershed for Scottish international football, because the next man brought a humility and orderliness to the job which was just a part of himself.

Jock Stein was Scotland's most successful club manager of all time and it was only fitting that he should eventually attain the highest position in football – manager of the national team. And, as expected, he once again proved how good he really was by taking them to two World Cup finals – Spain in 1982 and Mexico in 1986. I had the great pleasure of working with him for a year until that tragic night in Cardiff and found him to be the most humble of men.

Considering he had achieved such success, he was always reluctant to discuss or elaborate upon any of his achievements, always turning the conversation to his players who, he said, made his success. Jock Stein had the quality of greatness. Few people have it. In Jock's time he was prepared to recognise a home based player and if you examine his teams in the period he was manager you will appreciate that he did a lot for Scottish football.

I felt the 1986 campaign was a qualified success for Scotland, but that was the end of an era really. Souness, Dalglish, Willie Miller, Davie Cooper – players of that calibre are not easily replaced. This loss of players of such vast experience and international stature created a tremendous void. I was aware that, losing so many great players, we were destined for a barren period. This isn't in any way a criticism, but a fact.

Andy Roxburgh replaced me. Initially he was hampered by a lack of big club experience and this gave him some problems early on. He certainly made the best of the resources he had available and earned respect by his honest and open approach to management.

1990 opened with a disappointing loss to Costa Rica – typical Scotland. We redeemed ourselves with good performances against Sweden and Brazil. The process of laying the foundations for a good team is cyclical; experienced players finish their playing days and new ones replace them.

The Scottish football scene has always been distinguished by the enthusiasm of the support from the fans, even for a new team going through a rebuilding process. This was typified by the tremendous support in the European Championship of 1992, when the team and its supporters were acclaimed for their good behaviour and nature – a fantastic tribute.

The 1994 World Cup campaign fell a bit flat. The five goals we conceded against Portugal stands out as a low point. No team is going to make it to the finals if they give away five goals in a qualifying game. When I saw the qualifying pool for 1994 I feared that Scotland would not make it. There were too many grey areas and unfortunately I was proved right.

Despite the disappointment of missing USA '94, there are many reasons for optimism for the future. Exciting players such as Duncan Ferguson of Rangers and Gary McAllister, who has distinguished himself as a midfield player of international stature and has been rewarded with the captaincy of his country. There is a genuine opportunity for a fine team to grow and develop together.

I could go on and on and wax lyrical about all of the great players we have had and all the great names that Scotland have played in the past, but the best piece of advice I can give you is to read the book which will fully elaborate the achievements of Scotland in World Cup football.

Alex Ferguson
Old Trafford, April 1994

INTRODUCTION

For Scotland – as for England, Wales and Northern Ireland – active involvement in the World Cup did not commence until after World War II. By then, three tournaments were already consigned to history, those of 1930, 1934 and 1938. The four Home soccer associations, however, had spent much of the inter-war years disaffiliated from FIFA (Fédération Internationale de Football Association) and rendered themselves ineligible to compete – even if they had a mind to. Differences of opinion over permitting official fixtures with defeated World War I enemies; mistrust at the motives of continental professionalism eating into the amateur ethos; and general suspicion towards 'foreign' interference in a game considered to be British to the bootlaces all contributed to prolonged periods of estrangement between British and world football.

It took the more enlightened prospects for international cooperation, brought about by the ending of World War II, before permanent reconciliation was effected. The British associations rejoined FIFA in 1946 and expressed their preparedness to compete in the first post-war World Cup competition, to be held in Brazil in 1950 – where the scheduled 1942 tournament would have been held but for the war.

It is difficult to gauge how Scotland might have fared had they taken part in the World Cups of the 1930s. It was not until 1929 that Scotland dipped their toes into the waters of foreign competition. By then, England had been playing, and beating, continental upstarts for over twenty years. Scotland's undisputed supremacy in the Home International Championships of the 1920s – winning it seven times – was no guarantee that they would have overcome the unfamiliar styles and tactics employed by the emerging continental sides.

Even so, Scotland's pre-war results against continental opposition look healthy. Fifteen fixtures produced just two defeats, both recorded in the space of four days in May 1931, when Scotland were dumped 0-5 in Austria and 0-3 in Italy against two of the dominant teams of the decade.

Unaccountably, Scotland's international form deteriorated in the immediate post-1945 period. Of their first eleven peacetime fixtures just two were won, with defeats posted in Brussels (1-2), Berne (1-2) and Paris (0-3), not to mention Wrexham (1-3) and Belfast (0-2), and worst of all at Hampden against the English (0-2).

Several factors accounted for this slump. The selectors had resorted to *potpourri*, calling up players willy nilly, many of whom knew little about each other. Opponents unsportingly performed at their peak – Tom Finney reckoned his goal at Hampden to be the best of his career. And referees did the dirty. According to George Young, when Switzerland scored their winner the official danced with delight and congratulated the scorer. Peeved by these setbacks, fans scratched their heads and demanded the selectors pick Rangers' 'iron curtain' defence and Hibernian's 'famous five' forwards. Then all would be well.

In fact, post-1945 Scotland teams beat no British opponents until the seventh attempt (Wales 3-1). By then it was October 1948, and three months later the qualifying procedures for the 1950 World Cup were announced.

1

THE 1950 WORLD CUP

Let bygones be bygones. FIFA, it would appear, sought to placate the British soccer nations, both in recognition of their historical influence on the game and their decision to step into line. FIFA's qualifying arrangements were generous, to say the least. At the demand of the British associations, FIFA spared the home countries the indignity of the preliminary rounds. British footballers would not be asked to soil their boots in far off fields against foreigners. Instead, the Home Internationals of season 1949-50 doubled as Britain's World Cup qualifying zone. The champions would qualify automatically for Brazil.

Even then FIFA's beneficence was not spent. They invited Britain's top *two* teams to travel, only to be rebuffed by the Scottish FA. Nowadays, appearing in the finals of the World Cup is accorded the status of a national imperative, with no effort being spared to attain that objective. But in those days there was no great enthusiasm in Britain – especially in Scotland – for dabbling in what were felt to be sub-standard, meddlesome foreign competitions. The SFA reiterated its earlier declaration, that a Scottish playing party would not journey to Brazil unless they did so as British champions. In other words, if Scotland finished as British runners-up they would forfeit FIFA's invitation to compete.

At the time, the SFA's statement did not arouse much comment. The Welsh and Irish FAs had made similar declarations, though in their case with greater justification. Qualification for either of them would strain their financial and playing resources. Neither the Welsh nor the Irish were prepared or equipped for the rigours of a World Cup. Wales' sum experience of non-British football amounted to visits to Paris in 1931 and 1939. Since the war they had never played across the English Channel, let alone in South America. As for the Irish, they had yet to play anybody outside Britain. Even when the 1958 World Cup came around, their continental experience amounted to a 1-3 defeat in France in 1952.

Scotland's decision, however, could not so easily be shrugged off. It was probably taken, in part, through false modesty, in the belief that Scotland were not yet strong enough to do themselves justice – though they had emerged from their post-war trough to register a clean sweep in the British Championship of

1948-49. But the rebuff smacked of insensitivity. The SFA apparently expected FIFA to defer final scheduling until after the Home Internationals. Only then would it be known whether Britain would be sending one representative or two. A last-minute replacement might be needed, but by then the World Cup finals would be just two months away.

England were unruffled by the whole charade. They, it seemed, would be going to Brazil whatever, either as British champions or in company with them.

Strictly speaking, FIFA's arrangements were unfair as well as generous. It is standard practice that in World Cup eliminators teams play each other twice – home and away – or, in the event of a play-off, on neutral territory. The Home Internationals in any given season were not so arranged. Each nation played the others once only. In the season in question Scotland and Wales would enjoy the unmerited advantage of two home fixtures out of three – one of which would be against England. Despite Scotland's self-imposed restrictions, the fixture schedule smiled on them.

Qualifying Pool I

NORTHERN IRELAND v SCOTLAND
Saturday, 1 October 1949   *Belfast – 50,000*

All things considered, Scotland journeyed in good spirits to Windsor Park for the first international of the new season. They had followed up their triple British success with a 2-0 Hampden win over France, and were now seeking a fifth straight victory. Scotland had been beaten in Belfast, 0-2, on their last visit in 1947. Following the creation of the Republic of Ireland, the Northern Irish were no longer able to call upon players from the South. The Republic had recently beaten England 2-0 at Goodison Park. Of the 1947 Northern Ireland side, just three players remained – Jack Vernon, Sammy Smyth, and David Cochrane. Of these, Leeds' David Cochrane had played against England back in 1939. Seven of the remaining places were filled by debutants, one of them Barnsley's Danny Blanchflower.

The Scottish team was a near-replica of that victorious (3-1) at Wembley in April. Jimmy Cowan of Morton had donned the green jersey for eighteen months and would remain first-choice keeper until 1952. He had performed heroics at Wembley and been carried from the pitch. Then, as now, he was protected by Rangers' centre-half Willie Woodburn and full-backs Sammy Cox and George Young, the Scottish captain. The side showed just one 'Anglo', Billy Steel of Derby County. The solitary newcomer, earning his first and last cap in place of Billy Houliston, was East Fife centre-forward Henry Morris. Morris had a difficult game in prospect, being opposed by the worthy Irish pivot, Jack Vernon, of West Bromwich Albion.

The game proved to be a walkover for the Scots. Irish goalkeeper Pat Kelly (once of Aberdeen, now with Barnsley), was among those experiencing the strains of international football for the first time. He must have suffered nightmares for many a night, being responsible for up to five Scotland goals. The match, declared the *Glasgow Herald*, sternly, 'was the most remarkable International of our time', mainly because Scotland 'were inferior in several positions and played less combined football than the opponents they routed.'

Scotland were two goals up in four minutes. Henry Morris's international call-up was swiftly justified with a headed goal from Waddell's centre. Vernon might have headed clear but for Kelly, who, leaping for the ball, succeeded only in knocking his centre-half to the ground. Morris was left with an unguarded net. Waddell followed up with a splendid solo goal, bearing down on Kelly along the goal-line. The goalkeeper expected a pull-back that never came. He edged outwards and Waddell shot through the gate.

Ireland appeared to have absorbed these setbacks and had their opponents on their heels. Cowan changed direction in mid-air to keep out Bobby Brennan's header, then parried a Cochrane shot. The outcome was sealed when Scotland scored another pair midway through the opening half. Steel's lob from the edge of the area befuddled Kelly, who clutched spectacularly at thin air. From the restart, Lawrie Reilly took Waddell's pass to score emphatically. Kelly must have felt relieved. No one could blame him for that one!

The half-time tally showed one more. The ball was driven hard against Vernon's arm from a couple of feet and the referee awarded Scotland a penalty, converted by Waddell. Four of Scotland's goals could be attributed to men in black or in green.

Ireland commenced the second half as if set on scoring six to win. Six Irish players soon combined in the best move of the match, helping Sammy Smyth pull a goal back. The tall Wolves inside-forward was giving Bobby Evans and George Aitken a torrid time. Near the hour Smyth scored again, powering home John McKenna's corner. Scotland's cushion was now down to three. They began to fret until poor Pat Kelly settled their nerves. The ball was belted downfield towards the Irish goal. Morris started to chase but gave it up as a lost cause. It should have been, but Kelly, coming to collect, inexplicably stopped in his tracks. Morris spurted forward to score.

Ten minutes from time Jimmy Mason jinked his way through to walk the ball into the net. But Pat Kelly's nightmare afternoon was not over. This is how the *Glasgow Herald* described Scotland's eighth goal. 'Morris, off his balance, swung his boot and just managed to trundle the ball at Kelly, whose lamentable effort to save was received in complete silence. Not even the most raucous-voiced of the tartan-bedecked Scots desired any such goal.' At the end Jimmy Cowan tried to console his distraught opposite number. Not since 1901 had Scotland scored more than eight, when they thumped eleven past the sad Irish.

NORTHERN IRELAND (0) 2   SCOTLAND (5) 8
   Smyth 50, 59   Morris 2, 70, 89, Waddell 4, 40 pen,
                                        Steel 24, Reilly 25, Mason 80

N IRELAND: Kelly (Barnsley), Bowler (Hull), McMichael (Newcastle), Blanchflower (Barnsley), Vernon (WBA), Ferris (Birmingham), Cochrane (Leeds), Smyth (Wolves), Brennan (Birm'ham), Crossan (Blackb'n), McKenna (Hudd'field).
SCOTLAND: Cowan (Morton), Young (Rangers), Cox (Rangers), Evans (Celtic), Woodburn (Rangers), Aitken (East Fife), Waddell (Rangers), Mason (Third Lanark), Morris (East Fife), Steel (Derby), Reilly (Hibs).

SCOTLAND v WALES
Wednesday, 9 November 1949   *Hampden – 73,782*

The following month it was up to Wales to try to interrupt Scotland's winning ways. Although the Welsh had just suffered a 1-4 home reverse at the hands of England, they had proved, of late, to be more than a handful for the Scots. Matches between the two nations dated back to 1876. Of these, the Welsh had won only a dozen – although they had won six of the last ten. Wales had won 2-1 on their last visit to Hampden, in 1947, and had been tagged as something of a Scottish bogey team.

The Welsh retained seven of that 1947 winning eleven. These included mighty Trevor Ford in attack, but other positions were filled by players earning their crust in the obscurity of reserve or lower-division English football. In goal, twenty-one year old Keith Jones of Aston Villa was making his debut. In his prayers he must have pleaded for greater divine protection than that shown to Ireland's debutant, the luckless Pat Kelly.

Scotland's No. 7, 8 and 9 shirts found new occupants, the wearers in Belfast having to vacate them through injury. Alec Linwood of Clyde, called up at the last moment, pulled on the centre-forward jersey for the first time. Linwood eschewed brawn for skill, and would not relish the harsh attentions of veteran Welsh stopper, Trevor Jones. Another newcomer to international football, John McPhail, lined up with Celtic team-mate Bobby Evans. A second Anglo was selected, alongside Billy Steel – Billy Liddell of Liverpool stepping in for Willie Waddell.

Hampden was dank and misty. Its terraces were charged with noise, though the game was unexceptional. Scottish aggression was unleashed from the first whistle to the last, yet goalscoring opportunities were at a premium. Pick of the Scottish players was the fleet-footed, diminutive Billy Steel, who had tempted Derby County to break the British transfer record when signing him for £15,000. Not even he could carry the home attack single-handed on a day when the wingers, Liddell and Reilly, were well contained.

At the other end, Woodburn's no-nonsense approach upset Mr Law – the English referee. The match turned against Wales when, from a Welsh corner, Woodburn lunged at the ball, missed, and swiped Trevor Ford instead. Mr Law's whistle stayed silent, infuriating the red shirts, especially when Scotland scored soon afterwards. Steel skipped past Barnes to despatch a teasing cross that the young goalkeeper slapped against the crossbar. The ball fell sweetly for McPhail to prod home.

The longer the game went on, the more dominant Scotland became. Cowan was rarely troubled by a punchless Welsh attack, and the potentially eye-catching duel between Woodburn and Ford fizzled out. Yet Ford featured in the game's second, decisive, incident. Just after the hour Ford's volley looped off George Young's boot, spun high in the air and plopped sweetly against the face of the crossbar. Griffiths was first to the ball, controlling it instantly. The angle was tight but the goal was empty. Perhaps he was trying to score: perhaps to centre to a colleague, but Griffiths could only watch mortified as he side-footed the ball beyond the far post. The Hampden sigh was audible. The Welsh challenge was not yet exhausted, but one Scottish paper was moved to concede: 'Scotland had all the luck of this hard, gruelling struggle.'

Twelve minutes from time a fortuitous bounce enabled Linwood to escape from centre-half Trevor Jones and hook an excellent goal. Wales were hanging on now, and at the death McPhail missed a golden chance to increase the lead.

Alec Linwood had taken his chance well, but he now suffered the fate of Henry Morris – scoring on his debut to become an international outcast. Young Keith Jones had not disgraced himself either, but he too would never be picked for his country again.

It came as no surprise to Pat Kelly to learn that he was not included in the Irish team to face England later in November. A namesake – Hugh Kelly – won his first cap hoping for better things. He was to be disappointed. England cocked a snook at the Scots and went one better. They scored nine.

SCOTLAND (1) 2   WALES (0) 0
    McPhail 23, Linwood 78

SCOTLAND: Cowan, Young, Cox, Evans, Woodburn, Aitken, Liddell, McPhail, Linwood, Steel, Reilly.
WALES: K Jones (Villa), Barnes (Arsenal), Sherwood (Cardiff), Powell (Villa), T G Jones (Everton), Burgess (Spurs), Griffiths (Leicester), Paul (Swansea), Ford (Villa), Clarke (Man C), Edwards (Cardiff).

SCOTLAND v ENGLAND

Saturday, 15 April 1950   *Hampden – 133,300*

By the following April the full consequences of the SFA's policy of conditional participation were embarrassingly apparent. Now, as the climactic moment drew near, honourable defence of that policy was hard to find. It was rumoured that Scotland's 'grand slam' the previous season had encouraged the SFA's 'champions or nothing' edict. Scotland would obviously retain the British Championship and had nothing to fear from England or anybody else.

If FIFA's original proposal had been accepted, the issue would now have been settled: Wales and Northern Ireland had already been swept away and Scotland and England could prepare for the trip. But the SFA's intransigence meant that the coming match assumed high drama. 'The Match of the Century' it was billed – the sixty-eighth meeting between Scotland and England, and the most vital. The world's oldest soccer fixture had traditionally been a private affray designed solely for British consumption. But not now. The eyes of the world were turned on Hampden. Representatives from FIFA, Brazil and the English FA beseeched the SFA to reconsider. It seems almost comic now: Scotland had received an unconditional invitation to compete in the World Cup, and were refusing to budge.

Both teams had four points. Goal figures in those days played no part in the British Championship or World Cup, so for Scotland the issue was crystal clear. They must at least draw, for that would enable both countries to share the championship. Honour would then be satisfied and Scotland could travel on their own terms.

One cannot envy the Scottish players for the weight of expectation bearing down upon them. To their habitual relish of beating the auld enemy were now added extra, unwanted, pressures that could hardly assist their cause. England had won at Hampden on their last two visits – in 1939 and 1948 – and the previous month nine of the current England eleven had featured in an English League XI that beat their Scottish counterparts 3-1 at Middlesbrough. That Scottish setback settled the minds of many doubters. Bookies reported that the sharp money was on an England win.

Of England's two illustrious wingers, Tom Finney was included though Stanley Matthews was in the wilderness. Stylish full-back Alf Ramsey would step out at Hampden for the first time. He would mark Billy Liddell, the part-time 'Liddellpool' winger who filled his spare time as an accountant, Sunday School teacher, and later as Justice of the Peace.

The Scottish line-up showed several changes. Three players would win their first caps in the cauldron of Hampden Park on the occasion of Scotland's biggest match in memory. Of these, Bolton's Willie Moir topped the English first division score-charts, Hearts' Willie Bauld seized the No. 9 shirt, while Ian

Cowans belly-flops, but Mortensen's 'goal' is offside. (v England)

McColl at right-half boosted the Ibrox contingent to five. Four Anglos (Alec Forbes of Arsenal being the fourth) took the field in a side clearly weighted in favour of battlers. For lovers of trivia, all five Scottish forwards were named William. Fittingly, the English goalkeeper was Williams.

The match was all-ticket. Over 133,000 bodies crammed into Britain's largest stadium. Within two minutes Bauld pounded a shot straight at Bert Williams, the Wolves and England keeper. By the interval Scotland seemed to have lost their way, particularly on the right, where Moir found himself dwarfed by the occasion, and the doubts about Waddell's fitness seemed vindicated. Each time he crossed the ball he had to pull it back on to his left foot. Steel was also having a quiet game.

Early in the second half an English 'goal' was disallowed for offside. Bauld then fired the wrong side of Williams' post, but after the hour England took the lead. The Scottish defence expected Bob Langton to pass wide to Wilf Mannion; instead he slipped it square to Roy Bentley. The Chelsea forward had hitherto been well-marshalled, but now he turned and shot before Woodburn could tackle, and from twelve yards the ball cannoned off Cowan into the net.

Hampden was struck dumb. Scotland had to find the target, but England would not cooperate. Liddell's volley was somehow kept out by Williams, and near the end poor Willie Bauld, clean through, lashed the ball against the underside of Williams' bar. The ball bounced out, not in, and Scotland had lost. The *Scotsman* confessed: 'The Englishmen were just value for their win,' and The *Glasgow Herald* went further, unable to 'recall any international side so superior to another in ground passing and in accurate head work as Saturday's England eleven. We should not now be too proud to learn; we are no longer the masters.'

The begging did not cease with the final whistle. Arms continued to be twisted. Whatever the private thoughts of SFA members, pride was now at stake, and they would lose face if they now repudiated their earlier repeated declarations solely as a result of losing. So Scotland knocked themselves out of the 1950 World Cup.

FIFA would exact revenge. The Scottish vice-president of FIFA would not be re-elected. Nor was the Scottish public in a mood to forgive. The archaic organisation of Scottish international football was exposed to scathing criticism. Willie Moir, for example, the most inconspicuous player afield, had somehow been picked over the heads of the selection committee, several of whom had never seen him in action for Bolton. Scottish wounds, entirely self-inflicted, would not be quickly healed.

The only consolation was that England were headed for even greater humiliation, beaten 0-1 by the no-hopers of the USA and then by Spain, and sent crashing out of the Brazil World Cup. It is a mischievous thought: if Scotland had triumphed at Hampden it would have been them to face the USA.

SCOTLAND (0) 0   ENGLAND (0) 1
                                        Bentley 63

SCOTLAND: Cowan, Young, Cox, McColl, Woodburn, Forbes, Waddell, Moir, Bauld, Steel, Liddell.
ENGLAND: Williams (Wolves), Ramsey (Spurs), Aston (Man U), Wright (Wolves), Franklin (Stoke), Dickinson (Portsmouth), Finney (Preston), Mannion (Midd'bro), Mortensen (Blackpool), Bentley (Chelsea), Langton (Bolton).

Qualifying Pool I

	P	W	D	L	F	A	Pts
ENGLAND	3	3	0	0	14	3	6
Scotland	3	2	0	1	10	3	4
Northern Ireland	3	0	1	2	4	17	1
Wales	3	0	1	2	1	6	1

Other group results
Wales v England   1-4   England v N Ireland   9-2   Wales v N Ireland   0-0

Scotland appearances and goalscorers
World Cup qualifying rounds 1950

	Apps	Goals		Apps	Goals		Apps	Goals
Cowan J	3	–	Evans R	2	–	Linwood A	1	1
Cox S	3	–	Liddell W	2	–	Mason J	1	1
Steel W	3	1	Reilly L	2	1	McColl I	1	–
Woodburn W	3	–	Waddell W	2	2	McPhail J	1	1
Young G	3	–	Bauld W	1	–	Moir W	1	–
Aitken G	2	–	Forbes A	1	–	Morris H	1	3

33 apps   10 goals
26 Scottish League
7 English League
18 players used

2

THE 1954 WORLD CUP

FIFA saw no reason to change the British qualifying procedure for the next, 1954, World Cup. Two places were again on offer – the only qualifying zone so favoured – and this time Scotland, to no one's surprise in view of their chastening experience in 1950, quietly complied.

Mind you, circumstances in 1954 were more agreeable. The World Cup finals were not on the other side of the world but in nearby Switzerland, with obvious advantages in preparation and travelling.

Results had been patchy since losing to England in 1950. The Scots had – to their chagrin – recorded a six-point maximum in the British Championship a year too late, but in the midst of these victories had suffered a major setback. Back in 1931, Austria had been the first continental country to defeat Scotland. The same opponents now, in December 1950, completed the double, becoming the first foreigners to win in Scotland. On a bone-hard pitch Cowan extracted the ball from his net only once, but that was enough. Scotland thereby became the first British nation to surrender their invincibility at home. Nor could the result be dismissed as a fluke: five months later Scotland tasted Austrian hospitality and were thumped 0-4.

No sooner was the Austrian shock digested than Sweden repeated it, winning 3-1 in Stockholm in May 1952 and 2-1 at Hampden a year later. This latter reverse was Scotland's last fixture before being pitched into the World Cup eliminators. Scotland entered the new campaign without an international victory for a year.

Qualifying Pool III

NORTHERN IRELAND v SCOTLAND
Saturday, 3 October 1953   *Belfast – 58,248*

Despite the lapse of four years, four Scottish players – George Young, Sammy Cox, Willie Waddell and Bobby Evans – survived to meet Northern Ireland a second time in the World Cup. John McPhail was also recalled for his second

World Cup campaign, having faced Wales in 1949. Jimmy Cowan had lost his place in goal and signed for Sunderland, relinquishing his international jersey to George Farm of Blackpool. Scotland's attack had an experimental, makeshift look about it, as if the selectors were at sixes and sevens. Excluding the five players embarking on their second World Cup, the other six could scrape up ten previous caps between them. It was East Fife's Charlie Fleming's one and only cap.

Since the Irish dark days of 1949, when they had lost eight goals to Scotland and nine to England, they had clearly acquired some backbone. They had restricted the Scots to six in 1950, three in 1951, and the following year had the temerity to draw 1-1 at Hampden. The Irish were desperately in need of a fillip. They hadn't beaten anybody for six years, since accounting for Scotland in 1947.

Yet the signs were that Northern Ireland were on the up. Shrewdly coached by Peter Doherty, they couldn't keep losing, not with the trio of exceptional young players now at their disposal. Danny Blanchflower had been only a child when winning his first cap in the 2-8 horror of 1949. Now with Aston Villa, he was developing into one of Britain's classic half-backs. He would shortly be snapped up by Tottenham and climb higher mountains. Wilbur Cush and Billy Bingham were of similar age and not far short on talent. Despite their youth, all three had been fixtures in the Irish side for some years, and would provide the mainstay of the national team for another decade. With Northern Ireland improving and Scotland becalmed, few Scotsmen banked on victory.

If the navy shirts had been flattered by events in Belfast in 1949, they were entirely in the lap of the gods in 1953. The Irish had Scotland on the ropes from the start and battered them for practically the whole match. Scotland scarcely managed to cross the halfway line as Blanchflower and Cush welded an iron curtain across the pitch. Bingham repeatedly escaped the attentions of Cox, and Charlie Tully's lissom skills gave Celtic team-mate Bobby Evans a first-half runaround, until Tully took a knock. The heavy, ponderous-looking Scottish eleven were brushed aside by Irish speed and touch-play.

Attacks rained down on Farm, the busiest man on show. The goalkeeper leapt this way and that, eliciting gasps from the crowd as he kept out rasping shots from Jimmy McIlroy and Ibrox Irishman Billy Simpson. Defenders hacked clear whenever Farm was beaten.

Two minutes into the second period Scotland for once broke into the Irish half. McPhail headed on to Fleming, who survived Cush's tackle to drive past Smyth. According to the *Glasgow Herald*, Scottish supporters were so embarrassed that McPhail 'did a dance of delight and made more noise than all the thousands of his fellow countrymen, who found the occasion suitable for nose-blowing, scarf-adjustment and shoe-lace tieing'. Northern Ireland returned to bombard the Scottish defence, unleashing 'a dozen shots worthy of a goal'.

After seventy minutes Scotland darted upfield to score a second. Fleming's header from Waddell's centre was blocked by Smyth's legs. In keeping with the run of the ball that day, the rebound bobbled to Fleming, who gleefully scored again.

The two-goal advantage was quickly halved. Newcastle's Frank Brennan impeded Simpson with a bear-hug. It did not go unnoticed by Mr Bond, the English referee, and Norman Lockhart netted from the penalty spot. Scotland were hanging on, but played the ball upfield once more. Jim McCabe's miscued clearance was his one mistake, but it gave Jackie Henderson the chance to shoot inside Smyth's near post. That goal, claimed the *Scotsman*, 'made the score almost farcical.'

The Scottish press concurred on the ill-fortune of the Irish. The *Aberdeen Press and Journal* described the Scotland team as 'slow, inept, unenterprising, and altogether a very unimpressive lot'. The *Scotsman* admitted 'in every respect but the vital one of finishing, Ireland enjoyed much the better of the play'. The *Glasgow Herald* put its hand on its heart: 'not one of the thousands of Scots who attended the Windsor Park match will disagree with the view that if ever there was a travesty of justice this was it. Had Scotland lost 1-3 and yet played as well as Ireland did all of us would have been in a much happier frame of mind.'

NORTHERN IRELAND   (0) 1   SCOTLAND   (0) 3
Lockhart 75 pen   Fleming 47, 70, Henderson 85

N IRELAND: Smyth (Distillery), Cunningham (St Mirren), McMichael (Newc'tle), Blanchflower (Villa), McCabe (Leeds), Cush (Glenavon), Bingham (Sunderland), McIlroy (Burnley), Simpson (Rangers), Tully (Celtic), Lockhart (Villa).
SCOTLAND: Farm (Blackpool), Young (Rangers), Cox (Rangers), Evans (Celtic), Brennan (Newcastle), Cowie (Dundee), Waddell (Rangers), Fleming (East Fife), McPhail (Celtic), Watson (Huddersfield), Henderson (Portsmouth).

SCOTLAND v WALES
Wednesday, 4 November 1953   *Hampden – 71,378*

Scotland had to wait only a month for the opportunity to secure qualification for Switzerland. Victory over Wales – if followed by an Irish defeat by England – would guarantee Scotland at least second spot in the British league table. And that would be enough.

Wales, however, could be expected to take defeat no more lightly than had Ireland. The Welsh had been monstrously unfortunate against England, shredding their illustrious opponents with their spirited play and leading 1-0 until their defence was disrupted by injury. The final result – 4-1 to England –

was as nonsensical as Scotland's scoreline in Belfast. Wales fielded an unchanged team. Trevor Ford was still sidelined, so that the redoubtable 6ft 2in John Charles of Leeds United retained the No. 9 shirt.

Notwithstanding their defeat in 1949, the Welsh still had the 'Indian sign' on Scotland. They had returned in 1951 to snatch a late winner, and since the war could point to two Hampden wins out of three. A third now, with just the Irish to come, in Wrexham, would leave Wales well poised to qualify.

The Scottish selectors were no more deceived than the press by the result in Belfast. Six players were axed, including the entire forward line. Charlie Fleming became the latest Scottish centre-forward to score on his debut and be exiled thereafter. For Jimmy Watson and John McPhail, too, it was the end of the international trail. The players brought in were a mixture of old and new. Experienced hands – Lawrie Reilly and Bobby Johnstone of Hibs, Billy Liddell, and Allan Brown of Blackpool – were recalled. Another veteran, Willie Waddell, made way on the right wing for Partick's John McKenzie, one of two new caps. The other was St Mirren's brick-wall stopper, Willie Telfer.

Scotland began the stronger in an entertaining game played at high speed. They might have scored as early as the first minute, but Brown couldn't capitalise on McKenzie's opening. But a home score was only postponed. The Blackpool forward had only recently returned to action after breaking a leg, but there was no sign of his injury as he collected from Reilly and fired past Howells. Before half-time Scotland scored a second, even better goal. Johnstone switched the ball from one foot to the other before hooking home.

Wales had defended stubbornly, with their wing-halves, Paul and Burgess, prominent. Three minutes after the turnaround, however, Wales climbed back into the match with a stunning strike. John Charles, for all his reputation, had shown little. But now he collected Foulkes' cross, swivelled, and hit a thunderbolt past the hapless Farm.

The game rattled along. It was with a roar of relief that Hampden greeted Scotland's third goal. Liddell slipped the ball to Reilly, Ray Daniel challenged but lost his footing, and the Hibs No. 9 – three times top scorer in the Scottish League – was presented with a clean shot. But Wales, despite being under the cosh, once again underlined their fondness for Hampden. The blond Ivor Allchurch gathered the ball deep and survived one, two, three, four challenges before hammering his shot into the net from twenty yards.

The closing seconds were packed with incident and controversy. The ageless Welsh full-back, Wally Barnes, clumsily chested the ball back to his goalie. The contact was sufficiently near the arm to provoke a spontaneous roar of 'penalty'. The referee did not think so, and was already racing upfield to follow the belted clearance. The ball sailed deep into the Scottish half. Telfer was possibly congratulating himself on a flawless baptism, but preparing to pass back to Farm he was caught in possession. John Charles whipped the ball away and with Farm in limbo scored a dramatic Welsh equaliser. Telfer, desperately trying to retrieve his error, ended up in the net with the ball.

If Scotland felt aggrieved, they soon felt doubly sore. From the restart Reilly outstripped Daniel for pace. Reilly might have scored another of his renowned last-minute goals had Daniel not clipped his heels just outside the Welsh penalty box. The free kick came to nothing. To use a well-worn cliché, Scotland had played much worse and won – and had done so the previous month.

SCOTLAND (2) 3	WALES (0) 3
Brown 19, Johnstone 41,	Charles 48, 88, I Allchurch 65
Reilly 57	

SCOTLAND: Farm, Young, Cox, Evans, Telfer, Cowie, McKenzie, Johnstone, Reilly, Brown, Liddell.
WALES: Howells (Cardiff), Barnes (Arsenal), Sherwood (Cardiff), Paul (Man C), Daniel (Sunderland), Burgess (Spurs), Foulkes (Newcastle), E R Davies (Newcastle), Charles (Leeds), I Allchurch (Swansea), Clarke (Man C).

SCOTLAND v ENGLAND
Saturday, 3 April 1954   *Hampden – 134,544*

A week later England unconvincingly beat the gallant Irish at Goodison Park to seal their place in the World Cup. The outcome of Scottish qualification dragged on till the spring. Wales would entertain the Irish four days before England were due at Hampden. If Wales won, as expected, Scotland would have to avoid defeat, and all the tensions of 1950 would be reactivated. Happily, Ireland chose that occasion to end their seven-year winless sequence. The World Cup slots were now filled, Scotland and England were uncatchable. Nothing was at stake at Hampden except prestige and the British title.

Actually, this was not entirely true. As in 1950, the British champions were to be seeded in the World Cup finals. The draw had already taken place. In the first round the seeded British champions were scheduled to play the modest opposition provided by Belgium and Switzerland, while the British runners-up would be left with the daunting prospect of Uruguay and Austria. Scotland's dropped point against Wales meant that nothing less than a victory would do – to head the Home International table and tread the gentler path in Switzerland.

England had troubles enough. Against Wales and Ireland they had looked dreadful. Disaster was brewing. Massacred by the Hungarians at Wembley in November, the England team was promptly despatched to the knacker's yard. There was no international future for Alf Ramsey, Stan Mortensen, and many others. It was an England eleven containing four new caps that stepped out into the unfamiliar and intimidating atmosphere of Hampden Park.

The hosts, too, made changes. George Young missed his first ever World Cup game, providing a first (and last) cap for his Celtic rival Mike Haughney. Hibernian's Willie Ormond made his debut at outside-left. Willie Telfer was left to ponder that agonising moment when Wales equalised, for it had helped consign him to international oblivion. Newcastle's Frank Brennan returned for what would be his last cap. It was as well that Bobby Johnstone was versatile. He had previously worn the Scottish No. 7 shirt and the No. 11. Now he borrowed No. 9, pitting him against England's untried 6ft 3in centre-half, Harry Clarke. England were seeking a fifth successive Hampden victory: Scotland had not beaten them at home for seventeen years.

In preparation for the World Cup finals the SFA had appointed a part-time team manager to minister to Scotland's affairs. Andy Beattie – full-time boss of Huddersfield Town – must have been encouraged as his team enjoyed the early play and the early goal. It was scored in the eighth minute at the second attempt by Allan Brown, the ball bouncing off Gil Merrick and squeezing through Ron Staniforth's legs.

Playing against pounding wind and rain, England equalised out of the blue. Tom Finney, back in the side after a lengthy spell out of favour, returned the ball to Ivor Broadis, who accelerated past Cox to shoot past Farm.

As England's new boys gradually settled, the flow of play towards their goal was stemmed, then reversed. The supply to McKenzie and Ormond was throttled and Finney stamped himself as the game's principal authority.

Scotland emerged for the second half with several players not having changed into clean shirts. Finney rebuked them for their untidiness, leaving Cox for dead and crossing for the incoming Nicholls. Farm might have claimed the cross, but he didn't and Nicholls headed England in front. The scorer formed part of the West Brom partnership with Ronnie Allen that had scored over sixty goals that season. Midway through the second half it was Allen's turn, climbing to head England's third from Mullen's free kick.

Hampden had been quiet for some time. Now the trickle for the exits became a stampede. The remaining twenty-odd minutes were superfluous. The *Glasgow Herald* railed against Scotland's lack of fight: 'Half-way through the second half Scotland were disheartened, disillusioned and defeated.' Those who left early missed two more goals. Finney rubbed salt into Scottish wounds, taunting Cox from one end of the pitch to the other before crossing onto Mullen's head for number four. The goal was a landmark. England had never before scored four goals in Scotland. In the final seconds Ormond's swirling centre under the English crossbar saw Merrick and Byrne collide, leaving the ball to squirm gently over the line.

The Scottish verdict was depressing. The *Glasgow Herald* could 'recall no worse forward line, as a line, having worn Scottish colours. England, a far from brilliant England, have exposed our deficiencies to the full.' The *Scotsman* resorted to poetry: 'shiver'd was fair Scotland's spear and broken was her shield.'

SCOTLAND (1) 2	ENGLAND (1) 4
Brown 8, Ormond 88	Broadis 14, Nicholls 52,
	Allen 69, Mullen 81

SCOTLAND: Farm, Haughney, Cox, Evans, Brennan, Aitken, McKenzie, Johnstone, Henderson, Brown, Ormond.
ENGLAND: Merrick (Birmingham), Staniforth (Huddersfield), Byrne (Man U), Wright (Wolves), Clarke (Spurs), Dickinson (Portsmouth), Finney (Preston), Broadis (Newcastle), Allen (WBA), Nicholls (WBA), Mullen (Wolves).

Qualifying Pool III

	P	W	D	L	F	A	Pts
ENGLAND	3	3	0	0	11	4	6
SCOTLAND	3	1	1	1	8	8	3
Northern Ireland	3	1	0	2	4	7	2
Wales	3	0	1	2	5	9	1

Other group results
Wales v England   1-4   England v N Ireland 3-1   Wales v N Ireland 1-2

World Cup finals – SWITZERLAND   **June-July 1954**

Scotland were set to taste the fruits of their first World Cup finals, though hardly in the most confident frame of mind. The competition would be held in the congenial surroundings of Switzerland, an appropriate venue in those cold war years.

But if the hosts were inviting, FIFA left a bad taste with indefensible organisation. Half the sixteen finalists were seeded, two put into each group, and were then asked to play only the two non-seeds. That is to say, everyone would play just twice. The seeded teams avoided each other, likewise the non-seeds. Never in the history of the World Cup had seeding status carried greater rewards. In Pool III, defending world champions Uruguay and the powerful Austrians were named as the two seeds. Making up the numbers were Scotland and Czechoslovakia, neither of whom might pick up points off the other. Departing from 1950, the top *two* teams would proceed to the quarter-finals.

FIFA's denunciation of drawn games compounded the tournament's eccentricities. For no obvious reason, if the scores in group matches were level, extra time would be imposed to try to break the deadlock. Extra time for

McKenzie should look happy. Ormond's last-minute cross has found the net. (v England)

knock-out matches is one thing; for a league format quite another.

The Scottish players could do with some winning practice. They had won just once at Hampden in seven games, and that a canter against the USA. Three fixtures were arranged against undemanding Scandinavian opponents. Scotland managed to beat Norway, 1-0 at Hampden, with a performance so dire that the crowd cheered the Norwegians. Scotland went on to draw 1-1 in Oslo and – wearing the colours of Lord Rosebery – beat Finland 2-1 in Helsinki. Nothing emerged from these matches to diminish the view that Scotland would struggle against Uruguay and Austria.

The Scottish Football Association had recovered from its humiliation of 1950, only to invite another four years later. The eighteen players called upon in Oslo and Helsinki would evidently provide the basis of the World Cup squad. Twenty-two players were permitted. The SFA, however, had already intimated it would send just *thirteen* players. These, perchance, might have to survive five matches if Scotland reached the Final. They would have to play through injury or loss of form, for only in an emergency could replacements be flown out and inserted 'cold' into the team. Perhaps the SFA had a crystal ball, knowing the team was being thrown to the lions. The thirteen-man squad set up base in Lucerne on 12 June.

Name	Position	Club	Age	Caps	Goals
Fred Martin	Goalkeeper	Aberdeen	25	2	–
Willie Cunningham (c)	Full-back	Preston	29	3	–
John Aird	Full-back	Burnley	28	2	–
Bobby Evans *	Wing-half	Celtic	26	17	–
Tommy Docherty	Wing-half	Preston	26	5	–
Doug Cowie	Wing-half	Dundee	28	6	–
Jimmy Davidson	Centre-half	Partick Thistle	28	2	–
John McKenzie	Winger	Partick Thistle	28	4	1
Willie Ormond	Winger	Hibernian	27	3	1
George Hamilton *	Forward	Aberdeen	36	5	4
Allan Brown	Forward	Blackpool	27	12	6
Neil Mochan	Forward	Celtic	27	1	–
Willie Fernie	Forward	Celtic	25	1	–

* Would not appear in 1954 finals.		*Averages*	27.5	4.8	

The other names submitted to FIFA on a stand-by basis were:

John Anderson (Leicester)   Jackie Henderson (Portsmouth)
Ian Binning (Queen of the South)   Ian McMillan (Airdrie)
Bobby Combe (Hibernian)   David Mathers (Partick Thistle)
Ernie Copland (Raith)   Alex Wilson (Portsmouth)

The size of the travelling party did not attract much flak at the time. After all, this was all new for Scotland. England, too, declined to send a full complement, though their seventeen made more sense than Scotland's thirteen. More controversial was the make-up of the Scotland squad, which contained just one goalkeeper and no recognised centre-forward. The selectors, chaired by Mr T Reid of Partick Thistle, had seemingly plucked the most callow footballers they could find and then shoved them off to do a man's job. The players had amassed a mere sixty-three previous caps between them. Over a quarter of these had been earned by Bobby Evans, and he was injured. In other words, the team virtually picked itself.

A long list of experienced names had been passed over. Lawrie Reilly was recovering from pleurisy and Bobby Johnstone had to pull out through injury. Other players were axed permanently following the defeat by England, which seems to have had the same broom-sweeping effect on the Scottish selectors as Hungary had on England's. A sign of the low esteem in which the World Cup was held was the decision by Glasgow Rangers to tour North America, ruling out any Ibrox player from participating. The absence of George Young and incapacitation of Bobby Evans meant someone else had to captain the side. The job fell on Willie Cunningham of Preston North End, possessor of three caps. For good measure, the SFA omitted to include any training kit for their players, who had to train in whatever they had with them.

AUSTRIA v SCOTLAND
Wednesday, 16 June 1954   *Zurich – 25,000*

Scotland could hardly have found themselves in a tougher section. If anybody was going to wrest the Jules Rimet trophy off the Uruguayans, the obvious candidates were Hungary or Austria. The Austrians had faced the Hungarians in a warm-up match, and been a trifle unfortunate to go down 0-1. Their ominous domination of Scotland was firmly inscribed in the record books. Scotland had not beaten them in five attempts, the most recent of which, in Vienna in 1951, had seen the Scots trounced 0-4.

Austria had only contested one previous World Cup, when their earlier great team had reached the 1934 semi-finals, there to be knocked out by the hosts and eventual winners, Italy. Some of their current players were widely known and widely feared, foremost amongst them their roaming pivot, Ernst Ocwirk and his fellow half-backs Happel and Hanappi. The muscular Ernst Happel had been selected by FIFA for a 'Rest of Europe' team, skippered by Ocwirk, that had played at Wembley the previous autumn. The Austrians had qualified for the finals by beating Portugal, improbably, 9-1 in Vienna. This, in spite of the fact that Austria were considered a waning force, past their prime. But few Scots took comfort from that. Whichever way you looked at it, the match bore all the signs of pitching men against boys. Scotland were set fair for a good hiding.

They were also set for a good blushing. When Ocwirk shook hands with Cunningham in the centre circle and presented him with a commemorative pennant, Cunningham found himself with nothing to give in return.

That was the least of Scotland's problems. The team that Andy Beattie was asked to field was ludicrously unseasoned. No fewer than six players had made their international debuts against Norway and Finland, and two more – John McKenzie and Willie Ormond – during the British qualifiers.

Beattie could manufacture neither instant teamwork nor experience, but he could instil enthusiasm and aggression, both of which Scotland unleashed from the start in Zurich's Sportzplatz Hardturm. During the opening quarter the Austrians were hustled out of their elegant stride, disconcerted by the Scots' physical challenge. During this spell both McKenzie and Neil Mochan fired over – the latter from no more than six yards.

Aberdeen's Fred Martin was probably the most surprised goalkeeper to find himself in the World Cup finals, but he was assuredly gaining confidence.

Scotland were giving as good as they got, and when Mochan by-passed Happel only to be crunched in an Austrian sandwich, he must have felt aggrieved at winning merely an indirect free kick from Belgian referee Laurant Franken. Scotland felt even more aggrieved when Austria shortly scored a classic goal. Probst slipped the ball out to Alfred Körner, sprinted for the return, and shot past Martin from a tight angle.

Such a goal could reasonably be expected to open the Austrian flood gates. Instead it was Scotland who raised their game. At half-time Scotland could feel ill-served by the scoreline, and afterwards set out with gusto to redress it. Neil Mochan took the eye, roaming across the Austrian defence. Austria were discomfited by the tigerish tackling of Docherty, Davidson and Cowie. Schmied in the Austrian goal was busier than Martin in the other, and Austria resorted to foul play to protect their lead.

These methods served them well, for despite their second-half offensive the Scots rarely broke through. Ormond's header and Mochan's drop-shot passed over Schmied's crossbar, leaving Scotland to rue their missed first-half chances. The game was dying when Mochan turned on a sixpence, shot through a jungle of limbs and watched Schmied vault across his goal to gather at the second attempt.

Scotland were as close as that. Not to a draw, but to forcing the lunacy of thirty minutes extra time. Even in defeat, their performance won praise. They were now in the mood to take on Uruguay.

AUSTRIA   (1) 1   SCOTLAND   (0) 0
   Probst 33

AUSTRIA: Schmied, Hanappi, Barschandt, Ocwirk, Happel, Koller, R Körner, Schleger, Dienst, Probst, A Körner.
SCOTLAND: Martin, Cunningham, Aird, Docherty, Davidson, Cowie, McKenzie, Fernie, Mochan, Brown, Ormond.

URUGUAY v SCOTLAND
Saturday, 19 June 1954   *Basle – 34,000*

Uruguay. The mere name in 1954 had a debilitating effect on European ears, much as 'Brazil' would have for later generations. If it seemed that Uruguay were invincible, it was because they were. They had entered the World Cup twice previously, in 1930 and 1950, and won it both times. They had yet to sample their first defeat, and were now bidding to win the Jules Rimet trophy for a record third time, which, if successful, would entitle them to keep it outright. What was remarkable about these double world champions was how a tiny country with a population half the size of Scotland's could compete and dominate at the highest levels. Uruguay, like Scotland, lived in the lee of powerful neighbours, in her case Brazil and Argentina. That did not impede Uruguayan excellence. It was food for thought.

Uruguay were captained by Obdulio Varela, at thirty-nine the oldest player in the competition, one of five World Cup winners still around from 1950. The others were Máspoli in goal, Andrade, Míguez, and Juan Schiaffino, goalscorer supreme, who would shortly sign for AC Milan for a world record fee of £72,000. Defender José Santamaria would in due course anchor the great Real Madrid teams of the late 1950s.

The one factor in Scotland's favour was that Uruguay's triumphs had been in South America. This was their first excursion to Europe and their first experience of playing Scotland. But in dismissing Czechoslovakia 2-0 in their first match, Uruguay did not seem put out by their alien environment.

Such was the logic of the competition that Scotland were virtually excluded after their first match. To avoid returning home after their second, they obviously needed to beat the world champions, to join them on two points. But though goal figures would separate first place from second, they did not separate second from third. Teams tied on points had to play off. Assuming Austria beat Czechoslovakia, Scotland would need to defeat Uruguay *twice* to make the quarter-finals.

This was liable to prove an insuperable obstacle. Odds on Scotland's survival – shortened by their fighting display against Austria – lengthened when Andy Beattie announced hours before kick-off that he would resign at the final whistle, no matter the outcome. Not for the first time, a Scottish manager was ill-prepared to be strait-jacketed by the selectors. They, once skipper Willie Cunningham's X-rayed shoulder showed no break, nominated an unchanged Scottish team for the first time in memory. But then they had no choice.

The temperature in Basle's St Jakob Stadium was more suited to the Sahara. The pale blue shirts of the Uruguayans minimised the effects of the heat, the heavy shirts and boots of the Scots magnified it. Still, having dutifully stood to verse after verse of the interminable Uruguayan national anthem, they set about their opponents as they had left off against Austria. Early on, both Mochan and Allan Brown caught a glimpse of goal.

Scotland, once again, attempted to mark man-for-man. For their part, Uruguay performed 'bolt' tactics, as had Austria. One full-back played as central defender with the other supporting him. The wing-halves marked the wingers, leaving the nominal centre-half to do, and go, as he pleased. This role – performed for Austria by their captain, Ocwirk – was allocated by Uruguay to their own skipper, Varela.

The system may have been the same, but Scotland hadn't budgeted for Uruguay's speed. Abbadie skipped contemptuously round Aird and crossed for the other winger, Borges, to put his team ahead. On the half-hour, central attacker Omar Míguez capitalised on Docherty's wayward pass to extend the lead.

A two-goal half-time deficit was maybe a mite harsh. Perhaps the kilted pipers who entertained the crowd hoped to inspire the Scots. But from the restart they were in for an unpleasant surprise. Uruguay simply changed up a gear – or three. They freed themselves from Scotland's man-marking by seeking space before the ball was passed, and Abbadie and Borges began to treat Aird and Cunningham like the international novices they were. Docherty's slack pass set up another goal. Borges sped past the static Cunningham, homed in on Martin, and finished off with another mighty shot.

To Scotland's disquiet, Uruguay now turned it on. It was murder in the sun. Míguez claimed a second, to prevent Borges and Abbadie monopolising the scorecard. The crowd whistled and hooted at the Scots' inability to resist. Ninety minutes is a long time in football. After the Austria match Scotland's international standing had probably never been higher; now, never lower. Amidst the carnage Scotland still managed to create, and miss, opportunities of their own, but the real lessons were all being learned at the other end. In truth, it could have been even worse.

URUGUAY (2) 7   SCOTLAND (0) 0
  Borges 17, 48, 55, Míguez 30, 80,
  Abbadie 57, 85

URUGUAY: Máspoli, Santamaria, Martínez, Andrade, Varela, Cruz, Abbadie, Ambrois, Míguez, Schiaffino, Borges.
SCOTLAND: Martin, Cunningham, Aird, Docherty, Davidson, Cowie, McKenzie, Fernie, Mochan, Brown, Ormond.

It was a dispirited Scotland team (it could hardly be called a squad) that arrived home. The memory of one close result was obliterated by the ensuing disaster. Having overcome one British team, Uruguay completed the double, knocking out England in the quarter-finals 4-2. In the semis Uruguay came unstuck (after extra time) against the Hungarians in a match that should have graced the climax. Austria fell at the same stage to West Germany, who went on to inflict Hungary's first defeat in over thirty matches in the Final. Austria found partial compensation in the third/fourth place play-off. There they faced Uruguay in the match they evaded in Pool III. The Austrians, somewhat unexpectedly, won 3-1.

Final positions – Pool III

	P	W	D	L	F	A	Pts
URUGUAY	2	2	0	0	9	0	4
AUSTRIA	2	2	0	0	6	0	4
Czechoslovakia	2	0	0	2	0	7	0
Scotland	2	0	0	2	0	8	0

Scotland appearances and goalscorers
World Cup qualifying rounds and final competition 1954

	Apps	Goals		Apps	Goals		Apps	Goals
Brown A	4	2	Aird J	2	–	Aitken G *	1	–
Cowie D	4	–	Davidson J	2	–	Fleming C	1	2
McKenzie J	4	–	Docherty T	2	–	Haughney M	1	–
Cox S *	3	–	Fernie W	2	–	Liddell W *	1	–
Evans R *	3	–	Brennan F	2	–	McPhail J *	1	–
Farm G	3	–	Johnstone R	2	1	Reilly L *	1	1
Ormond W	3	1	Martin F	2	–	Telfer W	1	–
Cunningham W	2	–	Mochan N	2	–	Waddell W *	1	–
Henderson J	2	1	Young G *	2	–	Watson J	1	–

* Appeared in 1950 World Cup.

55 apps   8 goals
35 Scottish League
20 English League
27 players used

3

THE 1958 WORLD CUP

It was with the 1958 World Cup, held in Sweden, that the competition finally came of age. Previous tournaments had all been disfigured by the non-participation – for whatever reason – of some of the world's strongest nations. These handicaps did not mar the 1958 finals, nor any thereafter.

Lobbying behind the scenes ensured the scrapping of British patronage, the right to two of the final sixteen places. The arguments based on sentiment were outweighed by those of form. Nothing in the World Cups of 1950 and 1954 suggested Britain *deserved* two teams in the finals. Nor, it must be said, even one. There was idle talk about Britain having to field one team in future. For this downward reappraisal of British football, Scotland were not exactly blameless, witness the hullabaloo in 1950 and the debacle against Uruguay.

Not that the SFA mourned the passing of the British qualifying zone. They had never approved of interference in the Home Internationals in this fashion. From now on the four British nations would take their chances, being thrown into the wider European lottery. All four might make it, all four might not. When the draw was announced, Scotland found themselves pooled with Spain and Switzerland, with just one team to qualify.

Scotland's international progress since 1954 was cause for concern. Sixteen internationals were played prior to the 1958 qualifiers, only six won. The only notable scalps were those of deteriorating Austria, for whom defeat in Zurich was avenged, in a sordid, brutal match, 4-1 in Vienna. Against this stood some worrying defeats, the worst being a 2-7 hiding by England. Hungary did to Scotland was they had done to England, beating them twice in the space of six months, though mercifully the margins of defeat were narrower. Hungary's 4-2 success at Hampden provoked accusations of over-zealous Scottish tackling, Tommy Docherty being held especially guilty. In Scotland's final outing before the new campaign, they succumbed 1-2 at Wembley.

Significantly, the SFA made no attempt to replace Andy Beattie. Scotland would drift managerless from one World Cup to the next.

Qualifying Pool IX

SCOTLAND v SPAIN

Wednesday, 8 May 1957   *Hampden – 89,000*

In the mid and late 'fifties no British football fan could fail to be unaware of the glamour of Spanish football. Spain's great reputation at that time lay less with her international team than with the aura surrounding Barcelona and, above all, Real Madrid. Real had won the first ever European Cup, in 1956, and had just expelled Manchester United from the 1957 semi-finals. Centre-forward di Stefano and outside-left Gento were two of the greatest names in club, Spanish, and European football. Di Stefano, an Argentine by birth, was eligible – according to FIFA statutes at the time – to play for his country of residence. As for Barcelona, they were already *en route* to lifting the first European Fairs' Cup. Five of the Spanish side at Hampden were plucked from Barcelona, among them goalkeeper Ramallets – still around after frustrating England in Brazil in 1950 – and Hungarian-born inside-forward Kubala.

In post-war World Cups, Spain had finished fourth in 1950, having disposed of England, but missed the 1954 finals on the toss of a coin after failing to overcome Turkey in a play-off. The paths of Scotland and Spain had never before crossed. Spain had opened their account in Pool IX by being held 2-2 by Switzerland in Madrid. Notwithstanding, Spain remained favourites to qualify.

Three years on from the Uruguayan nightmare, the Scottish side had been entirely remodelled. Hard-man Docherty was the sole survivor, though 'Corky' Young had returned to lend his massive experience, having switched from right-back to centre-half. Now aged thirty-four, and Scottish 'Player of the Year' in 1955, he had announced his retirement from international football with effect from the return match in Spain. This would be his Hampden swansong, eleven years after he had first pulled on the navy shirt.

Scotland's new goalkeeper was Liverpool's bulky Tommy Younger, now winning his thirteenth consecutive cap. All eyes, however, focused on the forward line, where Blackpool's Jackie Mudie switched from inside-forward to centre-forward. Only John Charles had outscored Mudie in the English first division. Mudie's slight build would be offset by the inclusion of Rangers' burly Sam Baird. Nine of the side beaten at Wembley in April retained their places. Lawrie Reilly was one of the two unfortunates. He would never force his way back in, and thereby missed by one game the distinction of appearing in three World Cups.

A twenty-four hour deluge turned Hampden into a habitat for ducks, not for footballers from sunny Spain. But nothing could drown the skills of Gento, though the raw Eric Caldow slowly took his measure. The first goal, midway through the half, fell to Scotland. Shots in rapid succession by Sam Baird and

Gordon Smith engineered a corner kick. Mudie headed it onto the crossbar and netted the rebound.

Scottish joy was quickly tempered. Gonzales' sloppy pass was followed by Kubala's sloppy shot and Younger's sloppy attempt to save. 1-1. Play grew fiercer by the minute. Gento was felled inside the box by Young. No penalty. An indirect free kick to Scotland inside the Spanish penalty area required three takes before Tommy Ring thumped it over the bar. When the same player set off in pursuit of Docherty's pass, he was brought down in the box by Olivilla. South African John Hewie was only playing because of injury to Alec Parker. Hewie's penalty kick almost cut Ramallets in two.

Upon the resumption Mudie once more headed against the bar. This time there was no happy rebound and Spain shortly equalised. Di Stefano's backheel set up Gento, whose shot was parried by Younger. Suarez poached the loose ball.

Now Scotland surged forward, the Hampden roar pounding in their ears. On the left Ring teased and tormented Olivilla. Wee Bobby Collins slipped the ball through the slime to Mudie who blasted home from the edge of the box. Ramallets stood stationary as if auditioning for Madame Tussaud's. Scotland had their tails up now and celebrated with the best goal of the match. McColl put Collins clear on the right, Mudie gathered the ball and contemptuously stuck it away for his hat-trick.

SCOTLAND (2) 4   SPAIN (1) 2
  Mudie 22, 70, 79, Hewie 41 pen   Kubala 30, Suarez 50

SCOTLAND: Younger (Liverpool), Caldow (Rangers), Hewie (Charlton), McColl (Rangers), Young (Rangers), Docherty (Preston), Smith (Hibs), Collins (Celtic), Mudie (Blackpool), Baird (Rangers), Ring (Clyde).
SPAIN: Ramallets, Olivilla, Garay, Verges, Campanal, Zarraga, Gonzales, Kubala, di Stefano, Suarez, Gento.

SWITZERLAND v SCOTLAND
Sunday, 19 May 1957   *Basle – 48,000*

In the World Cups of the 'fifties and 'sixties competing nations saw nothing amiss in piling fixtures one upon the other. In 1957 Scotland completed their first three in the space of nineteen days. They set off fresh from their Hampden victory for a continental tour. World Cup eliminators would be contested in Basle and Madrid, with a friendly in West Germany in between.

Switzerland had already taken a point off Spain, who were in dire straits following the loss of two more at Hampden. A Scottish win in Basle would put Scotland three points clear, with one foot propping open the door to Sweden.

Whether they achieved this victory depended in large measure on the mood of their hosts, historically – like their neighbours Austria and Hungary – a side of fluctuating fortunes. At their best the Swiss were acclaimed tactical innovators, at their worst – not surprising with part-timers – one of Europe's punch-bags.

When Tommy Docherty stepped out into the St Jakob Stadium he might have suffered memories of the last time he did so. But now the opponents were Switzerland, not Uruguay; the weather filthy, not scorching. The match was being transmitted on Eurovision, the second half live to Scotland. In those black and white days Switzerland's red and white strip was not easily distinguishable from the Scots' blue and white. Switzerland requested that Scotland change their shorts, but as they had brought no others the hosts provided a set of their own. These were bright orange, not the obvious complement to navy shirts and scarlet socks.

There had been no need, or cause, to fiddle with the Scotland eleven. If the players hoped to provide football as dazzling as their appearance, the Swiss had other ideas. Scotland were soon trailing. Caldow had almost presented the Swiss with a gift start, but his two suicidal back-passes had been salvaged. Now, Vonlanthen despatched the ball to Meier, whose fast, low, return pass was thrashed past Younger from fifteen yards.

The home side did not seem put out by the chilly weather or sodden pitch, and for most of the opening half were in unquestioned control. Meier, Ballaman and Schneiter slowed the game to their tastes, the Scots slipped and slithered, and Younger fumbled almost everything that came his way. Docherty stood out as the one Scot to resist.

The change in fortunes came twelve minutes from half-time. It owed everything to a corner awarded in error and Mudie's firm header that flashed past Parlier. It was well that Scottish viewers were not privy to that first-half, for they would not have been cheered. The second period was little better, except that the Swiss ran out of steam – the clinging pitch sapping part-time legs. Scotland were left to enjoy one crucial moment. Collins dived to meet Smith's corner, nodding the ball beyond Parlier where it wedged in the far stanchion.

There remained time for Collins' defenders to attempt hara-kiri, when McColl's back-pass was snatched by Younger at the far post. Switzerland couldn't pull rabbits from top-hats. Scotland ended the match with a three-point cushion, but the Scottish press were not deceived: 'Some Scottish players probably realised that they will never again play so badly and be on a winning side.'

SWITZERLAND (1) 1   SCOTLAND (1) 2
  Vonlanthen 12   Mudie 33, Collins 71

SWITZERLAND: Parlier, Kernen, Koch, Grobety, Frosio, Schneiter, Antenen, Ballaman, Vonlanthen, Meier, Riva.
SCOTLAND: Younger, Caldow, Hewie, McColl, Young, Docherty, Smith, Collins, Mudie, Baird, Ring.

SPAIN v SCOTLAND
Sunday, 26 May 1957   *Madrid – 90,000*

From Basle the Scottish party stopped off in Stuttgart, where they inflicted a memorable 3-1 victory over world champions West Germany. Boosted by back-to-back away victories, it was an understandably buoyant Scottish squad which descended on Madrid.

Two points from their final two matches would guarantee a place in Sweden, while a draw now would eliminate Spain. To qualify themselves, Spain needed to beat Scotland, and then pray that Switzerland avoided defeat at Hampden before entertaining Spain in a showdown.

The Scottish party settled into a mountain retreat at Escorial, twenty miles outside Madrid. George Young had hoped to bow out of international football in the Chamartin Stadium, but he had been omitted in Stuttgart in favour of flame-haired Bobby Evans. Evans now retained his place and Docherty the captaincy. Young was incensed. The only other change was at right-half, where Hearts workhorse Dave Mackay won a first cap, being thrown in at the deep end. For their part, Spain restructured a defence beaten four times at Hampden. It was a do-or-die week for the footballers of the Spanish capital. Four days later the city would host the final of the second European Cup – and celebrate its retention by Real Madrid.

It may have been complacence (having beaten the World Cup holders, why worry about Spain?), but from the kick-off only one side was likely to win, and that side wasn't Scotland. Even the slippery pitch was in Scotland's favour: wherever they played of late they brought torrential rain. From the start, the ball was propelled towards Younger as if laced with iron filings and his goal plated with magnets. Di Stefano was inspirational, and Kubala – quiet at Hampden – turned on his skills with a vengeance.

Younger kept Spain at bay until he was beaten by Mateos's unstoppable shot. Had Mudie's looping header then finished in the net, rather than brought a flying save, who knows what the outcome might have been. The question was academic, for Kubala shortly ran through to put the game beyond Scotland.

Scotland were now seeking to save not the game, but their dignity. Captain Docherty did his best to close ranks, Younger was seldom found wanting, but these were minor barriers to Spain's unstoppable momentum. Twelve minutes into the second half a goalmouth scramble saw Basora smash home a loose ball.

The match was beyond redemption. Mackay looked out of his depth, Mudie never escaped Garay's clutches, Ring was snuffed out by Segarra, and Gordon Smith achieved so little he would never play for his country again. The one moment of Scottish heat was generated by Baird, who did not take kindly to Gensana's foul. The pair swung insults, fists and boots until separated by English referee Mr R Leafe, who took Baird's name.

Smith did salvage a goal, though not his career, with a header from Ring's cross. This insult to Spanish supremacy was cancelled out when Basora took a flying hack at the ball and saw it dribble past Younger. The goalkeeper was due his one moment of frailty: his team-mates were in his debt. Over ninety minutes Scotland had got off lightly, and this was not lost on the *Scotsman*: 'Spain played with Scotland as a cat would a mouse, to win much more convincingly than the margin would indicate.'

SPAIN (2) 4	SCOTLAND (0) 1
Mateos 13, Kubala 20,	Smith 79
Basora 57, 85	

SPAIN: Ramallets, Quincoces, Segarra, Gensana, Garay, Verges, Basora, Kubala, di Stefano, Mateos, Gento.
SCOTLAND: Younger, Caldow, Hewie, Mackay, Evans, Docherty, G Smith, Collins, Mudie, Baird, Ring.

SCOTLAND v SWITZERLAND
Wednesday, 6 November 1957   *Hampden – 58,811*

Scotland were glad of a six-month respite before tackling their decisive fixture. FIFA required all qualifiers to be done by Christmas, not dragging on till late spring as in 1950 and 1954. If Scotland won, they were home and dry. If they drew, and Spain won in Switzerland, Scotland would play-off with Spain on neutral territory. After their humbling in Madrid, even the most patriotic Scot would not relish that. As for Switzerland, wins over the Scots and Spanish in turn would take them to Sweden. In short, both teams had to win, and a cracker was on the cards.

The Scots were probably the only people on earth rooting for their team. Real Madrid's retention of the European Cup made them the most talked about and romanticised of European clubs. With the greatest footballing show on earth about to take place, neutrals the world over yearned to see Spain's stars where they belonged, onstage at the World Cup finals.

The selectors made several changes, the team having recently achieved the dullest of draws in Belfast. Falkirk's Alec Parker partnered Caldow at full-back. Willie Fernie's inconsistency was preferred to Dave Mackay's inexperience.

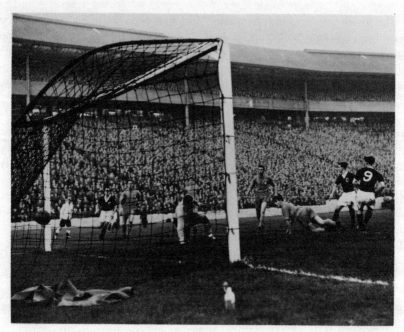

A white-blazered ref turns away after Mudie (second from right) scores. (v Switzerland)

Fernie's previous caps had been at inside-forward or on the wing: now he was asked to play wing-half. Alec Scott of Rangers succeeded Gordon Smith and Archie Robertson stood in for Sam Baird, giving the left side of attack an all-Clyde look. Switzerland lined up with nine of the side that had fallen away in Basle. It might have been eight. Travel bungles almost deprived them of key forward Vonlanthen, who played in the Italian League.

If the attacking spirit of the match was predictable, the all-round quality of the Swiss was not. In Basle they had looked skilful, if short on stamina. Clad in all-orange, they looked no less adroit at Hampden. Ballaman was in a class by himself and the wingers had the beating of the home full-backs. Against the run of play Scotland scored first. Docherty made the chance for Robertson to side-foot under Parlier.

Switzerland did not dwell on their disappointment. Docherty's passing was again a critical factor, but this time Riva cut out his slack clearance, evaded one tackle on merit, another when Evans stumbled, and prodded an equaliser.

Seven minutes into the second half, Fernie's fast, low centre was swept home by Mudie. In Basle, Switzerland had capitulated when falling behind a second time. This time they would not. Mudie's goal signalled a Swiss offensive of such intensity that the *Glasgow Herald* reporter was moved to comment: 'Midway in the second half Switzerland had Scotland in a state of

Alec Scott, surely offside, sprints through to score Scotland's third. (v Switzerland)

disintegration, the defence panic-stricken, and the forwards disillusioned and devoid of ideas.'

The match was settled by two moments of high drama. Chiesa surged past Docherty and Evans, Younger took the sting out of the shot, and Parker raced back to clear off the line. With Hampden agog, Scotland swept upfield. The Swiss had anticipated Collins' through-ball and moved out *en bloc*. Scott was so palpably offside that he hesitated himself, and only put the ball into the net as a gesture, assuming play had been halted.

Mr Leafe of England, who had officiated during Scotland's defeat in Madrid, allowed the goal. He did so at some risk to his personal safety, for the Swiss were outraged. To their credit, Switzerland kept pressing. Riva nodded down a corner kick that Younger might have claimed and Vonlanthen lashed the ball inside a post. Hampden then held its breath as Chiesa broke clear again, this time to be thwarted by a goal-line clearance. At the end, officials of both sides concurred that Switzerland had been unfortunate – but they were out, and Scotland were through.

SCOTLAND (1) 3   SWITZERLAND (1) 2
   Robertson 29, Mudie 52,   Riva 35, Vonlanthen 80
   Scott 70

SCOTLAND: Younger, Parker, Caldow, Fernie, Evans, Docherty, Scott, Collins, Mudie, Robertson, Ring.
SWITZERLAND: Parlier, Kernen, Morf, Grobety, Koch, Schneiter, Chiesa, Ballaman, Meier, Vonlanthen, Riva.

Qualifying Pool IX

	P	W	D	L	F	A	Pts
SCOTLAND	4	3	0	1	10	9	6
Spain	4	2	1	1	12	8	5
Switzerland	4	0	1	3	6	11	1

Other group results

Spain v Switzerland   2-2   Switzerland v Spain   1-4

World Cup finals – SWEDEN   June 1958

So Scotland had qualified – none too convincingly – but qualified none the less. Yet Scotland's was part of a wider British assault on Sweden. The detractors of the British game were in for a shock. England had already made sure of their place at the expense of Denmark and the Republic of Ireland. Now it was Northern Ireland's turn, famously defeating Italy in Belfast. Wales had not been so fortunate – Czechoslovakia pushing them into second place – but in the space of a climactic few days in February 1958 the fortunes of all four countries were turned topsy-turvy.

In the Asia-Africa qualifying zone no country would agree to play Israel. FIFA would permit nobody except the hosts and holders to compete in the finals without first beating somebody. All the runners-up in the European sections were subjected to a lottery for the right to meet Israel. Wales' name was drawn. Her footballers won 2-0 in Tel Aviv and on 5 February by the same score in Cardiff, allowing the unlikely name of Wales to be pencilled in as the Asian-African representatives in Sweden. After all the fuss about scrapping the British qualifying zone, one quarter of the final places would now be filled by British teams. Britain looked forward for a mass assault on the World Cup, but the day after Wales qualified disaster struck.

The Münich air-crash of 6 February 1958 did more than destroy Manchester United's bright young team. It claimed the lives of four England players and ended the career of Northern Ireland's centre-half Jackie Blanchflower. Wales and Scotland lost no players, but were disrupted at managerial level. Jimmy Murphy, who doubled as Manchester United's second-in-command and Welsh team manager, had to devote his main energies to Old Trafford, inevitably to the detriment of Wales. The club's manager, Matt Busby, had recently agreed to oversee the Scotland squad in Sweden. Alas, his injuries proved too severe.

Scottish pride had taken a battering in 1950 and 1954. Even so, they prepared for Sweden with no greater thoroughness or professionalism. Team selection was still an unending saga of musical chairs. Now, as the finals approached, no replacement for Matt Busby was sought. Trainer Dawson Walker found himself in charge. Scotland had lost one manager during the 1954 finals and four years later set off without another, follies that spoke ill of the SFA and instilled little confidence in the players.

Nor did a 0-4 trouncing at Hampden by a hastily reassembled, post-Münich England team. Much of the flak was directed at skipper Tommy Docherty, who found himself dropped for the duration of the World Cup. Without a manager it was not clear who was responsible, but it was now decided that bereft of Docherty's crunching tackles Scotland would switch to a short-passing style. By way of preparation Scotland drew 1-1 at Hampden in a fiery clash with post-revolution Hungary and, a week before the gloves came off, won 2-1 in Poland in another unfriendly 'friendly'.

Geographical seeding was employed for the 1958 World Cup. The sixteen finalists were neatly batched into four regions: Britain, Western Europe, Eastern Europe, Latin America. One country from each would be placed in each pool. Fate smiled on Scotland, who found themselves bracketed with Yugoslavia, Paraguay and France. None of the three had any track record in the World Cup, none had a habit of beating Scotland, and none seemed likely to prevent Scotland's march to the quarter-finals. The crazy experiment in 1954 – of playing just two group matches – was abandoned. Scotland would face all three opponents, doubtless preferring them to England's – Brazil, the Soviet Union and Austria.

The Scotland squad was mercifully raised to the permitted twenty-two.

Name	Position	Club	Age	Caps	Goals
Tommy Younger (c)	Goalkeeper	Liverpool	28	21	–
Bill Brown	Goalkeeper	Dundee	26	–	–
Eric Caldow	Full-back	Rangers	24	10	–
Alec Parker	Full-back	Everton	22	14	–
John Hewie	Full-back	Charlton	29	11	1
Harry Haddock *	Full-back	Clyde	32	6	–
Eddie Turnbull	Wing-half	Hibernian	35	5	–
Tommy Docherty *	Wing-half	Preston	30	22	1
Ian McColl *	Wing-half	Rangers	31	14	–
Doug Cowie	Wing-half	Dundee	32	18	–
Dave Mackay	Wing-half	Hearts	23	1	–
Bobby Evans	Centre-half	Celtic	30	34	–
Graham Leggat	Winger	Aberdeen	24	5	2

Tommy Ewing *	Winger	Partick Thistle	21	2	–
Alec Scott *	Winger	Rangers	21	5	2
Stuart Imlach	Winger	Nott'm Forest	26	2	–
Archie Robertson	Inside-forward	Clyde	28	4	2
Sam Baird *	Inside-forward	Rangers	28	7	1
Jimmy Murray	Inside-forward	Hearts	25	3	–
Bobby Collins	Inside-forward	Celtic	27	19	6
Johnny Coyle *	Inside-forward	Clyde	27	–	–
Jackie Mudie	Centre-forward	Blackpool	28	14	8

| * Would not appear in 1958 finals. | *Averages* | 27.1 | 9.9 |

Though fully-manned, the squad had unusual features. Tommy Younger was named as captain, the first goalkeeper to skipper Scotland since Partick Thistle's Kenny Campbell in 1921. Bobby Evans was listed as the only centre-half, and Jackie Mudie, despite his lack of inches and deep-lying style, the only centre-forward.

The Scottish selectors' chopping and changing over the years manifested itself in the paucity of caps. The average per man – less than ten – was even lower than that of England, whose squad had had to be rebuilt following the Münich air-crash.

YUGOSLAVIA v SCOTLAND
Sunday, 8 June 1958   *Västerås – 9,591*

The Scottish party set up camp in Eskiltuna, within easy access of their three World Cup venues in eastern Sweden. The team for Yugoslavia was that which faced Hungary and Poland and contained five players unused in the qualifying rounds. Tommy Docherty was not the only wing-half to lose his edge: McColl, Mackay and Fernie were also sidelined. Eddie Turnbull, thirty-five, enjoyed a recall to international colours after an eight-year gap. He was partnered by a veteran of 1954, Dundee's Doug Cowie. Two fresh wingers had been unearthed in Aberdeen's Graham Leggat and Nottingham Forest's diminutive Stuart Imlach. They were instructed to provide the ammunition for Mudie, who had played so spiritedly in the qualifiers. Joining action-man Bobby Collins at inside-forward was Hearts' Jimmy Murray. Leggat, Imlach and Murray had all won their first caps that spring.

Scotland could take heart from their past record against Yugoslavia. The countries had met twice in recent times, drawing 2-2 in Belgrade in 1955, Scotland winning 2-0 at Hampden a year later. Whether Yugoslavia's recent 5-0 trouncing of England said more about Yugoslavia or their opponents remained to be seen, though Yugoslavia fielded ten of that side. The indications were that Yugoslavia's national eleven were less formidable than their top club, Red Star Belgrade, who had reached the semi-final of the European Cup in 1957 and the quarter-final (whence knocked out by Manchester United) in 1958. Neither Yugoslavia nor Scotland could claim to be in form: Yugoslavia had won just four of their last nine matches; Scotland, only two from seven. Nevertheless, Yugoslavia, who qualified by beating Romania 2-0 in Belgrade, looked to be the strongest team in Pool II. A win here, or even a draw, would do nicely for Scotland.

In the event, Scotland participated in a fast, undistinguished match of the kind which commentators are apt to say was 'of two halves'. Scotland wore English white, and Yugoslavia started off treating them as they had the English. They went ahead after just six minutes. Imlach had already been slowed by a knock to the knee when Veselinovic bamboozled Cowie on the right and presented Petakovic with time and space. Younger might have made more of an effort to save, and Caldow, lunging back, only narrowly failed to clear.

Yugoslavia took the game by the scruff. Caldow belted a shot from Milutinovic off the line. New boys Imlach, Leggat and Murray struggled to impose themselves. Scotland contrived just two chances before the interval. Murray shot wide and Collins, intercepting a back-pass, poked the ball straight at Beara in goal.

Shortly after the turnaround Petakovic struck Younger's post, but within minutes Scotland were level. Caldow's free kick was flicked on by Turnbull, leaving Jimmy Murray to head through the keeper's hands for Scotland's first ever goal in the World Cup finals.

Yugoslavia's earlier skills had flattered to deceive. Scotland stayed in the driver's seat till the end. The admirable Evans policed one end, while at the other Mudie and Collins constantly threatened the evergreen Zebec, who had played for FIFA against Britain eleven years earlier. The Yugoslav wing-half, Boskov, so prominent in the first half, was outshone by Turnbull in the second.

Yugoslavia did not take kindly to seeing their initiative drain away. Collins would afterwards complain of a couple of teeth loosened by Sekularac. For all Scotland's improvement, it was Yugoslavia who came nearer to breaking the deadlock when Veselinovic's thunderous drive dented an upright. Caldow earned his wages when his despairing lunge snatched the ball off Milutinovic's toe in shooting stride. Scotland's moment of hope came when Beara dropped a cross under pressure from Mudie. The ball rolled into the net but the Swiss referee, Paul Wyssling, had blown for a foul on the goalkeeper. Mudie did not agree.

Scotland had escaped defeat in the World Cup finals for the first time. They did not know it, but they would wait sixteen years to repeat that feat.

YUGOSLAVIA   (1) 1   SCOTLAND   (0) 1
    Petakovic 6   Murray 51

YUGOSLAVIA: Beara, Sijakovic, Crnkovic, Krstic, Zebec, Boskov, Petakovic, Veselinovic, Milutinovic, Sekularac, Rajkov.
SCOTLAND: Younger, Caldow, Hewie, Turnbull, Evans, Cowie, Leggat, Murray, Mudie, Collins, Imlach.

PARAGUAY v SCOTLAND
Wednesday, 11 June 1958   *Norrköping – 11,665*

Paraguay were the unknown quantity in Pool II. They were certainly unknown as far as Scotland were concerned. On the one hand, any country of one and a half million people that could beat Uruguay 5-0 and boot them out of the World Cup had to be taken seriously. On the other, Paraguay had opened their account in Sweden by letting slip a 3-2 lead to be crushed 3-7 by France. If Scotland could defeat Paraguay, which the Scottish press dismissed as a formality, they stood a healthy chance of making the quarter-finals.

The selectors, chaired by Mr Waters of St Mirren, made three changes, all necessitated by injury. Imlach's knee was still swollen, so in came Willie Fernie for his second World Cup finals. At full-back, Alec Parker (now of Everton) replaced John Hewie, while goalscoring hero Jimmy Murray saw his place taken by Archie Robertson. Fernie and Robertson were lightweights embarking on a heavyweight contest.

It was a sunny evening in Norrköping, reminding the Paraguayans of home. They lined up, short and stocky, in thick-striped shirts, with Scotland permitted to return to their accustomed navy. If the Scots, eyeing the French result, expected Paraguay to wilt, they were quickly disabused. From the off, Paraguay carved through the Scottish rearguard. Parker swiped and missed, allowing Aguero a shot that passed through Younger's legs. For the second time in the competition, Scotland would have to claw their way back from losing an early goal.

First, they needed to grow wings. Scotland seemed quite unprepared for the South Americans' fleetness of foot. The Scottish half-backs, composed entirely of thirty-somethings, had not been found out by Yugoslavia's pedestrian style. But Paraguay treated them with the disdain youthful hooligans might employ on ageing school janitors.

Encouragingly, Paraguay looked anything but secure at the back. Mudie and Collins put in testing shots, and Echague blocked Robertson's mis-hit on the line. Scotland levelled when Leggat's angled drive was parried by a flashing limb, only to rebound to Mudie, who beat Paraguay's new goalkeeper, Aguilar. Collins might then have put Scotland in front, but his shot was too high.

Back on terms, the last thing Scotland needed was to lose a goal before half-time. Younger's save from Romero seemed to have averted that fate, but with the referee checking his watch Paraguay dashed upfield. A sequence of rapier passes left Aguero to skirt Parker's effete challenge, cut inside and score. Younger half-saved, but the ball squeezed inside a post. Younger and Parker eyed each other angrily.

Paraguay needed to hold out for forty-five minutes. They were not bothered by scruple. From the restart, Lezcano scythed down danger-man Mudie. The Blackpool forward was carried off for repairs and was never the same threat when he returned. Shots passed over at either end, but the fists were more accurate when Evans and Aguero took a mutual dislike. With Fernie and Robertson ill-equipped for a physical battle, and Mudie half-crippled, it was difficult to anticipate a second Scottish equaliser. Leggat, playing with an as-yet undiagnosed broken wrist, came nearest when shooting into the side-netting.

Indeed, Paraguay increased their lead. Younger claimed a high ball, lost it, and Paraguay's outstanding player – Parodi – pounced. Younger hung his head, then lifted it as Collins leant into a twenty-yarder that screamed past Aguilar. 3-2. As the statutory ninety minutes expired Mudie and Fernie saw point-blank shots charged down, with the goalkeeper sprawled on the deck and the goal gaping.

Afterwards the blame was heaped on Younger and Parker. Someone might have mentioned the Paraguayans' speed.

PARAGUAY   (2) 3   SCOTLAND   (1) 2
  Aguero 3, 44, Parodi 75   Mudie 23, Collins 76

PARAGUAY: Aguilar, Arevalo, Echague, Achucaro, Lezcano, Villalba, Aguero, Parodi, Romero, Re, Amarilla.
SCOTLAND: Younger, Parker, Caldow, Turnbull, Evans, Cowie, Leggat, Collins, Mudie, Robertson, Fernie.

FRANCE v SCOTLAND
Sunday, 15 June 1958   *Örebro – 13,554*

While Scotland were eating humble pie against Paraguay, Yugoslavia were topping Pool II, a late goal defeating France 3-2. Reaching the quarter-finals now looked a tall order for Scotland. They needed to beat France, sure enough, and hope Yugoslavia disposed of Paraguay. If Yugoslavia did not, a play-off was the best Scotland could hope for. For their part, France could not afford a draw for fear of being dragged into a play-off themselves. Both teams had to go for goals.

Notwithstanding their later accomplishments, France entered the Sweden tournament with proper humility, hanging on to qualify with a goalless draw in Belgium. France had made no impact in previous World Cups and their pre-Sweden form was so wretched that their win over Paraguay was their first victory for many months. Further, France's all-time record against Scotland offered little encouragement, the Scots claiming five wins out of six.

As Scotland pondered their inability to *create* seven chances against Paraguay, let alone *take* seven, they might have considered the key to French success. France might not appear to have much of a team, but she boasted some awesome players – especially in attack. Raymond Kopa played in the same Real Madrid forward line as di Stefano and Gento, and on the eve of the World Cup had helped the Spanish giants win the European Cup for a third time. Just Fontaine, the swarthy, Moroccan-born, inside-forward entered the World Cup as a footballing nobody, but would leave it a footballing legend. To set things rolling he had notched a hat-trick against Paraguay, followed by a pair against Yugoslavia.

Now was the time for Scotland to ring the changes. Tommy Younger's one miserable match in two dozen marked the end of his World Cup and the end of his international career. He was replaced by his long-term understudy, Dundee's Bill Brown. The captaincy passed, not before time, to Bobby Evans. Alec Parker was shown out of the door as quickly as he was shown in – Hewie returning. Dave Mackay took Cowie's place in the engine room; Murray returned for the wrist-damaged Leggat; and Sam Baird stood in for Robertson. Mudie and one or two others selected were clearly not fit. Once again Scotland played in white.

In the leafy setting of Örebro, France's attacking flair was soon confirmed. Less than two minutes had elapsed before Brown was called into action. Further sweeping French moves ended with one shot into the side-netting and Brown thwarting Fontaine. It surprised no one when the French finally broke through. Fontaine danced round Hewie and turned the ball back into the path of Kopa, who volleyed past Brown.

Long shots by Turnbull and Baird hardly threatened an equaliser, but suddenly Scotland had a penalty. Mudie had been manhandled as he advanced to challenge the goalkeeper. When Argentine referee Juan Brozzi pointed to the spot the French went berserk. Responsibility for the kick was entrusted to Charlton's Springbok left-back, John Hewie, but it smacked against a post and rebounded into play, whereupon a frightful brawl ensued. Hewie lay prostrate, surrounded by galled Frenchmen, with Scottish reinforcements steaming to the rescue. All three of Scotland's matches had now invited improper use of fists and boots, not a distinction of which to be proud.

Following the example of Paraguay, France scored a second, killer, goal on the stroke of half-time. The scorer was Just Fontaine, fastening on to a long ball, speeding past Evans and Hewie and beating Brown as the goalkeeper came off his line. Fontaine had now scored six goals in two and a half matches. Not bad.

Scotland would be remembered for two aspects of their play during the 1958 World Cup finals. The first was the violence that flared in each of their matches; the second, their sterling second-half fight-backs. For fifteen minutes France were driven back, during which time the struggling Mudie might have levelled. The likes of Fontaine, however, could not easily be suppressed. His was a snap-shot pushed onto the bar by Brown. The save was vital, for Scotland at last scored. Baird collected Murray's pass, wriggled-free, and shot in off a post.

One sensed a glimmer of hope. Abbès swooped to snatch the ball off Mudie's toe, but France still carried the greater menace. Time and again Brown came to the rescue, never more spectacularly than when turning Piantoni's free kick against his bar. When all was said and done, Scotland could have few complaints.

FRANCE   (2) 2   SCOTLAND   (0) 1
Kopa 20, Fontaine 45   Baird 58

FRANCE: Abbès, Kaelbel, Lerond, Penverne, Jonquet, Marcel, Wisnieski, Fontaine, Kopa, Piantoni, Vincent.
SCOTLAND: Brown, Caldow, Hewie, Turnbull, Evans, Mackay, Collins, Murray, Mudie, Baird, Imlach.

So Scotland were out, once again bottom of their group, still without a win in the finals of the World Cup, and with four defeats stacked against them. The three other British teams needed play-offs to determine their fate. England went out, but Wales and Northern Ireland – to the pleasure and surprise of both – reached the quarter-finals before returning home. The Irish were dumped 0-4 by France, who emerged as the revelation of the tournament, alongside Brazil, its winners. In finishing third, France amassed twenty-three goals from six matches, with Just Fontaine claiming thirteen, an all-time record. If only he had played for Scotland.

Final positions – Pool II

	P	W	D	L	F	A	Pts
FRANCE	3	2	0	1	11	7	4
YUGOSLAVIA	3	1	2	0	7	6	4
Paraguay	3	1	1	1	9	12	3
Scotland	3	0	1	2	4	6	1

Scotland appearances and goalscorers
World Cup qualifying rounds and final competition 1958

	Apps	Goals		Apps	Goals		Apps	Goals
Caldow E	7	–	Ring T	4	–	McColl I	2	–
Collins R	7	2	Smith G	3	1	Murray J	2	1
Mudie J	7	6	Turnbull E	3	–	Parker A	2	–
Younger T	6	–	Cowie D *	2	–	Robertson A	2	1
Evans R *†	5	–	Fernie W *	2	–	Young G *†	2	–
Hewie J	5	1	Imlach S	2	–	Brown W	1	–
Baird S	4	1	Leggat G	2	–	Scott A	1	1
Docherty T *	4	–	Mackay D	2	–			

* Appeared in 1954 World Cup.
† Appeared in 1950 World Cup.

77 apps   14 goals
52 Scottish League
25 English League
23 players used

4

THE 1962 WORLD CUP

Scotland had failed to illuminate the World Cups of Switzerland and Sweden. If they hoped to do better in 1962 they would have to do so in South America, in Chile. To qualify, Scotland would need to dispose of Czechoslovakia and the Republic of Ireland in Group 8, their first three eliminators to be played within twelve days in May 1961.

Scotland's results post-Sweden were the usual motley of the good and the bad. 1959 had yielded an encouraging victory (3-2) over West Germany; 1960, depressing defeats by Poland (2-3 at Hampden), Austria (1-4) and, would you believe, Turkey (2-4)! Horror of horrors, at Wembley in April 1961 Scotland disintegrated and were swept aside 3-9, their most crushing defeat in history. The World Cup qualifiers were a mere three weeks away, a state of affairs unlikely to boost the hopes of Scotland's new manager, Ian McColl.

A convalescing Matt Busby had taken over in the wake of the 1958 World Cup, but his health soon proved unequal to the task of managing both a club and a country. Andy Beattie, forgotten man of 1954, stepped back into the breach until he, too, fell foul of the competing obligations to club and country. Nottingham Forest needed him more than Scotland, and Beattie resigned a second time.

Scotland's third manager, McColl, was given no more of a free hand than his predecessors. The word 'manager' was still a euphemism for 'part-time coach working under the whip of the Scottish selectors'. McColl was initially appointed on a game-to-game basis, and at first struggled to have any of his choices picked. He had not yet hung up his own boots, having been a reliable servant of Rangers and Scotland, for whom he featured in World Cup qualifiers against Spain and Switzerland in 1957. He stepped from trooper to sergeant-major with no administrative or managerial experience behind him, less a case of *Jim'll Fix It* than rude confirmation of the SFA's obsolescent philosophy. Mind you, Walter Winterbottom of the English FA laboured under similar restrictions. McColl was still only thirty-four and combined his nominal responsibilities for Scotland with running his own garage business. Now, in the wake of the Wembley holocaust, he had some heads to lift.

Eight years previously, England's 3-6 torment by Hungary had truncated six international careers. Scotland's numbing reverse resulted in no comparable persecution. Only two players, one of them keeper Frank Haffey, would never be given the chance to make amends. Three others would be temporarily 'rested', the others had to pick themselves up and pull themselves together.

England was responsible in another sense for Scottish discontent. Players in the English League had rid themselves of the indignity of the maximum wage. Their income was now negotiable, and England captain Johnny Haynes (of Fulham) had become British football's first £100 a week footballer. This revolution unsettled senior players in Scotland, where the maximum wage was retained. They listened wistfully to the talk of big money earned by their colleagues down south. Several Scottish players procrastinated over signing new contracts, in the hope of receiving lucrative invitations from England. The combination of a crushing defeat and financially frustrated players did not bode well for the coming World Cup campaign.

Qualifying Group 8

SCOTLAND v REPUBLIC OF IRELAND
Wednesday, 3 May 1961   *Hampden – 50,000*

This was Scotland's first-ever hello to the Irish Republic. The whipping by England notwithstanding, the Scots would have expected to cruise through. The Irish had been paired with England in the qualifying stages of the previous World Cup, losing 1-5 at Wembley, drawing 1-1 in Dublin. The Irish team, managed by Johnny Carey, all earned their living in the English League and was not short on talent. It could call upon full-back Noel Cantwell and winger Johnny Giles – both of Manchester United – and uncompromising Sunderland centre-half Charlie Hurley.

The Scottish side had been thrown into the melting pot. The selectors named a squad of fifteen players for the two Ireland matches. Only Eric Caldow, the new captain, remained from 1958. He was the last of that famous generation of Rangers defenders. Lawrie Leslie of Airdrie kept goal in place of the disgraced Frank Haffey. Bobby Shearer retained his place, winning his second cap alongside Ibrox club-mate Caldow. With Dave Mackay set to play for Spurs in the FA Cup Final the following Saturday, his place went to a Celtic new boy, Paddy Crerand. His wing-half partners were both winning second caps – Celtic's Billy McNeill and Rangers' Jim Baxter. Few could foresee it, but this half-back trio now combining for the first time would stand comparison with Scotland's best.

Curiously, it was two Wembley forwards – Denis Law and Ian St John – who were asked to 'take a rest'. Their shoes were filled by Ralph Brand of

Rangers, for his second international, and David Herd of Arsenal, the solitary Anglo, for his fourth. Three other forwards were retained – Motherwell's Pat Quinn, plus the wingers John McLeod of Hibernian and Davie Wilson of Rangers. The Ibrox contingent was five.

On a bright, sunlit evening, Scotland's early pressure soon paid off. Hurley headed out Caldow's free kick to Brand, who killed the ball and drove it back inside Noel Dwyer's right post. The lead was nearly sacrificed when George Cummins' free kick was misjudged by Leslie and slapped against the face of the bar.

Scotland doubled their advantage late in the half. Crerand and Herd created the goal, scored by Brand with a fierce shot. There was time before the intermission for Herd, who enjoyed a memorable duel with Hurley, to connect firmly with Wilson's cross. Dwyer turned the header against a post.

That save gave Ireland hope, for the Scots were not yet over the horizon. The visitors began the second half impressively, fired up by salvaging a quick goal. Giles escaped from Baxter – who would commit several unseemly fouls on his first Hampden appearance – to cross beyond the far post. Joe Haverty eluded Shearer to shoot past Leslie.

Ireland had snatched the initiative and threatened to snatch the match. They might have done so but for a magnificent Scotland goal on the counter-attack. The score read 2-1 for just eight minutes when a silky-smooth Scottish build-up was topped by an unstoppable drive by David Herd.

The Irish continued to play neat football, but a scoreline a mite harsh was forced on them in the closing stages. Davie Wilson's header brought another fine save from Dwyer, but the ball spilled from his hands and Herd tapped in.

The victory was sound enough, but learned discussion afterwards dwelt less on the score than on savouring the exciting potential shown by the wing-halves, Crerand and Baxter. The partnership would survive unbroken for eleven matches.

SCOTLAND (2) 4   REPUBLIC OF IRELAND (0) 1
Brand 14, 40, Herd 59, 85   Haverty 52

SCOTLAND: Leslie (Airdrie), Shearer (Rangers), Caldow (Rangers), Crerand (Celtic), McNeill (Celtic), Baxter (Rangers), McLeod (Hibs), Quinn (Motherwell), Herd (Arsenal), Brand (Rangers), Wilson (Rangers).
IRELAND: Dwyer (Swansea), McNally (Luton), Cantwell (Man U), McEvoy (Blackburn), Hurley (Sunderland), Saward (Huddersfield), Giles (Man U), Fogarty (Sunderland), Curtis (Ipswich), Cummins (Luton), Haverty (Arsenal).

REPUBLIC OF IRELAND v SCOTLAND

Sunday, 7 May 1961   *Dublin – 45,000*

Aches and pains had four days to disperse before Scotland set off for the return in Dublin. It was Scotland's first full international in that fair city since 1913. The need was to harvest two more points, giving them a head start of four over the Czechs, who had yet to commence their programme. Victory would not be easy: of nineteen games at Dalymount Park since the formation of the Republic, Ireland had lost but four.

Scotland had hoped to field an unchanged team, but David Herd was taken unwell at the last minute, enabling Alex Young of Everton – in time to become a Goodison legend – to reclaim the No. 9 shirt. Ireland brought in four new faces, among them Leeds' Peter Fitzgerald at centre-forward. Fitzgerald had played for Sparta Rotterdam against Rangers in the European Cup.

The ground was hard, the wind was high, and the game was a mess. Scotland played into the gale. In the third minute Brand appeared to be pulled down in the box from behind. The referee, a portly, elderly Belgian by the name of Grandain – who put one in mind of Agatha Christie's distinguished detective, Hercule Poirot – saw nothing wrong. Nor did he a minute later when Scotland went in front. Brand held off Noel Dwyer and Charlie Hurley and his flick was nodded into the net by Alex Young. Brand himself was arguably offside, Young manifestly so – as the flagging linesman confirmed. Irish shirts buzzed dementedly around the Belgian detective, but he took no notice.

Scotland's second goal was also dubious, through this time the Irish shot themselves in the foot. Rather than belt the ball anywhere, Phil Kelly lost out to Davie Wilson on the touchline. Kelly looked suitably red-faced when Wilson bore down on Dwyer, forced him to come out and squared for Young to notch his second 'open' goal.

Scottish-Irish relations were further strained when Cummins took a swipe at Crerand, who exceeded the 'eye for an eye' principle and put the boot in. Monsieur Grandain contented himself with the mildest of admonitions. The more legitimate activity of the half saw Fitzgerald's shot-on-the-run whizz over Leslie's bar; while Fagan's effort struck Leslie amidships and left him winded. At the other end, a Wilson shot was kept out by an Irish goalpost.

The second half was even drearier than the first. The conditions didn't help. Crerand and Baxter successfully deflated Ireland's attempted resurrection, though Haverty seemed to have got clear until caught by McNeill.

It was all too much for the paying Irish customers. Boos and slow handclaps resounded round the stadium. Twice the ball landed in the crowd, and twice it stayed there. That the referee was no Irishman was demonstrated near the end when McNeill up-ended Fitzgerald inside the box and saw Ireland given a free kick five yards outside.

The game was dead long before Brand's final fling, screwing the ball past Dwyer from a tight angle.

REPUBLIC OF IRELAND   (0) 0   SCOTLAND   (2) 3
Young 4, 16, Brand 86

IRELAND: Dwyer (Swansea), Kelly (Wolves), Cantwell (Man U), McEvoy (Blackburn), Hurley (Sunderland), Meagan (Everton), Fagan (Derby), Giles (Man U), Fitzgerald (Leeds), Cummins (Luton), Haverty (Arsenal).
SCOTLAND: Leslie, Shearer, Crerand, Caldow, McNeill, Baxter, McLeod, Quinn, Young, Brand, Wilson.

CZECHOSLOVAKIA v SCOTLAND
Sunday, 14 May 1961   *Bratislava – 50,000*

A week later Scotland flew to Bratislava for the third and last of their crammed fixtures. Little was it guessed, but over the next sixteen years Scotland and Czechoslovakia would be twinned time and again. At the time, the Czechs paraded an undistinguished record in the World Cup, other than reaching the 1934 Final which they lost 1-2, dubiously after extra time, to the thuggish hosts, Italy. Czechoslovakia had belonged to Scotland's group in Switzerland, 1954, but FIFA's mischievous organisation kept them apart. Czechoslovakia duly lost seven goals to Austria and Uruguay; Scotland, eight. In Sweden four years on, the Czechs sustained two defeats by Northern Ireland, the second in a play-off. Though the Czechs would present a sterner test than the gentlemen of Dublin, they seemed nothing out of the ordinary. Ominously, however, in the inaugural European Nations Cup, Czechoslovakia overcame a 0-2 defeat in Dublin to claim third place.

The current Czech side boasted two outstanding half-backs, Josef Masopust, now thirty, and the stocky Pluskal. They provided a stern yardstick by which to compare Crerand and Baxter. What Scotland quickly learnt was that the Czechs also possessed flying wingers, who tormented the full-backs from the off. It would have been a cool, pleasant evening, but for the roasting Pospichal and Masek gave Caldow and Shearer.

Czechoslovakia wanted an early goal and their wish was Pospichal's command. Baxter stood off Scherer, permitting him time and space to bring the ball deep before laying it off to Pospichal. The winger's shot from the edge of the area flew low inside Leslie's left post. Five minutes later the dazzling Czechs scored again. This time Baxter was even more culpable. His untidy challenge on Kadraba was worth half a penalty; his elbow nudging the ball another half. The Austrian referee, Herr Steiner, knew his fractions, and Kvasnak scored from the spot.

For Scotland the game was up. The Czechs looked stronger and faster in all departments. Poor Crerand came down to earth with a bump. In Dublin he was magical, in Bratislava mundane. He and Baxter learned the lesson of their lives. Ten minutes before the break Crerand and Kvasnak indulged in a bout of fisticuffs and the referee pointed dramatically to the stand. Play was held up for two minutes, partly due to the recalcitrant offenders, partly due to the referee unknowingly pointing in the wrong direction.

When order was restored, the twenty remaining players carried on as though nothing had happened, Czechoslovakia driving forward, Scotland driven back. There had been two changes to the Scottish forward line. Alex Young's double in Dublin was enough to see him dropped from the international team for five years. In the short-term, David Herd took over. Perhaps the Scottish selectors operated in five-year cycles, for Ian McMillan of Rangers – who claimed the inside-right berth ahead of Pat Quinn, bringing the Ibrox representation up to six – had been previously banished for five seasons. For Herd and McMillan, the sentence for the team's feeble collapse in Bratislava would be international banishment, not for five years, but for eternity.

Herd, at least, showed some self-respect. Two minutes before the break his solo run and shot offered a rare gesture of defiance. His disappointment at Schroiff's save was compounded by the keeper's long punt downfield. The ball dropped to Kadraba, who sped through a flimsy McNeill challenge to score dramatically from twenty yards.

The Scottish changing room at half-time must have resembled a mortuary, appropriate perhaps to the Slovan Stadium surrounded by tall, stately cypress trees. The Czech style – slow, patient, boring, until they reached the penalty area, when all was fast and furious – could not be contained, let alone countered. The second half was little more than shooting practice for the Czechs, every Scottish pass derisively cheered by the home crowd. Herd took a knock, and spent the last quarter of the match receiving treatment or hobbling on one leg. The Scottish left was ruthlessly exposed. Baxter was no defender, and behind him Caldow was overrun. Five minutes from time Pospichal blasted number four. Scotland licked their wounds, but Czechoslovakia had looked good – really good.

CZECHOSLOVAKIA (3) 4   SCOTLAND (0) 0
  Pospichal 7, 85, Kvasnak 12 pen,
  Kadraba 44

CZECHOSLOVAKIA: Schroiff, Safranek, Tichy, Pluskal, Popluhar, Masopust, Pospichal, Scherer, Kadraba, Kvasnak, Masek.
SCOTLAND: Leslie, Shearer, Caldow, Crerand, McNeill, Baxter, McLeod, McMillan, Herd, Brand, Wilson.

SCOTLAND v CZECHOSLOVAKIA
Tuesday, 26 September 1961   *Hampden – 51,590*

Mixed feelings must have plagued the Scottish camp at the thought of the Czechs' trip to Hampden – eagerness, to exact revenge, apprehension, at the thought of a second drubbing. The Scottish selectors plied the knife. Leslie, Shearer, McLeod, McMillan and Herd would not play international football again. Ralph Brand and Pat Quinn topped the scoring charts in the new season. Neither was picked.

There were recalls for Bill Brown, now of Tottenham, and for Celtic full-back Duncan McKay. The half-backs, despite the mauling in Bratislava, were retained. Four fresh forwards were introduced to bolster the solitary survivor, Davie Wilson. Three of these – John White of Tottenham, Liverpool's Ian St John, and Denis Law, now of Torino – had teamed up two years previously.

This combination was selected mindful that Czechoslovakia might come to defend. A draw would leave the Czechs needing just three points off Ireland to qualify. Certainly, they did stiffen their defence, making three changes. These included the return of full-backs Bomba and Novak, the Czech captain, now winning his sixty-fifth cap.

Given the hype, and the fact that the match was staged under Hampden's new floodlight pylons, it was hoped the elements would smile. Instead, a vicious wind gurgled round Hampden, marginally favouring the Czechs in the first half. Early goals had detonated all Group 8 matches to date, and this was no exception. In the sixth minute a back-heel from Masopust, a lay-back from Kadraba and a fierce shot from Kvasnak put the visitors in front. It was an incisive goal and the white-clad Czechs danced a ghostly tango in delight.

Like all east European teams, Czechoslovakia had been scathingly dismissed as dour, one-paced, unimaginative. The stereotype had its source in political propaganda, not footballing analysis, and was hopelessly misplaced. The Czech forwards constantly interchanged, and the whole side bristled with imagination and power. Not for one moment had they come to defend. Now, a goal behind, the calibre of the Scottish team was held up for inspection.

The Scots could not compete with their opponents' technical wizardry but they could, and did, combat Czech steel. The game surged from end to end. One moment Brown was leaping at the feet of Scherer; the next, shots from Scott and will-o'-the-wisp John White were charged down in front of Schroiff.

Scotland levelled when Law back-headed White's cross to St John, whose header ought to have been saved. Schroiff allowed it to squeeze under his body. The goal was hardly an epic, but it was all Scotland needed. They powered forward, though the Czechs continued to break out at lightning speed. Scherer's slide-rule pass set up Kadraba for a shot that Brown turned behind for a corner.

Soon after the changearound Scotland lost a dreadful goal. Popluhar's belted clearance found Scherer, who to his disbelief was permitted to stroll forty yards into the Scottish nerve centre and beat Brown with ease. It was the sort of goal to have coaches and managers tugging at their hair.

With the wind at their backs and the Hampden roar in their ears, Scotland dug deep for a spell of frenzied attacking. St John tussled with the giant Popluhar and Denis Law was a constant thorn in the Czech rump. It was Law who equalised, drilling White's cross into the net. Hampden was a cauldron, Scotland turning the screw against a cool, calm defence that refused to panic. Falling rain could not dampen Scotland's ardour. St John was felled but won an indirect free kick, not a penalty. Wilson collided with Schroiff and was crudely flattened by Kvasnak. Czechoslovakia seemed as impressive on the defence as on the offence, but with seven minutes to go Scotland took the lead for the first time. White was again the instigator, sparking the move that climaxed with Denis Law swerving clear of two tackles and rifling the ball past Schroiff at the far post.

In view of the quality of the opposition, the win was a testament to Scottish football. Denis Law had enjoyed his finest hour. If Czechoslovakia should drop a point to the Irish, Scotland would qualify. To no one's surprise the Czechs won 3-1 in Dublin, 7-1 in Prague, and would now meet Scotland for the third and decisive time – in a play-off.

SCOTLAND (1) 3   CZECHOSLOVAKIA (1) 2
  St John 21, Law 62, 83   Kvasnak 6, Scherer 51

SCOTLAND: Brown, McKay, Caldow, Crerand, McNeill, Baxter, Scott, White, St John, Law, Wilson.
CZECHOSLOVAKIA: Schroiff, Bomba, Novak, Bubernik, Popluhar, Masopust, Pospichal, Scherer, Kadraba, Kvasnak, Masek.

CZECHOSLOVAKIA v SCOTLAND
Wednesday, 29 November 1961   *Brussels – 7,000*

Czechoslovakia's twin victories over Ireland locked themselves and the Scots on six points. Goal tallies, as such, didn't count, otherwise the Czechs would have been through with something to spare. But if the play-off ended all-square, even after extra time, then goal difference would come into play. Put like that, Scotland had to win, Czechoslovakia only to draw.

The SFA tried to pull a fast one. When asked to suggest a neutral venue they came up with 'Wembley'. Perhaps they hoped the Czechs knew now't about geography, or that Scotland played there every other season. The Czechs shook their heads crossly, and Brussels was agreed upon as the site to determine the fifteenth of the sixteen final places in Chile. There were also arguments over the ball to be used and the order in which the national anthems would be played.

In the interim, Scotland had taken pleasing victories against Northern Ireland (6-1) and Wales (2-0). In the spring they would beat England to land the British Championship outright for the first time in eleven seasons.

Torino had dug their heels in, refusing to release Denis Law for the Irish and Welsh matches, though relenting for the Czech play-off. But it was touch and go. The wingers Wilson and Scott were ruled out by injury and replaced by Ralph Brand, playing out of position, and Dundee's Hugh Robertson. Bill Brown was also unfit, handing his jersey to Eddie Connachan of Dunfermline. For Connachan and Robertson, it would be their first and last cap. The other newcomers, both introduced against Wales, were right-back Alec Hamilton and centre-half Ian Ure – both from a Dundee outfit on its way to the Scottish title. The average age of the Scotland eleven was just twenty-three.

Three of the Czechs' four changes were in defence, Hledik becoming the third right-back to face Scotland in as many matches. As before, the bulk of the side were drawn from the Czech champions, the Army team, Dukla Prague.

Brussels' Heysel Stadium enticed no more than 7,000 spectators, among them a contingent of Scottish soldiers, to view a game that, with so much at stake, could euphemistically be described as 'hard'. The Czechs were equipped for all contingencies. If they needed to play, they could play; if they needed to kick, they required no lessons from anyone.

For once, the game did not conjure an early goal. Law's electric showing at Hampden guaranteed that he was securely padlocked. Half-time was barely ten minutes distant when St John was fouled – not for the first time – by Popluhar. Baxter took the free kick and St John, spurting forward, headed home.

Now the Czechs had to attack. The game grew rougher, too rough for the lightweight John White, whose skills on a heavy pitch were neutralised by the iron men of the red army. Ian Ure emerged as equally ferric, stamping himself with his conspicuous fair hair as Scotland's most visible source of resistance. St John splendidly held the line, despite the lack of service from his shackled wingers. Early in the second half he found room for a shot, but the ball flew straight at Schroiff.

The rain-sodden minutes were slowly consumed, but twenty still remained when the Czechs drew level. A backs-to-the-wall Scottish defence conceded a string of corners. From the fifth, right-back Hledik planted a header past Connachan. The goal was a near-replica of St John's, and had an astonishing sequel. Less than a minute later Scotland were awarded a disputed free kick. Brand flighted the ball for St John to side-foot into the net.

It was, or should have been, a killer goal. Czechoslovakia had to start all over again. Had they the heart to emulate the Scots and twice come from behind? Eight minutes remained when Scotland learned the answer. Kvasnak's shot ricocheted around the penalty area. It was partially cleared to Scherer who slammed it into goal, whence it flew out off a stanchion. 2-2.

Scotland were giving their all. Law drove inches too high, and in the first minutes of extra time the ill-treated White summoned the energy to whack the ball from twenty yards against the junction of post and bar. White's near-miss would provide Scotland with an agonising 'if only', for Czechoslovakia were now firing on all cylinders. It surprised few neutrals when Pospichal volleyed past Connachan, nor when on the stroke of half-time Kvasnak blasted a long range shot in off the bar. The second period of extra time was superfluous.

Scotland had done themselves proud. They had been just eight sickening minutes from Chile. But the outcome was just. Ian McColl was honest enough to admit: 'Even when we were ahead twice we were never in command in the same way we had been at Hampden while we were behind.' *The Times* confessed: 'The Czechs came out like thoroughbreds when it really mattered. The best side won, and won worthily.' It was *The Times*, too, which, by implication, offered the finest praise for Scotland and the most astute prophecy: 'Czechoslovakia will take some stopping in Chile.'

CZECHOSLOVAKIA (0) 4	SCOTLAND (1) 2
Hledik 70, Scherer 82,	St John 35, 71
Pospichal 95, Kvasnak 105	*After extra time (2-2 after 90 minutes)*

CZECHOSLOVAKIA: Schroiff, Hledik, Tichy, Pluskal, Popluhar, Masopust, Pospichal, Scherer, Kvasnak, Kucera, Jelinek.
SCOTLAND: Connachan, Hamilton, Caldow, Crerand, Ure, Baxter, Brand, White, St John, Law, Robertson.

Czechoslovakia did indeed take some stopping in Chile. They forced a draw with defending champions Brazil, who went on to eliminate England 3-1 at the quarter-final stage. The Czechs overcame Hungary, then Yugoslavia in the semis to face Brazil again, this time in the World Cup Final. The Czechs took the lead, too, before eventually succumbing 1-3. Measured by these standards, Scotland's exclusion was easier to take.

Qualifying Group 8

	P	W	D	L	F	A	Pts
CZECHOSLOVAKIA *	4	3	0	1	16	5	6
Scotland	4	3	0	1	10	7	6
Republic of Ireland	4	0	0	4	3	17	0

* Czechoslovakia qualified after play-off with Scotland.

Other group results
Rep Ireland v Czechoslovakia 1-3   Czechoslovakia v Rep Ireland   7-1

Scotland appearances and goalscorers
World Cup qualifying rounds 1962

	Apps	Goals		Apps	Goals		Apps	Goals
Baxter J	5	–	Shearer R	3	–	Hamilton A	1	–
Caldow E *	5	–	Herd D	2	2	McKay D	1	–
Crerand P	5	–	Law D	2	2	McMillan I	1	–
Brand R	4	3	Quinn P	2	–	Robertson H	1	–
McNeill W	4	–	St John I	2	3	Scott A *	1	–
Wilson D	4	–	White J	2	–	Ure I	1	–
Leslie L	3	–	Brown W *	1	–	Young A	1	2
McLeod J	3	–	Connachan E	1	–			

* Appeared in 1958 World Cup.

55 apps   12 goals
45 Scottish League
8 English League
2 Italian League
23 players used

5

THE 1966 WORLD CUP

The 1966 World Cup finals were to be staged as near as could be, in England. For that reason above all others, it was imperative for Scotland to qualify. Never before or since would any British team be so favoured to shine, or even to win the Jules Rimet trophy. Wembley, of course, was a second home to Scotland's international footballers. They played there bi-annually. The half dozen supporting stadiums to be called upon were familiar stomping grounds to those players earning their crust in the English League.

Scotland had come so close to qualifying for Chile that they keenly awaited news of the current opposition. They found themselves allocated to the same group as Finland, Poland and Italy, with just one to qualify. Italy, the seeded team, were probably happier with the draw than Scotland.

Scotland's international exhibitions since those stirring battles with Czechoslovakia gave few grounds for cheer – with one dazzling exception. In 1962 Scotland lost at home to Uruguay, then in 1963 strung together a sequence of results that made sense only to a psychologist. In April they won worthily at Wembley with ten men after Eric Caldow's international career was ended by a broken leg. In May they defeated Austria at Hampden 4-1 in an abandoned match, the latest in a string of ill-tempered clashes between the two nations. In June Scotland embarked on an excursion to Norway, the Irish Republic, and Spain. They slumped to a 3-4 defeat in Bergen, against one of Europe's weakest sides; followed this by losing 0-1 in Dublin (permitting the Irish belated consolation for two recent World Cup defeats); and then, extraordinarily, demolished Spain 6-2 in Madrid. To this day that scoreline stands out as probably Scotland's finest.

Other notable scores were Scotland 6 Norway 1, which made the defeat in Bergen all the more culpable, and West Germany 2 Scotland 2 in Hanover. In two years' time the Germans would reach the World Cup Final.

It was a pity Ian McColl could not expose his team to competitive action, for alone of the British nations Scotland turned her back on the 1964 European Nations Cup. He led his troops into the new World Cup campaign just a couple of weeks after they had slipped to a 2-3 defeat in Cardiff.

Qualifying Group 8

SCOTLAND v FINLAND

Wednesday, 21 October 1964   *Hampden – 54,442*

The Scotland team that failed honourably against Czechoslovakia was not one to be lightly discarded. Of the players who carried Scotland so near in 1961, nine were still pulling on the navy in 1964 and beyond. Of these, Alec Hamilton, Jim Baxter, and Denis Law (happily ensconced with Manchester United) were named to face Finland at Hampden. Baxter, now twenty-five, was already being talked about as one of Scotland's greats. Slim Jim's ball skills had taunted the English at Wembley in 1963, and any player to do that was taken to Scottish hearts. This would be Baxter's last season at Ibrox, a season prematurely terminated by a broken leg sustained in Vienna in the European Cup.

As for Denis Law, he was already a footballing phenomenon. Whereas Baxter's memory would be cherished only north of the border – the player failing to live up to expectations when moving south – Law's monument straddles Scotland, Italy and England. Still only twenty-four, the audacious, crowd-pleasing, salmon-leaping Law had first been capped in October 1958 when he was just eighteen. He scored on his debut, naturally. Six years on, he was in sight of Hughie Gallacher's twenty-three goal record for Scotland.

As for the mortals around him, Campbell Forsyth of Kilmarnock kept goal and Jim Kennedy of Celtic enjoyed a run at left-back. Paddy Crerand still had some international mileage in him, but for this match his shirt went to another of Scotland's crop of wing-halves, John Greig of Rangers. In attack, Celtic's Stevie Chalmers and Jimmy Johnstone were both winning second caps. No. 8 was Davie Gibson of Leicester, while No. 11 was none other than Alec Scott, now with Everton, about to see action in his third World Cup.

There was one debutant, centre-half Jackie McGrory of Kilmarnock – Billy McNeill, Ian Ure and Ron Yeats all injured. The 'Killies' dual representation was a tribute to the side that finished second in the league twice running and which would shortly finish first. The selectors were evidently looking to the future: six players had fewer than five caps to their names.

As for the Finns, they were expected to be the whipping boys of Group 8. The best that could be said of them was that they had just claimed the Scandinavian Championship for the first time in fifty-six years – though in doing so they had contrived to lose to Norway. Scotland had faced Finland just the once, when they had scraped through 2-1 in Helsinki in preparation for the 1954 World Cup finals. The Finnish side showed only one professional, Peltonen, who played for Hamburg in the West German Bundesliga. The side was handicapped by the unavailability of both first-choice wingers. That meant

6ft 3in centre-forward Tolsa was likely to be starved of service.

Finnish frailty was exposed after just two minutes, thanks to a goal of comic proportions. Scott took a corner, Halme missed it, and Law swung a hopeful boot. The ball looped gently goalwards where two line-bound defenders were perfectly positioned to clear. They somehow failed to do so.

The Finnish goal endured siege conditions. Halme saved at Law's feet, Rinne came perilously close to putting through his own net, and Chalmers fired wide from close in. To kill off any thoughts of a fight-back, Scotland scored twice more in the closing minutes of the half. Gibson's cross was headed home by Chalmers. When Law was presented with a gaping goal he hit the bar. Law's frustration was eased when Gibson's shot seemed to take Halme by surprise.

At 3-0 the game was over, but there remained an opportunity for Scotland to display a killer streak and stack up a mountain of goals. The opportunity was squandered. The Scottish players indulged in exhibition stuff, content to tickle the opposition rather than murder them. Baxter became casual beyond belief, and Denis Law, improbably, tried to score with a back-heel. Scotland had their impertinent faces slapped twenty minutes from time when Peltonen's swerving shot from nowhere bamboozled Forsyth, who helped the ball into the far corner. It wasn't cheers that greeted the Scottish players as they trooped off at the end, but whistles.

SCOTLAND   (3) 3   FINLAND   (0) 1
Law 2, Chalmers 38,   Peltonen 70
Gibson 42

SCOTLAND: Forsyth (Kilmarnock), Hamilton (Dundee), Kennedy (Celtic), Greig (Rangers), McGrory (Kilmarnock), Baxter (Rangers), Johnstone (Celtic), Gibson (Leicester), Chalmers (Celtic), Law (Man U), Scott (Everton).
FINLAND: Halme, Makipaa, Kautonen, Holmqvist, Rinne, Valtonen, Jarvi, Peltonen, Tolsa, Syrjavaara, Hyvarinen.

POLAND v SCOTLAND
Sunday, 23 May 1965   *Katowice – 95,000*

The first hurdle, small though it was, had been successfully cleared. Now the Scottish Goldilocks was about to tackle the medium-sized bowl in the shape of Poland. Seven months had passed, during which the Scots had played Northern Ireland (3-2) and England (2-2) in the Home Internationals and Spain in a 'friendly'. Spain avoided a repetition of the 2-6 spanking two years earlier by forcing a spiteful goalless draw at Hampden. Behind the scenes, however, trouble was brewing for Scotland. A week before the team faced Poland, as the squad prepared at Largs, Ian McColl was asked to resign – in plain man's language, sacked. His record was no disgrace. Enjoying a crop of fine players on which to draw, McColl's teams had won sixteen out of twenty-seven matches. Jock Stein, three months into managing Celtic, stepped forward on a caretaker basis. He agreed to administer Scotland's World Cup programme until a long-term successor to McColl was appointed.

Only three of the team that beat Finland survived to face Poland in Katowice – Hamilton, Greig and Denis Law, now acclaimed as European Footballer of the Year. Of the remainder, Forsyth, Kennedy and Gibson had hung up their international boots. Bill Brown was back to keep goal. An able replacement for Eric Caldow had been discovered in Chelsea's Eddie McCreadie. With Baxter still crocked, Paddy Crerand (now playing alongside Law at Old Trafford) filled in, with Billy McNeill again performing the stopper role. Wee veteran Bobby Collins, now a driving force with mighty Leeds United, was back for his last international, having first played for Scotland back in 1950! Willie Henderson of Rangers returned on the right wing. The ongoing search for a quality centre-forward alighted for the moment on Neil Martin of Hibernian.

Poland were another of those east European sides who blew hot and cold. After the dramas against Czechoslovakia, no way would the Poles be under-estimated. Past results were even: Scotland winning 2-1 in Warsaw in 1958; losing 2-3 at Hampden two years later. In 1962 Northern Ireland had beaten Poland home and away in the European Nations Cup. Unless Poland had improved dramatically, Scotland could reasonably expect some reward.

The weather was worse than foul. The Slaski Stadium in the heart of Poland's coalmining belt suffered a climatic interpretation of Dante's *Inferno*. The driving rain turned Poland's white shirts an insipid grey. Undaunted, it was the hosts who showed the early superiority, surging through the puddles like power-driven swans. In the first minute Pohl's shot skidded off Brown's chest. McNeill was on hand to clear. Scotland seemed content to contain, and their 4-3-3 formation, anchored by Collins, Crerand and Law in midfield, designed to that end. During this first period the only danger to the Polish goal came when McCreadie forced a save from the otherwise idle Szymkowiak.

A goalless first half did not displease Scotland, but the complexion of the game changed within five minutes of the turnaround. Lentner escaped the clutches of Greig and Hamilton to fire past Brown. There was now no profit in defence. Law, in any case, had stagnated in midfield, far from his natural habitat. Now he pushed forward. He had topped the scoresheets in the English first division and his country needed his magic.

With Martin and Hughes switching positions, the change in Scottish fortunes was spectacular. The one-way traffic was soon reversed. Law powered in a header from Henderson's cross, only to see Szymkowiak touch the ball onto the post.

Law did better next time. Collins' cross was only half-cleared. Henderson nodded the ball back in, the goalkeeper strained to reach it, and Law punished his mishandling. 1-1. There was little else to report. Long before the end the uncovered terraces were drained of people. Most of the bedraggled spectators had long since left for the warmth of their own homes.

POLAND   (0) 1   SCOTLAND   (0) 1
Lentner 50   Law 76

POLAND: Szymkowiak, Szczepanski, Ozlizio, Bazan, Gmoch, Grzegorczyk, Banas, Nieroba, Liberda, Pohl, Lentner.
SCOTLAND: Brown, Hamilton, McCreadie, Greig, McNeill, Crerand, Henderson, Collins, Martin, Law, Hughes.

FINLAND v SCOTLAND
Thursday, 27 May 1965   *Helsinki – 20,162*

The result in Poland was adjudged a point gained rather than lost, especially as the Italians had done no better themselves. The Scottish party embarked on an arduous journey by bus, train and plane to Helsinki for the return fixture with Finland.

Reflecting the example of Alf Ramsey in England, Jock Stein insisted on a greater say in team-selection. The manager engineered a more attack-minded formation. Thirty-two year old Bobby Collins stepped aside for Hibernian's Willie Hamilton, overlooking the pressing claim for inclusion of young, abrasive Billy Bremner. John 'Yogi' Hughes, suffering from a heavy cold, was replaced by Davie Wilson, for whom this would be the last of his twenty-two caps. The Finnish side, looking like prisoners with their uniform crewcuts, retained just five of the side beaten at Hampden.

Helsinki's Olympic Stadium saw Scotland, playing in white, suffer an immediate setback. After five minutes they might have been two goals up; instead they found themselves a goal behind. The home team's first attack brought a corner, from which Hyvarinen scored with defenders threshing around. Scotland scorned a chance to level when Henderson was tripped by Rinne and won a penalty. Law was entrusted with the kick, but his shot came back off the inside of a post.

The play was scrappy, though the Finns enjoyed their share of the good moments. Scotland looked uneasy, both at their own inability to score and at the threat presented by the blond Peltonen. It was left to Crerand and Law to inject any quality into Scotland's play. Eight minutes from half-time Crerand won the ball and spread it wide to Law. Willie Hamilton dummied Law's cross for Wilson to score.

At the start of the second half Nasman pulled off a flying save at the top corner from Willie Hamilton. After fifty minutes Crerand crossed for Law, who tee'd up the ball for Greig, twenty yards out, to smash Scotland's second goal. With Scotland now in control the game became more and more untidy. The East German referee blew his whistle frequently and capriciously. Finland were on the receiving end but Scotland, you might say, were unable to finnish the Finns. The hosts might have saved the game when a frightful mix-up in front of Brown threatened danger until Law cleared. Law would afterwards be voted 'man of the match'. His prize was a silver spoon. Better than a wooden one.

Stein was pleased with the result, less so with the referee and most of the Scottish forwards. The following month Italy arrived in Helsinki with Scotland hoping for an upset. Italy won 2-0.

FINLAND (1) 1   SCOTLAND (1) 2
Hyvarinen 5   Wilson 37, Greig 50

FINLAND: Nasman, Kautonen, Makipaa, Holmqvist, Rinne, Heinonen, Kumpalampi, Peltonen, Hyvarinen, Ruotsalsainen, Nuoranen.
SCOTLAND: Brown, Hamilton, McCreadie, Crerand, McNeill, Greig, Henderson, Law, Martin, Hamilton, Wilson.

SCOTLAND v POLAND
Wednesday, 13 October 1965   *Hampden – 107,580*

The new season did not commence auspiciously for Scotland, who succumbed to a 2-3 defeat in Belfast just eleven days before the Poles turned out at Hampden. Poland were in even worse spirits. Their 0-2 reverse in Finland made qualification nigh-on impossible. But with matches against Scotland and Italy to come, Poland could still be king-maker if not king. In terms of results so far, Scotland had done all that was required of them. With two matches against Italy to round off the group, it was vital that Scotland sealed Poland's elimination. In other circumstances, the Poles might have been content with a draw. The defeat in Finland meant only a win would keep their flickering hopes still flickering.

Jock Stein had sought to stabilise the Scottish line-up. Eight players were picked for their third World Cup match under his charge. Tottenham's Alan Gilzean had been in and out of the No. 9 shirt for two years. Now he pulled it on for the first time in the World Cup. Billy Bremner was given another opportunity to show he could do for his country what he could for his club. Presented with his international baptism on the left wing was eighteen-year old Rangers starlet Willie Johnston. He was preferred to John Hughes. The Poles made five changes from the first match.

Scotland began as if the occasion was too much. Brown came to the rescue three times in the opening minutes, with Faber out on the left looking especially troublesome. As Scotland steadied the ship, Law was given half a chance by Bremner, and after fourteen minutes McNeill put his team in front. Henderson's corner was bungled by Kornek, under pressure from Gilzean. The keeper slapped the ball towards McNeill who chested it down and hoofed it into the net.

Suitably encouraged, Scotland began to open up. Young Willie Johnston – who six months previously was playing in the Scotland youth side – led his full-back on a first-half merry-go-round. When Henderson was crash-tackled by Gmoch, the referee incensed the crowd by awarding an indirect free kick instead of a penalty. Then Kornek smothered the ball at Gilzean's feet, and on the half-time whistle Gilzean's header forced a springing save from the Polish goalkeeper.

Scotland had their tails up and looked good for more goals. But somebody must have put Mogadon in their orange juice. They emerged for the second half to play like zombies. All cohesion went, and Scotland were soon reduced to chasing frantically the shadows of their opponents. Poland sported socks with narrow hoops, giving them the appearance of miniature zebras scampering around the grasslands of Hampden. Playing 4-2-4, with Liberda reinforcing Nieroba in midfield, the zebras reduced Scotland to lumbering wildebeest. Crerand and Bremner, vital cogs in the Scottish boiler-room, lost the rhythm of the game, and Law dropped back to swap jobs with Bremner. Two goalbound shots by Pohl were intercepted – one by Brown's hands, the other by his knees. Law's despairing 'tackle' on Nieroba appeared a trifle high: it took the Pole on the neck.

The Hampden throngs rubbed their eyes in disbelief. Their frantic whistles grew in intensity. Somehow the Scottish goal was spared. As the game entered its final phase Scotland still clung to McNeill's earlier goal. Hampden chewed through its finger nails, eyes on watches rather than the field. Eight minutes to go, seven, six. Then Alec Hamilton lost possession to Faber. The winger's cross to the far post escaped McCreadie and found Liberda in sweet isolation. He pulled the ball down and blasted it over Brown's shoulder. 1-1.

Hampden grimaced at the prospect of a vital point dropped; the whistles instantly quelled. Scotland kicked off dejectedly. The ball bobbled out of play. When it returned, Sadek propelled himself through a bemused Scottish defence to shoot past Brown. The silence told its own story as the zebras celebrated with an abridged Polka. Somewhere up in the stands the watching Italian spies were hugging each other.

The performance – contrasting the two halves – was as unreal as anything most Scots could remember. The *Glasgow Herald* put its tears into words: 'From a first half of interest and enthusiasm, Scotland tumbled to a level of incompetence and a condition of total ruin which were incredible to see. A bed of nails is like a feather mattress to anyone who watches Scottish teams nowadays.' Not that anyone noticed, but Scotland's first home defeat in the World Cup for eleven years was the first by a side boasting a majority of Anglos. It was all the fault of England. More to the point, Denis Law had seriously crocked his right knee, and would never be quite the same again.

SCOTLAND (1) 1   POLAND (0) 2
   McNeill 14   Liberda 84, Sadek 86

SCOTLAND: Brown, Hamilton, McCreadie, Crerand, McNeill, Greig, Henderson, Bremner, Gilzean, Law, Johnston.
POLAND: Kornek, Szczepanski, Ozlizio, Anczok, Gmoch, Nieroba, Sadek, Szoltyski, Liberda, Pohl, Faber.

SCOTLAND v ITALY
Tuesday, 9 November 1965   *Hampden – 100,393*

Those two late goals had reduced Scotland's World Cup hopes to pulp. When Poland went on to crash 1-6 in Italy, some measure of Scotland's task against the *azzurri* became clear. Group 8 was complete apart from Scotland's two matches with Italy. If Scotland won both they would qualify. They needed three points to force a play-off. Anything less and it was goodbye England '66.

Jock Stein was not one for panicking, but drastic team surgery could not be gainsaid. Alec Hamilton's international career was terminated; so was the redoubtable Crerand's. For these crucial matches two new caps were awarded, to Ronnie McKinnon of Rangers – when Billy McNeill withdrew with a knee injury – and to Celtic's Bobby Murdoch. John Greig turned makeshift full-back. With McCreadie serving a suspension and replaced by Rangers' Davie Provan, the entire Scottish back line was recast.

Jim Baxter, of course, had broken a leg the previous year. He had transferred to Sunderland under the stewardship of Ian McColl but had found it difficult to acclimatise. This, however, was his stage. Slim Jim was irresistibly recalled and handed the captaincy. Denis Law, for all his knowledge of Italian football and the fact that he was now Scotland's top scorer in history, had gone off the boil. He found himself dropped for only the second time in three years, permitting Sunderland's Neil Martin to return for his final cap. The experience of John Hughes was preferred to the dash of Willie Johnston. All told, just five players were retained from the numbing Polish experience.

Italy had won the World Cup in 1934 and 1938 but, strangely, had failed to assert themselves since then. They had found themselves knocked out in the first round in 1950, 1954 and 1962, and in 1958 had failed even to reach the finals, when Northern Ireland had been their conquerors. This would be the first Scottish-Italian meeting for thirty-four years, since Scotland journeyed to a 0-3 defeat in Rome in 1931.

It was the strength and reputation of Italian clubs that impressed more than any tangible success of the national team. The two Milanese giants – AC and Internazionale – had carried off the European Cup in 1963, '64 and '65, and six of the current Italian side played for one or the other, including the renowned Facchetti, Mazzola and Rivera. Facchetti and Henderson would resume a personal acquaintance, having squared up twice in the European Cup.

The Italian side was managed by Edmondo Fabbri, who enjoyed the luxury of a month free from league distractions in which to prepare. Hampden's piercing floodlights beamed down on ninety minutes of Scottish passion. Given the shape of the group, it surprised no one to find Italy – broad hoop encircling their chests – funnelling back into defence; nor that Gilzean and Martin were marked so closely as to border on personal indecency. With no winger of his own to mark, Provan ventured up the left at will. His shot after sixteen minutes was sliced by Facchetti over his own bar. If more of the play was concentrated inside the Italian half, the more dangerous moments arose at the other end. The tall, nippy Barison gave Greig a hard time, and the speed of Sandro Mazzola kept McKinnon on his toes. Bremner fought to curb Gianni Rivera. Barison's header towards the top corner was nodded out by Greig. For Scotland, Baxter shone like a beacon light, illuminating all his team's inventive moves. The final memory of a stirring half was Baxter's pile-driver that speared inches wide.

After the break Italy continued to frustrate, soaking up shots, crosses, headers and lobs like a human sponge. Yet Italy had their moments. Lodetti's drive beat the thigh-strapped Brown but was thumped clear by Greig, and Mazzola's flick squeezed under the goalkeeper but past a post. Rivera then escaped Bremner to shoot into the side netting. Of the two keepers, Brown had come nearer than Negri to losing a goal.

Fans were drifting away as Scotland mustered one final surge. Gilzean's point-blank effort was parried by the goalkeeper. With less than two minutes on the clock, and the Italians content to hump the ball into the crowd, Baxter slipped a precision pass through the Italian defence. Greig, who had already distinguished himself with two goal-line clearances, galloped through to crash the ball low inside Negri's left post.

Hampden went potty. At the end the crowd refused to disperse, demanding an encore. The players returned to acknowledge the cheers and chaired Greig from the pitch. Scotland were, after all, still alive in the World Cup, but the *Glasgow Herald* was in no mood to get carried away: 'Before the blood rushes to one's head it is sobering to recall the pattern of the 88 minutes which went before the goal. There were very few of them in which Scotland looked capable of penetrating a superbly organised Italian defence.'

Joy for Scotland. John Greig scores a late winner. Lodetti, No. 7, looks dejected. (v Italy)

SCOTLAND (0) 1   **ITALY (0) 0**
  Greig 88

SCOTLAND: Brown, Greig, Provan, Murdoch, McKinnon, Baxter, Henderson, Bremner, Gilzean, Martin, Hughes.
ITALY: Negri, Burgnich, Facchetti, Guarneri, Salvadore, Rosato, Lodetti, Bulgarelli, Mazzola, Rivera, Barison.

ITALY v SCOTLAND
Tuesday, 7 December 1965   *Naples – 79,000*

Greig's life-saver meant that Scotland had achieved the first of two necessary victories over Italy. The second, away from home, was likely to be yet harder. Scotland would either have to win outright, or draw, and then beat the Italians in a play-off decider.

Stein was preoccupied by the question of which objective to aim for. Should he instruct his side to frustrate the Italians and play for a draw, or go for broke and hope for victory? This dilemma was eventually resolved by external factors. Brown and McNeill were already out, injured. They were joined on the casualty list by Jim Baxter, so influential at Hampden. On the Saturday, Bill

Shankly and Matt Busby – the Scottish managers of Liverpool and Manchester United – refused to release players from league engagements. Injuries that day were sustained by key members of the Scottish squad. None was more publicised than that to Denis Law, though it was doubtful in any case whether he would have been reinstated.

The Scotland manager found his squad of twenty-two cut down to fifteen – fourteen, when hours before kick-off Willie Henderson ruled himself out. Stein could still have fielded a side recognisable in terms of defence, midfield and attack, but he opted to withdraw Gilzean from the No. 9 shirt and hand it to Ron Yeats, the Liverpool centre-half. Fears that Yeats would act as a stopgap striker were removed once play began, when he took his place alongside McKinnon as a second orthodox stopper. There were no more doubts about the game Scotland would try to play.

From the start, the Scotland team looked unwieldy, a situation not entirely excused by the injury crisis. Adam Blacklaw had last played in goal for his country two and a half years previously. McCreadie's suspension had been served, allowing him to return and permit Greig to move back into midfield. Included in the side were two players – Charlie Cooke of Dundee and Jim Forrest of Rangers – who had made their debuts a month earlier in beating Wales. Forrest and Hughes were all Scotland had to show for an emasculated attack. If Scotland should lose a goal, goodness knows how they could make one themselves. Of the team as a whole, only John Greig had earned more than seven caps, an extraordinary state of affairs that did not augur well.

Edmondo Fabbri had made three changes, one of them in goal. Albertosi stood in for the absent Negri. Barison was dropped, punishment for allowing Greig to advance unattended to score at Hampden.

Naples, and its San Paolo Stadium, was regarded in Italy as something of a soccer outpost, far from the prosperous and fashionable cities to the north. On a wet, windy night, the early minutes passed without alarm for the white-shirted Scots. The visitors extracted the Italian sting to such an extent that the stadium was drained of atmosphere, the spectators huddled and hushed under a myriad of umbrellas. Scotland monotonously retreated, slowing the pace of the game. There was little action to report until the thirty-eighth minute. McCreadie shaped to clear Rivera's cross, only to miscue the ball, which fell for Pascutti to score from close in. Cushions rained down in celebration. McCreadie's inexplicable error had effectively put Scotland out of the World Cup, for they were hardly equipped to exert pressure on Italy's formidable defence. Before the goal, Italy had looked tense and irritable: now they imposed an iron grip. Scotland failed to create a whiff of a chance throughout the match.

Even so, only sixteen minutes remained when Italy settled the outcome. Blacklaw collided with a defender in punching clear. Before he could recover, Facchetti – twenty-five yards distant – flighted the ball back under the crossbar.

Blacklaw leapt upwards and back but the ball dipped beyond his groping fingers and into the net.

At the death Rivera's lateral flick was angled home by Mora to complete Scotland's anti-climactic exit from the 1966 World Cup. Afterwards, Albertosi, the goalkeeper, was asked what had been his most anxious moment. 'When Yeats dived on me,' he replied. Enough said. Up on the cold, wet terraces of the San Paolo Stadium the night was pierced by constellations of bonfires.

ITALY (1) 3   SCOTLAND (0) 0
Pascutti 38, Facchetti 74, Mora 85

ITALY: Albertosi, Burgnich, Facchetti, Rosato, Salvadore, Lodetti, Mora, Bulgarelli, Mazzola, Rivera, Pascutti.
SCOTLAND: Blacklaw, Provan, McCreadie, Murdoch, McKinnon, Greig, Forrest, Bremner, Yeats, Cooke, Hughes.

So, the euphoria of Hampden was followed by the despair of Naples. But Italy's jubilation would also be transient. Within seven months they were to know shattering defeat at the hands of North Korea and ignominious exit from the World Cup finals. Tomatoes and ridicule awaited their return home. Meanwhile, Scotland could only look on in frustration as England, playing every match at Wembley and latterly without wingers, lifted the World Cup. How far Scotland would have reached would remain a question without an answer.

Qualifying Group 8

	P	W	D	L	F	A	W	D	L	F	A	Pts
		Home					**Away**					
ITALY	6	3	0	0	15	2	1	1	1	2	1	9
Scotland	6	2	0	1	5	3	1	1	1	3	5	7
Poland	6	1	2	0	8	1	1	0	2	3	9	6
Finland	6	1	0	2	3	4	0	0	3	2	16	2

Other group results

Poland v Italy	0-0	Finland v Poland	2-0
Italy v Finland	6-1	Poland v Finland	7-0
Finland v Italy	0-2	Italy v Poland	6-1

Scotland appearances and goalscorers
World Cup qualifying rounds 1966

	Apps	Goals		Apps	Goals		Apps	Goals
Greig J	6	2	Baxter J *	2	–	Gibson D	1	1
Brown W *†	4	–	Gilzean A	2	–	Hamilton W	1	–
Hamilton A	4	–	McKinnon R	2	–	Johnston W	1	–
Henderson W	4	–	Murdoch R	2	–	Johnstone J	1	–
Law D *	4	2	Provan D	2	–	Kennedy J	1	–
McCreadie E	4	–	Blacklaw A	1	–	McGrory J	1	–
Bremner W	3	–	Chalmers S	1	1	Scott A *†	1	–
Crerand P *	3	–	Collins R †	1	–	Wilson D *	1	1
Hughes J	3	–	Cooke C	1	–	Yeats R	1	–
Martin N	3	–	Forrest J	1	–			
McNeill W *	3	1	Forsyth C	1	–			

---

* Appeared in 1962 World Cup.   *66 apps   8 goals*
† Appeared in 1958 World Cup.   *39 Scottish League*
                                                  27 English League
                                                  31 players used

---

6

THE 1970 WORLD CUP

If Scotland intended to win the World Cup in 1970 they would have to perform far from the familiar climate and conditions of Britain, and travel to Mexico with its hazards of heat and altitude. Not being seeded in their qualifying section, Scotland were also bound to face one of Europe's strongest sides. Too true. Scotland should get the better of Cyprus; they might get the better of Austria; but could they overcome West Germany? The Germans had contested the 1966 World Cup Final, taken England to extra time, and lost because a Russian linesman was deluded into thinking that Hurst's shot off the crossbar bounced behind the goal-line.

As seems distressingly familiar to report, there was much despondency in Scotland's results twixt World Cups. Of thirteen matches played prior to the curtain raiser against Austria in 1968, Scotland had won just four. These were against Northern Ireland, Wales, Denmark – and England at Wembley, where Scotland inflicted on the world champions their first defeat since their coronation. Scottish fans lived off the Wembley triumph, sucking it dry of any long-term meaning. It flattered to deceive that all was well, when the truth was more sobering. Scotland were embarrassed at Hampden by England, Holland, Portugal and the Soviet Union. This string of defeats said more about the worth of the Scottish team than did the isolated success at Wembley, which took on the qualities of an oasis in a Scottish desert.

Circumstances also soured the taste of that Wembley victory. Scotland had deigned to compete for the 1968 European Championship. British access to the quarter-finals was reserved for the Home International champions over two successive seasons, 1966-67 and 1967-68. In that context, Scotland's Wembley triumph was wiped out by defeat in Belfast, and England finished top of the pile.

What helped make 1967 memorable for Scottish football was that, no sooner had Scotland beaten England, than Celtic triumphed over Internazionale in that momentous Final of the European Champions' Cup. It came as little surprise that Celtic players would now be plucked *en masse* into Scotland's World Cup teams.

That same year the SFA also stepped into the modern world by appointing their first full-time manager. The last amateur ever to play for Scotland, during World War II, Bobby Brown was recruited from his post at St Johnstone, whom he had taken from the world of second division part-timers to the top flight. As manager of Scotland, Brown would enjoy greater autonomy than his predecessors. He might not enjoy job security, but he could pick his own teams.

Qualifying Group 7

SCOTLAND v AUSTRIA
Wednesday, 6 November 1968   *Hampden – 80,856*

Notwithstanding their inconsistent results, Scottish teams enjoyed a welcome continuity between 1965-68. Baxter may have gone, washed up before his time, but eight players who lined up against Austria had seen active service in the previous campaign. The three World Cup newcomers were also hardened internationalists. Each was, predictably, on Celtic's payroll. Goalkeeper Ronnie Simpson had made his debut at Wembley at the venerable age of thirty-six. Striker Bobby Lennox had been a Scottish regular for two years, full-back Tommy Gemmell for even longer.

With West Germany obvious favourites to head Group 7, it was vital Scotland took maximum points from Austria and Cyprus. History suggested Scotland might struggle against Austria, who had won 1-0 in the 1954 World Cup and whom Scotland had beaten just once in nine attempts since 1931. The statistics take no account of the heat generated by Scotland-Austria clashes. There was no love lost, epitomised by the 1963 fixture abandoned by the referee with Scotland 4-1 ahead.

Denis Law was the only current player to survive that bloodbath. Knee trouble had kept him out of the side for over a year. Now he was paired for the first time with Charlie Cooke, who had swapped the blue of Dundee for that of Chelsea. The Celtic duo, Jimmy Johnstone and John Hughes, played as flankers. 'Wee Jinky' Johnstone had graduated from Parkhead ballboy into a Celtic conjurer, whose torment of full-backs was matched only by his torment of managers. The driving force in the 4-2-4 midfield was Billy Bremner, who assumed the captaincy from John Greig.

For Austria, their plight was already desperate. Having crushed Cyprus 7-1, they had lost their critical home game with Germany 0-2. That seemed to rule them out, and defeat at Hampden certainly would. Austria, in fact, were a poor shadow of the team of their halcyon days in the early 'thirties and early 'fifties. Victories over Cyprus and Finland were their only successes in two seasons.

The game had an astonishing start, the visitors going in front after just two minutes. Tam Gemmell was caught in possession trying to dribble out of his penalty area. The ball was played out wide to Starek, who hit a swirler past Simpson.

If Hampden was stunned, it was soon ecstatic. Lennox won a corner, taken by Cooke, and finished by Law at the far post. With their dander up, Scotland might have scored a double-quick second. Cooke latched on to Bremner's pass to crash the ball against the bar.

The rest of the game could hardly live up to that electric opening, though with a draw suiting nobody, both sides pressed. Starek was 'late', whacked Hughes, and was booked. But Austria were holding their own. Starek was a gem in midfield, Hasel held the front line effectively, and Austrian touch play invited murmurs of approval.

Substitutes were at long last permissible in World Cup football. Austria brought on Kogelberger for Redl at the start of the second half. With the wind behind them, Scotland won the lion's share of possession. Hughes was 'sandwiched' without gaining a penalty. Law and Cooke, however, failed to harmonise, and it seemed as if any further goals would have to come from elsewhere. With twenty minutes left, wee Jimmy Johnstone hit the bar. Bremner dived to head home the rebound, but the effort was chalked off for offside.

Five minutes later, Law became the first Scottish player to be substituted in the World Cup. Gilzean deputised and Scotland immediately scored. Fuchsbichler had made several important interceptions, but now he failed to hold Greig's centre. In rugby terms, a ruck ensued, in the midst of which scrum-half Bremner forced the ball over the line.

Austria resumed their twinkling footwork. Scotland lived dangerously. Gilzean was the next to be booked, and Simpson took a knock diving at Kogelberger's feet. Chances fell to the home side to make the game safe, but they weren't taken and many a Scottish fingernail was shortened by the end.

The defeat effectively eliminated Austria but the *Glasgow Herald* gave them their due: 'The entertainment was provided mainly by the Austrians, a well-drilled and skilful side who at times made the Scots look out of their class.'

SCOTLAND (1) 2   AUSTRIA (1) 1
Law 7, Bremner 75   Starek 2

SCOTLAND: Simpson (Celtic), Gemmell (Celtic), McCreadie (Chelsea), Bremner (Leeds), McKinnon (Rangers), Greig (Rangers), Johnstone (Celtic), Cooke (Chelsea), Hughes (Celtic), Law (Man U) (*sub* Gilzean, Spurs), Lennox (Celtic).
AUSTRIA: Fuchsbichler, Gebhardt, Sturmberger, Eigenstiller, Pumm, Starek, Ettmayer, Metzler, Hasil, Siber, Redl (Kogelberger).

CYPRUS v SCOTLAND
Wednesday, 11 December 1968   *Nicosia – 10,000*

Five weeks later the Scotland party jetted to the strife-torn Mediterranean island of Cyprus. They travelled happy with their two points tucked away, but they might have been even happier. West Germany had recently played in the National Stadium in Nicosia. After ninety minutes the Germans had failed to break through. A dropped point would have been a godsend to Scotland, but as injury time ticked away the Germans netted the goal they so desperately needed.

If Germany could struggle in Cyprus, so could Scotland. Bobby Brown was evidently alive to this and made changes. Three Celtic players were ruled out by injury on the Saturday – Gemmell, Johnstone and Hughes – and the other two, Lennox and Simpson, were rested. Time had caught up with the evergreen Celtic goalkeeper. It was time to look ahead. His replacement might have been Bobby Clark, but Aberdeen had shipped eleven goals in a fortnight. Instead, Birmingham's Jim Herriot won a second cap.

Three players turned out for their second international: Doug Fraser in place of Gemmell, Tommy McLean of Kilmarnock deputising for Johnstone, and Colin Stein replacing Hughes. Bobby Murdoch, Celtic's sole representative, policed the midfield with Bremner, while Alan Gilzean wore the No. 10 shirt vacated by Law.

It was a journey into the unknown for Scotland, and a nightmare one at that. They had never played Cyprus before, nor had they any experience of a grassless pitch, based on clay with a gravel overlay, and which demanded the wearing of rubber boots. Bremner called correctly and set the opposition to face the setting sun. Fears that Cyprus would resist as they had the Germans were dispelled within three minutes, when Gilzean powered home McCreadie's cross. Cypriot spirits were further dampened when Pakkos, their one 'quality' player, went off injured.

Playing in white, Scotland threatened to score each time they ran at the motley amateurs. Murdoch flashed home number two from long distance. Gilzean had an effort disallowed before he notched his own second. Five minutes from the interval Stein's drive was deflected past Alkiviades by a hapless defender. There was still time for a Stein cross-shot to be helped home by an obliging home defence. By half-time Herriot had touched the ball twice.

Second-half rain dampened Scotland's attacking frenzy and reduced the playing surface to a concoction resembling mortar. McNeill took over from McKinnon and headed a corner too high. Near the end the hobbling Stein gave way to Lennox, but no more goals materialised. The hundreds of British servicemen in the ground were satisfied with the first half; bored with the second. Cyprus's sum achievement over ninety minutes was a solitary corner.

CYPRUS   (0) 0   SCOTLAND   (5) 5
                                  Gilzean 3, 30, Murdoch 23,
                                  Stein 40, 43

CYPRUS: Alkiviades, Iacovou, Theodorou, Koureas, Panayiotou, Michaeil, Eftimiades, Crystalis, Asprou, Pakkos (Markos), Stylianou.
SCOTLAND: Herriot, Fraser, McCreadie, Bremner, McKinnon (McNeill), Greig, McLean, Murdoch, Stein (Lennox), Gilzean, Cooke.

SCOTLAND v WEST GERMANY
Wednesday, 16 April 1969   *Hampden – 115,000*

So far so good, but now came the real test. Scotland needed to beat a West German team that contained six of the 1966 World Cup Final eleven. The team brimmed with the famous and the great – Schnellinger, Vogts, Beckenbauer, Schulz, Haller, and young Gerd Müller. The mere prospect was enough to raise goosepimples.

West Germany's World Cup record was awesome. They had first competed in 1954 when they had confounded all predictions to beat the Hungarians in the Final. They were fourth in 1958; quarter-finalists in 1962; and finalists in 1966. They had never lost a World Cup qualifier.

Nevertheless, Germany were, and are, curiously vulnerable against weaker nations. It had needed an injury-time goal to secure victory in Cyprus; and failure to win in Albania had eliminated the Germans from the 1968 European Championship. Germany had a poor track record against British opposition. In the past year they had twice drawn 1-1 with Wales, and beaten England for the first time. They had never beaten Scotland.

Scotland's team showed five changes. The main talking point was the return of fourteen-stone Liverpool goalkeeper Tommy Lawrence to replace Herriot, out with an injured hand. Lawrence's solitary cap had been earned six years back. Bobby Brown had hoped to field two wingers, but injury to Hughes meant a recall for Bobby Lennox. Law and Gilzean provided a spearhead of potentially devastating aerial power.

Surveying previous World Cups, Scotland had regularly conjured famous home wins over their main challengers – Spain in 1958, Czechoslovakia in 1962, Italy in 1966. They sorely needed to extend that sequence; otherwise the odds would be heavily stacked in Germany's favour.

The pattern of the game was soon established. The well-oiled German machine funnelled back as Scottish zest threatened to drive the visitors into the Clyde. Schnellinger stuck tight to Gilzean, Schulz swept up at the back, and Beckenbauer patrolled here, there and everywhere to keep his side on an even keel.

Alan Gilzean admires Bobby Murdoch's late thunderbolt. (v W Germany)

It was not a night for second-raters. Bremner and Murdoch relentlessly drove Scotland forward, and Law and Gilzean both directed headers on target. At the other end Müller had the ball in the net, but it had already passed out of play. When the overworked Wolter pushed out a cross to Johnstone, it only needed a clean return strike, but Johnstone's miscued effort was hacked away.

With the interval beckoning, Beckenbauer was fouled outside the Scottish penalty area. He pushed the free kick to Müller, who squeezed past McKinnon and Greig to shoot wide of Lawrence. It was a stunning goal. To rub salt into the wound, on the half-time whistle Wolter saved athletically from Murdoch.

For some reason the Germans sent out a new keeper for the second half. Scotland derived no advantage, for young Sepp Maier proved even more resilient than his predecessor. It must have been galling to Scotland that, even as their pressure intensified, the Germans never seemed to break sweat, and even their goalmouth clearances seemed to find a free team-mate.

Scotland's wingers were perhaps the least penetrating of the home players, denying Law and Gilzean the chance to shine. Murdoch surged through to flash a massive shot narrowly wide. The Hampden gasps of anguish hung in the air like the wail of the banshee. Lennox was pulled off in favour of Charlie Cooke, temporarily out of favour at Stamford Bridge. The Germans responded by bringing on Lorenz for Overath.

Sepp Maier is beaten and Denis Law points to the sky. Murdoch scores. (v W Germany)

If anything, the last ten minutes saw Germany breaking free of the Scottish stranglehold, but after eighty-eight minutes all was back in the melting pot. Scotland's substitution paid off. Cooke sold a dummy and stroked the ball into the path of the on-rushing Bobby Murdoch. The Celtic midfielder slipped past Patzke to send a blinding shot into the far top corner of the net. Maier was beaten and Hampden exploded with relief. It would have exploded a second time, but Bremner's last-gasp effort was headed off the line by Beckenbauer. The Germans' earlier composure deserted them. The ball was repeatedly belted into the terraces as the final seconds ticked away.

Bobby Murdoch was the toast of Hampden.

SCOTLAND (0) 1   WEST GERMANY (1) 1
    Murdoch 88   Müller 39

SCOTLAND: Lawrence, Gemmell, McCreadie, Murdoch, McKinnon, Greig, Johnstone, Bremner, Law, Gilzean, Lennox (Cooke).
W GERMANY: Wolter (Maier), Schnellinger, Vogts, Beckenbauer, Schulz, Patzke, Deerfel, Haller, Müller, Overath (Lorenz), Held.

SCOTLAND v CYPRUS
Saturday, 17 May 1969   *Hampden – 39,095*

The euphoria was understandable: the celebrations lasted long into the night. The cold light of reality, however, told that Murdoch's sterling effort was likely to prove futile. Germany had come for the draw and had achieved it. The programme was now half-complete. Both Scotland and Germany had five points from three games, but the Germans could now look forward to three home fixtures. Already it was clear that Scotland would need some improbable results in Hamburg and Vienna come next autumn.

The first task was to dispose of Cyprus. Scotland endured an undistinguished preparation. The increasing importance attached to clubs' European fixtures, played in midweek, exacerbated the problem of getting players released for internationals. This was now proving a major headache for the managers of Scotland, Wales and Northern Ireland. English clubs were obliged to release players for the England team but not for the other British teams. To ease the mounting problem of fixture congestion, the Home Internationals were shunted to the end of the season, being crammed into a week in early May when interest was at its lowest. Scotland's thrilling 5-3 win in Wrexham was followed by an abject 1-1 draw with the Irish at Hampden. The series concluded with Scotland walloped 1-4 at Wembley, before a live TV audience. That same day Germany went clear at the top of Group 7 by beating Austria. These were not results designed to boost Scottish confidence for the visit of Cyprus a week later.

Liverpool refused to release Tommy Lawrence, citing an important league engagement. Jim Herriot kept goal. Eddie McCreadie turned out for what would be his last international. Bobby Murdoch had shown signs of battle fatigue during the British Championship and was omitted in favour of Charlie Cooke. A clever, twisting young winger from Leeds United, Eddie Gray, introduced against England, retained his place. On the right, it was Willie Henderson's turn for a game at the expense of Jimmy Johnstone. The Cypriots were on a 'high', having scored a goal, despite losing 1-2 at home to Austria.

When Scotland failed to score quickly they became fidgety. Cyprus began to look composed, even cheeky. It was new-boy Gray who settled the nerves with a sizzling run and shot into the far corner. Tower-of-strength Billy McNeill, with few defensive responsibilities, then strode upfield, collected Greig's throw, and belted the ball past Alkiviades.

It was now that Colin Stein got into the act. It is doubtful whether he knew beforehand that no Scottish player this century had exceeded four goals in one game, and that the last person to score four was Hugh Gallacher in 1929. In the twenty-eighth minute Stein headed in Cooke's corner and he was on his way.

Cyprus brought on two fresh pairs of legs for the second half, endeavouring to keep the score respectable. It was slightly less respectable four minutes later, when Stein intercepted a slack back-pass and dribbled round the goalkeeper. Ten minutes later the score was less respectable still, as Henderson hared down the right to set up a chance for Stein.

Stein had his hat-trick, and thirty minutes remained for him to inflict further mayhem. When Alkiviades pushed away Gray's effort, Stein thrashed the ball home at the near post.

Jim Herriot must have been bored to death. So must the Scottish substitutes, neither of whom was invited to join in the party. Gilzean set up Henderson for the seventh goal, and with fourteen minutes left Scotland were awarded a penalty. Stein had equalled Gallacher's record, now was his chance to overtake it. Instead, responsibility was entrusted to the team's authorised penalty-taker, Tommy Gemmell. Why demean the cherished records held by the legendary heroes of old?

Scotland had equalled their World Cup record score of eight goals, established against Northern Ireland in 1949. More importantly, should they need a play-off with West Germany, Scotland looked like having the better goal difference. In that case they would not need to beat them, just draw. Scotland should have known better. Four days later Cyprus were butchered 0-12 by Germany, who thereby overhauled Scottish goal difference. But things were looking up for Cyprus. In Nicosia they had earned one corner: at Hampden they managed two.

SCOTLAND   (3) 8   CYPRUS   (0) 0
    Gray 15, McNeill 20,
    Stein 28, 49, 59, 67,
    Henderson 70, Gemmell 76 pen

SCOTLAND: Herriot, McCreadie, Gemmell, Bremner, McNeill, Greig, Henderson, Cooke, Stein, Gilzean, Gray.
CYPRUS: Alkiviades, Mertakis, Savakis (Fokk), Stephanis (Constantas), Koureas, Sotirakis, Panikos, Marcou, Crystalis, Mellis, Stylianou.

WEST GERMANY v SCOTLAND
Wednesday, 22nd October 1969   *Hamburg – 72,000*

The crunch came in October with a visit to the Volkspark Stadium in Hamburg. The Germans' win over Austria meant that Scottish backs were well and truly to the wall. This was the Germans' last fixture: the Scots had to travel to Vienna a fortnight later. Germany had nine points from five games, Scotland seven from four.

Defeat in Hamburg would put Scotland out. Nor could they afford to draw. True, that would keep them alive for the moment, but they would then need outright victories over Austria and Germany (in the play-off) to reach Mexico. Four years previously, when confronted by a similar dilemma, Jock Stein had gone for a draw in Italy rather than a win. Bobby Brown now faced the same choice, but his conclusion differed. The devil take the hindmost: Scotland would attack. If they pulled it off, they would need only to draw in Vienna.

It was a familiar-looking outfit that Brown sent out, with one exception. Hibernian's Peter Cormack picked up a rare cap, his hard running being required to bolster Bremner and Gray in midfield. A second unfamiliar face, that of Wolves' Hugh Curran, might have led the attack in place of Colin Stein. The Rangers striker was going through a lean spell, but Curran went down with flu on match-day and Stein kept his place. His scoring record for Scotland was exceptional, ten goals from six games, and only once had he failed to find the net. A goal in Hamburg would be priceless.

With the Germans employing twin strikers, Uwe Seeler and Gerd Müller, Brown matched them with twin stoppers, McKinnon and McNeill, only the second time they had lined up together. Greig switched to right-back. Given the importance of the match, it was shown live on Scottish TV with key Scottish League matches having to be postponed. The English League was less cooperative, but it was Germany who suffered most from foreign obstruction. Helmut Haller arrived late from Juventus, and AC Milan flatly refused to release world-class defender Karl-Heinz Schnellinger.

Scotland could not have dreamt of a better start. A weaving run by Eddie Gray after just three minutes ended with a shot-cum-centre that Maier, straining upwards, couldn't hold. Jimmy Johnstone, the smallest player on the field, could hardly believe it as the ball dropped sweetly for him.

Scotland made the Germans appear almost mundane as they played some of the most controlled football anyone could remember. Bremner won everything in midfield, while Gray and Johnstone teased and tormented the German full-backs. For half an hour Herriot barely touched the ball, though Beckenbauer's free kick did set up Haller to crash an almighty shot against the keeper's right post. Undeterred, Scotland had chances to make it 2-0, none better than when Gilzean hoisted the ball over Maier's crossbar.

Seven minutes from half-time the Germans levelled. McNeill's inattentive back-pass cost an unnecessary corner which eluded Herriot and flew around before Fichtel lashed it home. Gray's immediate riposte was to force Maier into a flying save.

The game was already one to be savoured; it increasingly became one unsuitable for faint hearts. The Germans came out fired up for the second half. Johnstone was a principal target: he spent as much time on his bottom as on his feet, yet Scotland twice came close to retaking the lead. Gemmell, wide on the left clipped the bar, before Bremner crashed a ferocious shot squarely against the woodwork.

Vogts is helpless as Maier boobs and Jimmy Johnstone puts Scotland ahead. (v W Germany)

By this stage the number of bookings exceeded goals, but on the hour the game exploded. Seeler, the German captain, winning his sixty-second cap, headed a free kick to Müller who hooked mercilessly past Herriot. But German celebrations were strangled in mid-cheer as Gilzean rose almost nonchalantly to nod McKinnon's cross past Maier.

Scotland sensed blood and forced the Germans to back-pedal. The names of Müller and Overath were added to the list of bookings, and Stein saw his best effort of the night headed out by Vogts. It seemed as though Scotland would leave with a famous, if probably futile, draw when the Germans pulled out their master punch. The fleet-footed Libuda had given Gemmell a trying time throughout. Less than ten minutes remained when Haller's diagonal pass out of defence found Libuda out on the right. The winger set off and evaded Gemmell yet again to score a sublime goal. The Scottish players collapsed where they stood. It was bad enough to lose when they scarcely deserved to, but ignominy was to follow. The frustrated Gemmell swung a criminal kick at Haller and was ordered off. Scotland could not save the game with eleven men, let alone ten, and made a tearful farewell.

WEST GERMANY (1) 3   SCOTLAND (1) 2
Fichtel 38, Müller 60, Libuda 81   Johnstone 3, Gilzean 64

W GERMANY: Maier, Höttges, Vogts, Beckenbauer, Schulz, Fichtel, Libuda, Seeler, Müller, Overath, Haller.
SCOTLAND: Herriot, Greig, Gemmell, Bremner, McKinnon, McNeill, Johnstone, Cormack, Gilzean, Gray, Stein.

AUSTRIA v SCOTLAND

Wednesday, 5 November 1969   *Vienna – 11,000*

So Scotland, once again, had been beaten in their group's most testing away fixture. In this respect, defeat in Hamburg accorded with those in Spain (1958), Czechoslovakia (1962) and Italy (1966). Yet this time there was honour in defeat. Seldom had Scotland played better and lost, but Reinhard Libuda would go on to destroy better teams in Mexico.

Whatever moral honours went to Scotland, they were out of the World Cup. Their visit to Vienna two weeks later was meaningless, an aggravation which they could have done without. All the match could offer, apart from pride, was an opportunity to experiment. Aberdeen's Ernie McGarr won a second and last cap. He would be the fourth keeper Scotland had called upon in six World Cup matches. The persistent failing over the years to find a settled keeper cannot have helped continuity or confidence in the Scottish defence.

At left-back Manchester United's Frances Burns made his one and only international appearance, in place of the suspended Gemmell. Making his delayed debut was Wolves' Hugh Curran, as Colin Stein stepped down. With Cormack injured, a recall awaited Bobby Murdoch, for what turned out to be his last game. There was no need for twin stoppers, so Billy McNeill gave way to Hibernian's Pat Stanton. Only three Austrian players remained from the side beaten at Hampden twelve long months before.

After the champagne, the beer. Scotland were as dreadful in Vienna as they had been impressive in Hamburg. The pitch was wet, the crowd small, and Curran didn't get a kick. Scotland fell behind after fourteen minutes, when Redl climbed above Burns to head home Parits' centre.

Scotland were finished from that moment. Greig became the focus of boos in the Prater Stadium when he crudely crunched the scorer, who needed lengthy treatment. A half-hearted shot from Cooke was the only effort on goal Scotland mustered throughout the first half.

It was not that Scotland were apathetic; they were simply bad. They tackled as fiercely as in any cup-tie, but could not prevent Austria increasing their lead after fifty-three minutes. Geyer, wide on the right, lost and regained possession several times as he forced his way past clumsy challenges. At last the ball ran to Redl who finished off a messy goal.

With a two-goal lead, Austria took a breather. Colin Stein substituted for Curran, and Leeds' Peter Lorimer won a first cap when he took over from

Cooke. Nothing transpired which either substitute would remember warmly. For Scotland, the 1970 World Cup was well and truly over.

AUSTRIA (1) 2   SCOTLAND (0) 0
  Redl 14, 53

AUSTRIA: Harraither, Wallner, Sturmberger, Schmidradner, Fak, Geyer, Hof, Parits, Kaiser, Ettmayer, Redl.
SCOTLAND: McGarr, Greig, Burns, Murdoch, McKinnon, Stanton, Cooke (Lorimer), Bremner, Gilzean, Curran (Stein), Gray.

The British jinx that had haunted German football had first been laid to rest in 1968, with a win over England at Hanover. Following the tense victory over Scotland in Hamburg, the Germans with proper sense of balance duly eliminated England, by the same score, from the quarter-finals in Mexico. The exhaustion imposed by that extra-time marathon was largely responsible for the Germans falling at the next hurdle, to the Italians, also after extra time. Italy, in turn, lost the Final to the magnificent Brazil.

Qualifying Group 7

| | | | Home | | | | | Away | | | |
	P	W	D	L	F	A	W	D	L	F	A	Pts
WEST GERMANY	6	3	0	0	16	2	2	1	0	4	1	11
Scotland	6	2	1	0	11	2	1	0	2	7	5	7
Austria	6	2	0	1	9	3	1	0	2	3	4	6
Cyprus	6	0	0	3	1	8	0	0	3	1	27	0

Other group results

Austria v Cyprus	7-1	W Germany v Cyprus	12-0
Austria v W Germany	0-2	Cyprus v Austria	1-2
Cyprus v W Germany	0-1	W Germany v Austria	1-0

Scotland appearances and goalscorers (substitute appearances in brackets)
World Cup qualifying rounds 1970

	Apps	Goals		Apps	Goals
Bremner W *	6	1	Law D *†	2	1
Greig J *	6	–	Burns F	1	–
Gilzean A *	5 (1)	3	Cormack P	1	–
McKinnon R *	5	–	Curran H	1	–
Cooke C *	4 (1)	–	Fraser D	1	–
Gemmell T	4	1	Henderson W *	1	1
McCreadie E *	4	–	Hughes J *	1	–
Stein C	3 (1)	6	Lawrence T	1	–
Gray E	3	1	McGarr E	1	–
Herriot J	3	–	McLean T	1	–
Johnstone J *	3	1	Stanton P	1	–
Murdoch R *	3	2	Simpson R	1	–
Lennox R	2 (1)	–	Lorimer P	– (1)	–
McNeill W *†	2 (1)	1			

* Appeared in 1966 World Cup.
† Appeared in 1962 World Cup.

72 apps   18 goals
38 Scottish League
34 English League
27 players used

7

THE 1974 WORLD CUP

The qualifying draw for the 1974 World Cup – the finals of which would be staged in West Germany – pitched Scotland into a welcome three-team group. Yet more welcome were the two opponents: Denmark and Czechoslovakia. There was no need to fear either, and for the first time since qualifying in 1958 Scotland could claim a genuinely kind draw.

They needed it. Scotland's form since being squeezed out by West Germany caused even the most enthusiastic fan to dig deep for excuses. Twenty-one internationals had been played, only seven won, only fourteen goals scored. Scotland had failed to surmount the first phase of the 1972 European Championship, their opponents being Denmark, Portugal and Belgium. Scotland had, predictably enough, beaten all three at home; equally predictably, lost to all three away.

And there lay the nub. Scotland's performances continued to invite diagnosis of schizophrenia. At Hampden, Scotland feared no one. Away from Hampden, no one feared Scotland. Since the 5-0 thrashing of Cyprus in Nicosia in 1968, Scotland had played eleven internationals overseas and hadn't won any.

To be sure, Scottish fortunes seemed to be improving following the galvanising effects of Tommy Docherty's appointment as team manager in the autumn of 1971. Bobby Brown had become increasingly bogged down by the 'club v country' unavailability of key players. Results suffered, and when Scotland lost 1-3 at Wembley the SFA lost patience.

Although Docherty's was an inspired choice, it was also a surprising one. A Scottish international himself, his brusque management style at Chelsea had raised his profile dramatically. He was a man who ruffled feathers, and seemed to sliding out of football altogether. He had just been appointed assistant manager to second division Hull City when the invitation from the SFA arrived. He began well. Only three of Docherty's first ten matches were lost.

On the club scene, Rangers captured the Cup-Winners' Cup, to take them out of Celtic's shadow. Provided Docherty could do something about that dire away record, Scottish qualification for West Germany seemed within reach.

Qualifying Group 8

DENMARK v SCOTLAND

Wednesday, 18 October 1972   *Copenhagen – 31,000*

Tommy Docherty's brief reign certainly stirred things up. Unhampered by even having to consult with a selection committee, he rang the changes and brought Scottish international football into the modern world. The post-Docherty era would never be as undistinguished as pre-Docherty. He did not flinch from overturning preconceived ideas. Docherty's managerial experience in England and on the continent (with Porto) had widened his horizons. He demanded the strongest possible Scottish team, even if that meant the wholesale inclusion of Anglos. Almost inconceivably, in Copenhagen only one Old Firm face took the field.

Scotland had enjoyed a healthy continuity in the World Cup campaigns of 1966 and 1970. But Docherty was determined to wipe the slate clean. Peter Lorimer and team captain Billy Bremner would be the only survivors of 1970. Aberdeen's Bobby Clark was now the first-choice goalkeeper. In front of him, Manchester United sweeper Martin Buchan partnered Sheffield United's Eddie Colquhoun. Full-backs John Brownlie of Hibs and Alex Forsyth of Partick Thistle completed the defence. Arsenal's George Graham contested midfield with Bremner. The wingers were Peter Lorimer and Manchester United's Willie Morgan; the central strikers, Lou Macari and Jimmy Bone – the Norwich player claiming his one and only cap.

Prior to June 1971, Scotland had won four out of four against Denmark. But that month they had gone down 0-1 in Copenhagen. Docherty knew his team needed a win, but he could not be blind to Scotland's endemic failings abroad. Docherty told the press: 'The game is becoming too academic. The ball is being treated too gently. I want it hit hard.' Today, such a statement seems prehistoric.

His players – kitted in white to assist the requirements of black and white television – perceived little distinction between ball and man. Danish footballers were harshly treated. Docherty had little interest in sporadic brilliance from his players, preferring cold, clinical professionalism.

Despite being 'softened up', the part-amateur, part-expatriate Danish team must have entertained early hopes of a repeat win in the Idraetspark Stadium. Most of Scotland's early efforts were confined to long-range.

This was little comfort when the likes of Peter Lorimer were in the opposing side. It was his venomous drive that, though turned for a corner, opened the lock. Taking the kick himself, Lorimer drove the ball waist-high across goal where Lou Macari stole in at the near post to head home. Seeking to capitalise, George Graham strolled through two minutes later to shoot hard against

Therkildsen's legs. Bone was in the right place to net the loose ball. Scotland led 2-0.

Such a score was just the tonic, and to keep the speedy Danes quiet Buchan crash-tackled Henning Jensen and found himself booked by Mr Bakhramov, the Russian referee. It was Bakhramov who, in the 1966 World Cup Final, had been the linesman who awarded Geoff Hurst his 'crossbar' goal.

The sprightly, red-shirted Danish team hit back. Eigil Nielsen cleared Forsyth's lunge and bore down on Clark, only to be floored by the full-back's covering tackle. Laudrup thumped the free kick high to Clark's right. The keeper got a touch but couldn't save. Scotland responded with a sequence of intimidatory challenges, and Bremner discreetly slowed the dangerous Eigil Nielsen. More worthily, Lorimer's mighty shot threatened to snap a post at the base.

The first half had been hard work. The second was equally dour, as Bremner continued to sort out the Danes. On the hour Graham almost restored the Scots' two-goal margin when hammering Brownlie's centre against the junction of bar and post.

Four minutes later, Bone was replaced by fellow-debutant Joe Harper, which doubled the Pittodrie representation. Harper was the Scottish first division's top scorer last season and this. With ten minutes remaining the wee man took Macari's back-heel to stroke the most casual of goals and tie up the points.

Harper was clearly in the mood. He too shot against a post. Lorimer lobbed the rebound onto Morgan's head for Scotland's fourth. Macari was pulled off, allowing a young man called Kenny Dalglish to experience his first taste of World Cup football.

Scotland might have had five or six by the end. But over ninety minutes the win had been harder, and less attractive, than the scoreline suggested. Never mind, a new-look national team had recorded Scotland's first victory on the continent for four long years.

DENMARK (1) 1
Laudrup 28

SCOTLAND (2) 4
Macari 17, Bone 19, Harper 80,
Morgan 83

DENMARK: Therkildsen, T Nielsen, M Jensen, Roentved, Ahlberg, Bjoernmose, J Hansen (B Jensen), Laudrup, Olsen, H Jensen, E Nielsen.
SCOTLAND: Clark (Aberdeen), Brownlie (Hibs), A Forsyth (Partick), Bremner (Leeds), Colquhoun (Sheff U), Buchan (Man U), Lorimer (Leeds), Macari (Celtic) (*sub* Dalglish, Celtic), Bone (Norwich) (*sub* Harper, Aberdeen), Graham (Arsenal), Morgan (Man U).

SCOTLAND v DENMARK

Wednesday, 15 November 1972   *Hampden – 47,109*

Strategically, Scotland set about trying to qualify for the 1974 World Cup as they had that of 1962. Then, as now, they and Czechoslovakia were joined by a piggy in the middle – the Irish Republic in 1962, Denmark now. Then, as now, Scotland opted to play their first two matches against piggy. Czechoslovakia would then follow suit, leaving the Scots and Czechs to round up the group with their own double-header. Following the example of 1962, Scotland hoped to have four points in the vault before the Czechs commenced their programme, putting maximum pressure on their east European rivals.

Scotland now sought to finish off the Danish challenge. Docherty made four changes, the Danes six – capitalising on the availability of exiles not released for the earlier match. The Leeds influence on the Scottish team was extended yet further. Though Eddie Gray was injured, Bremner and Lorimer were joined by the Elland Road goalkeeper, David Harvey. Born in England of Scottish parents, Harvey was among those taking advantage of FIFA's new ruling, that permitted a player to turn out for the country of his parents, irrespective of where he had been born. England, in other words, had had first claim on David Harvey's services. Fat chance, with Gordon Banks in his prime and Peter Shilton in the wings. Harvey, like Bob Wilson before him, knew which side his bread was buttered.

Bremner and Graham continued in midfield; Lorimer and Morgan on the flanks. Joe Harper and Kenny Dalglish, both subs in Copenhagen, lined up from the start – Dalglish gaining his opportunity when Macari called off. Traditionalists would have been mortified by the overall composition of the Scottish team. Only three players hailed from north of the border: the rest were Anglos – the most ever included in a Scottish World Cup fixture.

Any Scottish nerves dissipated in the second minute when they took a brisk lead. Lorimer, as with Scotland's opener in Denmark, won a corner which he took himself. The ball was cleared towards the opposite corner flag, and when Colquhoun despatched it back into the goalmouth, Kenny Dalglish was on hand to score his first international goal.

Spurred on by Bremner and Graham, the game was Scotland's for the taking. Lorimer and Morgan both might have scored, and the Manchester United winger proved a constant irritation to the prickly Danes. The visitors had been upset by Scottish 'tackling' in Copenhagen, and their current eleven included its share of hit-men.

Scotland sealed the result, sensibly, by repeating the lesson of the first half and scoring immediately play resumed. A substitute goalkeeper, Hildebrandt, awaited the Scots, but he could do nothing as Lorimer collected Graham's cross to the far post, held off a challenge, and whacked the ball into goal.

Denmark rarely threatened after that, and the game died as a contest. The rest of the second half produced its share of Scottish shots, and more than its share of Danish pass-backs. Denmark seemed concerned only to avoid losing a third goal. Harper, providing a Laurel and Hardy spectacle against the giant Munk Jensen, failed to impose himself legitimately and was booked for taking out his frustration on the substitute goalkeeper. Dalglish was pulled off, allowing a sixth and final cap to Coventry's Willie Carr. The referee made a note of two Danish names: Laudrup, a substitute, and Munk Jensen, for an unsporting assault on Lorimer. Lorimer appeared to be a marked man. Six minutes from time Roentved hacked him once too often, Lorimer swung an angry fist, and both were shown the way to the changing rooms. No sooner had they departed than Carr was fouled, Morgan took the penalty, and the ball sailed over the bar.

If the scoreline in Copenhagen flattered Scotland, that at Hampden did not. But afterwards, foe turned friend. Docherty needed Denmark to do Scotland a favour and avoid defeat by the Czechs. Three World Cups earlier, the Republic of Ireland had been unable to assist Scotland as required. But in May 1973 came the fantastic news: the Danes had drawn 1-1 in Copenhagen. The Czechs' 6-0 revenge in the return match could not rectify the damage. Scotland were poised to qualify.

SCOTLAND   (1) 2   DENMARK   (0) 0
Dalglish 2, Lorimer 48

SCOTLAND: Harvey, Brownlie, Donachie, Bremner, Colquhoun, Buchan, Lorimer, Dalglish (Carr), Harper, Graham, Morgan.
DENMARK: Therkildsen (Hildebrandt), Ahlberg, J Hansen, M Jensen, Roentved, Bjerre, Olsen, Michaelson, B Jansen, Christianssen (Laudrup), Le Fevre.

SCOTLAND v CZECHOSLOVAKIA
Wednesday, 26 September 1973   *Hampden – 100,000*

It would be ten months before Scotland embarked on the second phase of their campaign. Those ten months were disastrous from the point of view of building on the momentum generated by Tommy Docherty. Within weeks of sinking Denmark he had turned his back on SFA bronze in favour of Old Trafford gold. Docherty's successor was a complete contrast: where the Doc was loud, Willie Ormond was quiet; where Docherty had governed the rich and powerful, Ormond – like Bobby Brown – came straight from the pastures of St Johnstone.

Ormond's team lost five out of the first six, a sequence set in train when England crushed Scotland 5-0 on 14 February 1973 to 'celebrate' the centenary of the Scottish FA. Rarely had a 'St Valentine's Day Massacre' been so painful. Before the season was out, Northern Ireland and Brazil also came, saw and conquered at Hampden.

If the national stadium was proving an unhappy home for Scotland, they at least had the consolation that, come the World Cup, it would likely revert to being a veritable fortress. Only England (twice in the 1950s) and Poland had won there in fifteen World Cup matches. Scotland's win in Denmark, followed by the Czechs' draw, meant that Scotland could lose twenty goals in Bratislava and not care a fig – provided they beat the Czechs at Hampden. The Czechs, pale reflections of their 1962 team, had halted a nine-game run without a win when beating Denmark at the second attempt.

None of the current Czech team harboured active memories of Scottish-Czech skirmishes a dozen years back. But one Scot did – the inimitable Denis Law. He was now thirty-three, free transferred by Manchester United and in his second stint with neighbours City. Docherty had begun Law's international resurrection, which would now be consummated by Ormond. The legendary striker stepped up for his fourth World Cup, twelve years to the day since he smashed two goals past Czechoslovakia to earn that ill-fated play-off.

Ormond had dismembered the team he inherited from Docherty. Only Bremner, Dalglish and Morgan remained, though some of those overlooked would later be recalled. Celtic keeper Alistair Hunter earned a rare call-up. The full-backs were named as Sandy Jardine and Danny McGrain. They flanked Manchester United's young giant, Jim Holton, and the Scottish Football Writers' 'Player of 1973', George Connelly, winning his first cap. The second international baptism was for Coventry's flying winger, Tommy Hutchison. Bremner would police midfield with Celtic's tough-tackling Davie Hay.

For those unable to obtain tickets – restricted to 100,000 on police advice – the match was transmitted live on TV. Battle was brutal whether viewed from terrace or sofa. Scotland attacked: Czechoslovakia defended. Dalglish and Hutchison were instantly up-ended and Law announced his return to international duty with a dreadful foul on Bendl. Samek clattered Bremner and was booked; the crowed chanted 'animals', and Bremner whacked Kuna so fiercely that the Czech schemer could not resume and was subbed by Dobias. The game was not yet twenty minutes old.

Efforts by Bremner, Jardine and Morgan instilled hope before Ally Hunter, after thirty-three minutes, sent a wave of despair through the stadium and the nation. Adamec interrupted a raging Scottish attack with a punt downfield. It had no constructive intent: nor had Nehoda's aimless swipe at the ball. But Hunter flapped and flopped, and it squeezed inside a post. Silence.

Scottish tears took just seven minutes to dry. The omnipresent Law won a corner which big Jim Holton powered into the net.

The Czechs looked more impressive after the break. Pivarnik rolled the ball along Hunter's crossbar. Bremner continued to invite Czech displeasure, and

Panenka became the second player booked for crunching the Scottish captain. Ormond needed greater firepower, and midway through the half replaced the subtleties of Dalglish with the brute strength of Leeds' reserve striker, Joe Jordan. The substitute almost left his mark with a bullet header that flew too high, but Scottish adrenalin was now in full flow. Bremner received Morgan's free kick to thump leather on wood. The ball ran along the goal-line, past the far post, from where Morgan finally chipped it back into the bowels of the enemy. This time Jordan's header was straight and true. He had been on the pitch just eleven minutes. Pandemonium.

Czechoslovakia brought on Capkovic for Panenka and piled men forward. But Scotland were not to be denied. Ormond was carried shoulder high and Hutchison, Jordan and Law were the toast of the land. Scotland had become the first European team to qualify for West Germany and the singing lasted long.

SCOTLAND   (1) 2   CZECHOSLOVAKIA   (1) 1
Holton 40, Jordan 75   Nehoda 33

SCOTLAND: Hunter, Jardine, McGrain, Bremner, Holton, Connelly, Hay, Law, Morgan, Dalglish (Jordan), Hutchison.
CZECHOSLOVAKIA: Viktor, Pivarnik, Samek, Zlocha, Bendl, Bicovsky, Adamec, Kuna (Dobias), Nehoda, Stratil, Panenka (Capkovic).

CZECHOSLOVAKIA v SCOTLAND
Wednesday, 17 October 1973   *Bratislava – 15,000*

So Scotland were back in the World Cup finals, having avenged that crushing night in Brussels in 1961, when the Czechs had won a bruising play-off. The present match was about as meaningless as a bikini in Siberia.

The principal Scottish casualty of that golden Hampden evening was Ally Hunter, who would not sample international football again. In his stead, Harvey returned. Injuries compelled Ormond to reshuffle his team. Holton, Hutchison and Bremner were all unfit. Bremner had an ankle injury which there was no sense in aggravating. His withdrawal was seized upon by the Czech press as implying cowardice. Kuna had not yet recovered from Bremner's attentions. The talk was of an eye for an eye if the Scottish captain dared to play. Instead, Davie Hay was for the first time handed the honour of skippering his country. The two centre-backs were both newcomers: John Blackley of Hibernian gaining a first cap; Rangers' Tom Forsyth a second.

The Czechs retained a nucleus of players from the 1970 team that lost to England in Mexico: Viktor in goal, Hagar, Pollak, Vesely and Capkovic. Three others from that eleven – Adamec, Kuna and Dobias – had played at Hampden, though they would be missing from the return in the Telhalne Stadium.

To describe the game as tedious is to be generous. Scotland had every incentive to avoid unnecessary bookings, and their tactics seemed no more threatening than to retain possession. This they achieved without alarm until the seventeenth minute, when Nehoda carried the ball past Forsyth, who challenged untidily and handled into the bargain. Having manufactured the penalty, Nehoda was given the privilege of scoring from it.

The Scots showed no great enthusiasm to make good the deficit; the Czechs even less to increase it, or exact gratuitous retribution on their opponents. After an hour Ormond pulled off Law and awarded a first cap to Hearts' Donald Ford, Scotland's leading scorer this season. Ford came nearest to squaring the issue. In the last minute his shot from a tight angle cannoned to safety off Viktor's head. At the end a storm of whistling enveloped the stadium.

The Scottish players looked none too distressed, but later tuned in to extraordinary news. At Wembley Poland had knocked England out of the World Cup. Some Scots were disappointed, others ecstatic, but their own achievement was now all the more laudable. Scotland would hog the British limelight in West Germany.

CZECHOSLOVAKIA (1) 1   SCOTLAND (0) 0
Nehoda 17 pen

CZECHOSLOVAKIA: Viktor, Pivarnik, Samek, Dvorak, Hagara, Bicovsky, Pollak, Gajdusek, Vesely (Klement), Nehoda, Capkovic (Panenka).
SCOTLAND: Harvey, Jardine, McGrain, Forsyth, Blackley, Hay, Morgan, Jordan, Law (Ford), Dalglish, Hutchison.

Qualifying Group 8

	P	W	D	L	F	A	Pts
SCOTLAND	4	3	0	1	8	3	6
Czechoslovakia	4	2	1	1	9	3	5
Denmark	4	0	1	3	2	13	1

Other group results
Denmark v Czechoslovakia   1-1   Czechoslovakia v Denmark   6-0

World Cup finals – WEST GERMANY   **June-July 1974**

Scottish joy at qualifying for the first time in sixteen years was understandable; their current prospects realistically encouraging. The team had players of quality. Moreover, Scottish sides generally performed better when talked of in the language of understatement. Willie Ormond, fortunately, was not one for shooting his mouth off.

The eagerly awaited draw was not especially generous. Joining Scotland in Group 2 would be defending champions Brazil. Scotland had performed bravely in Rio two years previously, but had still lost 0-1. Probable defeat by Brazil in the finals should be balanced by victory over Zaïre. Allowing for over-simplification, this meant Scotland would contest the second qualifying place with Yugoslavia, whom they would face last.

Scotland's form in the build-up was as up-and-down as one has come to expect. Which was the real Scotland, that which beat England at Hampden, or that which lost to Northern Ireland in the same stadium? Ormond arranged home and away friendlies with the World Cup hosts, drawing at home (1-1), losing away (1-2). *En route* to the tournament the team stopped off to play Belgium and Norway. Scotland impressed in neither match, losing the first (1-2), laboriously winning the second (2-1). These preparations were notable more for off-the-field revelries than on-field sparkle. Jimmy Johnstone, having the previous month nearly been swept out to sea on a rowing boat at Largs, was involved in Oslo with Billy Bremner in an 'incident' in a student bar. Both players came near – perhaps very near – to being sent home. Team morale was further dampened by failure to settle lucrative commercial contracts. This World Cup, and those to come, were about making money. The Scottish players demanded their share.

Though Willie Ormond was not required to name his twenty-two man squad until eight days before the tournament, he saw no reason to delay, announcing his list almost a month before the gloves came off. The full party, which was not amended, was as follows:

No	Name	Position	Club	Age	Caps	Goals
1	David Harvey	Goalkeeper	Leeds	26	7	–
2	Sandy Jardine	Full-back	Rangers	25	16	1
3	Danny McGrain	Full-back	Celtic	24	12	–
4	Billy Bremner (c)	Midfield	Leeds	32	47	2
5	Jim Holton	Central defence	Manchester U	23	11	2
6	John Blackley	Central defence	Hibernian	24	3	–
7	Jimmy Johnstone	Winger	Celtic	29	22	2
8	Kenny Dalglish	Forward	Celtic	23	19	5
9	Joe Jordan	Forward	Leeds	22	11	3
10	Davie Hay	Midfield	Celtic	26	24	–
11	Peter Lorimer	Winger/Forward	Leeds	25	13	3
12	Thompson Allan *	Goalkeeper	Dundee	26	2	–
13	Jim Stewart	Goalkeeper	Kilmarnock	20	–	–
14	Martin Buchan	Central defence	Manchester U	25	13	–
15	Peter Cormack *	Midfield	Liverpool	27	8	–

16	Willie Donachie	Full-back	Manchester C	22	11	–
17	Donald Ford *	Forward	Hearts	29	3	–
18	Tommy Hutchison	Midfield/Winger	Coventry	26	8	–
19	Denis Law	Forward	Manchester C	34	54	30
20	Willie Morgan	Winger	Manchester U	28	19	1
21	Gordon McQueen	Central defence	Leeds	21	1	–
22	Eric Schaedler *	Full-back	Hibernian	24	1	–

* Would not play in the finals or in future. *Averages*   25.5 13.9

With Peter Cormack at the last moment replacing Newcastle's Jimmy Smith, the squad was youngish and, compared with the 1970 English twenty-two, internationally raw. Players had on average fewer than fourteen caps per man, a consequence of managerial upheavals and disruptions. Only Bremner and Law boasted more than two dozen caps, and doubt surrounded Law's likely contribution. It was a sign of changing times that just one Rangers player was selected, compared with five from Leeds United and another five from the two Manchester clubs.

ZAÏRE v SCOTLAND
Friday, 14 June 1974   *Dortmund – 27,000*

The inaugural match of the 1974 World Cup finals pitched the holders, Brazil, with their new, no-nonsense style, against Yugoslavia. The Scottish party did not care who won, so long as the match was not drawn. Whoever lost would be under pressure to keep afloat. The game ended goalless.

From their base at Erbismuhle in the Taunus mountains near Frankfurt, the Scotland squad prepared for a demolition job against Zaïre. When Scotland last contested the World Cup finals, in 1958, points were all that mattered. But goal difference now counted. Even before the first ball was kicked, it was realised that qualification might be reserved for those most ruthless against Zaïre. In this sense, Scotland were handicapped in meeting them first, when the Africans would be armed with the weapon of surprise. Brazil and Yugoslavia would be watching closely, to learn their secrets.

Zaïre were as familiar as Martians. Though coached by the ex-Yugoslavian goalkeeper, Vidinic, they had taken no prized scalps. They claimed Africa's one place in the finals, overcoming in the process a home defeat by neighbours Cameroon, whom they had to beat in a play-off.

Ormond named a predictable side for the task of beating Zaïre, preferably with something to spare. David Harvey had established himself in goal; Sandy Jardine and Danny McGrain were splendidly paired full-backs. The only

Peter Lorimer volleys Scotland's first World Cup finals goal since 1958. (v Zaïre)

doubts surrounded the identity of Jim Holton's partner in the back four (John Blackley); whether Denis Law would enjoy another Indian Summer (yes); and whether there was room on the flank for either Jimmy Johnstone or Tommy Hutchison (no).

Scotland received the first shock. Like the Paraguayans in 1958, Zaïre were nippier than expected. Perhaps they exerted themselves to keep warm. The Africans felt so chilled by the German summer that they donned vests under their lemon shirts. These, coupled with green shorts and brown skins, presented an image of humming-birds at play. Scotland's methods for softening-up these humming-birds did not endear them to the German neutrals in the half-empty Westfalen Stadium. Jordan offered no kid gloves to acrobatic keeper, Kazadi. The goalkeeper recovered from one early collision to save from Law. Nevertheless, it was Zaïre who could so easily have scored first. Kakoko missed his kick, had time for a second, and put his shot against a post and into the side-netting.

In due course, Scotland's superior strength began to tell. The obvious tactic of projecting high crosses towards Jordan and Law increasingly betokened a goal. It came after twenty-six minutes and was worth the wait. Jordan at the far post headed back McGrain's centre for Lorimer to strike a famous volley past Kazadi.

Scotland's fortunes seemed yet rosier six minutes later when they scored again, this time with a goal of less quality, less legitimacy, but much hilarity. Jordan, possibly offside, sprinted on to Bremner's chipped free kick. In oceans of space, Jordan had time to pick his spot. Instead, the header was tamely struck and plonked straight at the goalkeeper. Alas for Zaïre, Kazadi proved unequal to it, and in the manner of a grandmother spilling her handbag fumbled the ball into the net. Jordan was allowed to celebrate when he should have been cringing with shame.

Zaïre were far from crestfallen. Before the break Kidumi clobbered Bremner and became the latest in a growing list of players cautioned for their dislike of the Scottish captain. Kidumi then collected N'daye's pass in front of Harvey, only to dally and allow the keeper to block.

In the second half Scotland ground forward in the hope or expectation that the Africans would tire. They did not. Kazadi and Lobilo, the able centre-half, repelled all assaults. When Jordan felled Kilasu he found himself threatened within an angry black circle. Mayanga nearly punished the Scots, climaxing a diagonal run with a twenty-yard drive that Harvey turned aside. The floodlights were then extinguished, providing everyone with a four-minute breather. For a while play continued as if by candlelight, but as Zaïre substituted Mayanga for a fresh forward, Kembo, the lights were restored to full power.

It was as if the darkness had fallen from the Africans' eyes. For the last twenty minutes they carried the game to Scotland, much to the crowd's delight. Bremner, foolishly, seemed content on Scotland preserving, rather than seeking to increase, their lead. Long before the end he was urging caution among the players, seeking to slow the pace. Zaïre brought on a second fresh forward and Scotland gave the long legs of Hutchison a run out. Dalglish made way.

Chances fell at both ends. Lorimer's piledriver was turned onto the bar by Kazadi, but then N'daye screwed wide with one chance and obliged Harvey to touch over a second. The final score might have been 6-3 to Scotland. Scotland had managed their first ever win in the World Cup finals. Zaïre had been beaten but not slaughtered, and that might prove painful.

ZAÏRE   (0) 0   SCOTLAND   (2) 2
                                       Lorimer 26, Jordan 33

ZAÏRE: Kazadi, Mwepu, Mukombo, Buhanga, Lobilo, Kilasu, Mayanga (Kembo), Mana, N'daye, Kidumu (Kibonge), Kakoko.
SCOTLAND: Harvey, Jardine, McGrain, Bremner, Holton, Blackley, Dalglish (Hutchison), Hay, Lorimer, Jordan, Law.

BRAZIL v SCOTLAND
Tuesday, 18 June 1974   *Frankfurt – 62,000*

Under normal circumstances, a first World Cup victory – at the sixth attempt – would have been cause for cheer. There was little evidence of Scottish self-satisfaction, both because of the nature of the opposition and the already crystallising fear that Scotland had not done enough. One way to dispose of nagging doubts was to beat Brazil. That would guarantee a place in the last eight and almost certainly eliminate the nation which had won the Jules Rimet trophy three times out of the last four. Indeed, Brazil's third success, in 1970, meant that they kept the trophy for good. A new 'World Cup' was now being fought for.

But beat Brazil? The mere question was enough to raise goosepimples. Scotland had never beaten them. They had lost narrowly, 0-1, twice (at Rio and Hampden), and achieved a 1-1 home draw back in 1966. The indications in 1974 were that Brazil were inhibiting their prodigious flair in favour of European-style pragmatism. This was probably welcome to Scotland, who were better equipped to counter thuggery than magic. In any case, Brazil were depleted through the retirement of Pelé, Gérson and Tostão, and by injury of Clodoaldo, absentees that did Scotland no harm at all. Jairzinho, Piazza, and the moustachioed captain, Rivelino, were the sole survivors of the team that lifted the World Cup in 1970.

Denis Law had struggled against Zaïre's youthful zest, and now, having earned his fifty-sixth cap, he was finally pensioned off. Amazing to think that his international career had extended over sixteen years, commencing immediately after the 1958 World Cup finals. He was one match short of participating in *five* World Cups. In came Willie Morgan for his first full game in five weeks. The other change was to bring in Martin Buchan for Blackley. This brought the Old Trafford contingent up to three, one short of Leeds'.

As defending champions, Brazil had not been required to submit themselves to the indignities of qualifying. Indeed, as three-times champions, they had only once had to do so in twenty years.

Afternoon rain had softened the pitch in Frankfurt, but the match was played in evening sunshine in front of prime minister Harold Wilson and some 12,000 Scots in the packed Wald Stadium. Wilson turned a deaf ear to the whistling of 'God Save the Queen' and its substitution by the echoing stanzas of 'Flower of Scotland'. Nor could he have enjoyed the sight of Brazil threatening to sweep their opponents into the River Main. Scotland began as if with a massive inferiority complex. They hung on in desperation as Brazil rolled back the clock to their golden years. For half an hour Scotland walked the plank.

The champions endured one red-faced moment when keeper Leão slid a goal kick over his own goal-line. But the danger to Scotland's goal was real

Leão saves from Jordan in a crowded goalmouth. (v Brazil)

when a Rivelino 'special' from twenty-five paces forced Harvey into a flying save. From the corner, blond full-back Francisco Marinho's acrobatic volley left the crossbar quivering crazily and Harvey wringing his fingers. With Jardine clearing another effort off the line, Scotland were on the rack. The tartan army watched the action through closed fingers.

As Brazil failed to break through, they slowly lost their way and the Scottish pulse rate dropped. For the last fifteen minutes of the half Harvey breathed easier and his colleagues even began to cross the halfway line. As the tide turned Rivelino exhibited the shadow side of his character, forsaking his extravagant skills for skulduggery of every kind. He entered the referee's book for an unpleasant foul on – who else? – Bremner. At Hampden the previous year he had been likewise prone to incivility, and likewise Scotland were none too distressed. A devilish Rivelino was better than a divine one.

The attitude of both teams at half-time was shaped largely by news that Yugoslavia were six goals up against Zaïre. In the backs of their minds Scotland must have rued their goal-shyness, for it now looked as though they *had* to beat Brazil *or* Yugoslavia. As for Brazil, if they could hold out for forty-five minutes they would need only to beat Zaire 3-0 to make the quarter-finals.

Upon the resumption Brazil adopted a 'what we have we hold' policy as Scotland piled forward in a navy tidal wave. Bremner and Hay emerged as

Not a man to tangle with, but Jordan beats Luis Pereira to the ball. (v Brazil)

international giants as they put Brazil to the sword. Leão leapt to touch over Hay's effort and Lorimer's bullet free kick had the crowd roaring. The beat of Brazilian bongos was drowned by the chants of the tartan army. Midway through the half came the moment that would haunt Billy Bremner. Leão plunged at the ball, pushed it against Bremner's shins, and both players watched helpless as it rebounded agonisingly wide of a post. Scotland's attacks were now being thwarted by any means (though the final foul-count was roughly equal). For all their pressure, Scotland were unable to carve out the one clear chance that would steal the match, and they might yet have lost when a lightning Brazilian break-out was foiled by Harvey's smothering save. Upon the final whistle Brazil were all smiles and handshakes.

BRAZIL (0) 0   SCOTLAND (0) 0

BRAZIL: Leão, Nelinho, Luís Pereira, M Marinho, F Marinho, Piazza, Rivelino, P Cesar Lima, Jairzinho, Mirandinha, Leivinha (P Cesar Carpegiani).
SCOTLAND: Harvey, Jardine, McGrain, Holton, Buchan, Bremner, Hay, Dalglish, Morgan, Jordan, Lorimer.

YUGOSLAVIA v SCOTLAND

Saturday, 22 June 1974   *Frankfurt – 56,000*

Victory over Brazil would have been acclaimed as Scotland's greatest ever result. Even the draw was praiseworthy, except for its likely bearing on the outcome of Group 2. Brazil had come off worse from two goalless draws, but now looked like stepping effortlessly into the last eight. Yugoslavia, having scrutinised Scotland's failings against Zaïre, had taken the punch-drunk Africans apart. The final score, 9-0, equalled the record for the World Cup finals. For Scotland to qualify, one of two things had to happen. They either had to beat Yugoslavia, or, should they draw, Brazil must not exceed a one-goal win over Zaïre. The latter prospect was not worth banking on: Scotland had to win.

The Brazilian press acknowledged that Scotland had overrun Brazil for seventy minutes, and had praised Bremner as a 'small giant'. Ormond saw no reason to change such a team, although its chief shortcoming – an inability to carve out openings – invited suggestions that Kenny Dalglish be dropped. Dalglish had looked lacklustre throughout the Home Internationals and the pre-World Cup matches in Belgium and Norway, not to mention Scotland's first two matches in Germany. Danny McGrain's performances were up to his usual standard, but he had shed over a stone in weight and would shortly learn that he was diabetic. With hindsight, he might even have wished to be dropped, rather than exert himself to such an extent that his health was threatened.

Yugoslavia, coached by Miljan Milanovitch, had been the final team to qualify, needing a play-off before disposing of Spain. They were appearing in their first finals since 1958, when they drew with Scotland 1-1. They had, in fact, never beaten the Scots. For Yugoslavia, the present match was as good as a home fixture. Some 40,000 Yugoslavs lived and worked in Frankfurt. The national side was packed with star players – Buljan and Katalinski in defence, Oblak in midfield, Dragan Dzajic on the wing.

With one team needing to win, the other to draw, there was little doubt which goal would be the busier. Blistering temperatures did not prevent Scotland rolling up their sleeves and driving forward. Bremner and Hay, both prominent against Brazil, now turned on the performances of their lives. Free kicks – they numbered more than sixty, evenly divided – broke up every move. By the end there were also five bookings, Hay and Jordan from Scotland. The heading ability of the Leeds forward had been a frequent talking point in Germany, and the Yugoslavs ensured he was given little opportunity to exercise it. Scotland's inability to create telling openings continued to frustrate their otherwise sterling efforts. Dalglish once again (by his own admission) struggled to make any impact, and he was pulled off to make way, a second time, for Tommy Hutchison.

Joe Jordan appears to be held off as Maric collects. (v Yugoslavia)

Dalglish later summed up the match: 'The Yugoslavs didn't allow us to play.' McGrain added: 'The match was a dreadful anti-climax for Scots players and fans alike. Despite heavy pressure from the opening whistle we could not find a way through a nine man defensive barrier.' Yet news of Brazil's progress at Gelsenkirchen offered unexpected salvation. Brazil stood 1-0 at half-time. As both matches entered their final ten minutes Scotland were still breathing. Brazil were winning only by two, giving them an identical record to Scotland.

Then the world caved in. Although Scotland did not yet know it, Brazil scored a third when Valdomiro's slack shot from the tightest of angles crept into the net under the Zaïre goalkeeper. Back at Frankfurt, Yugoslavia surged out of packed defence. Substitute Karasi began a move continued by Dzajic on the right. Karasi spurted forward, dived for the cross in front of Jardine, and headed cleanly past Harvey. Scotland were out of the World Cup.

Yet the causes of subsequent anguish and debate were still to come. Ormond prepared to install Jimmy Johnstone but failed to attract the referee's eye. The flying winger, who five years previously had shredded the Red Star Belgrade defence in the European Cup, dejectedly re-took his seat. One of the greatest wingers in British football would never kick a ball in the World Cup finals.

With two minutes remaining, Hutchison's twisting run past Buljan yielded a fast, low centre across the goalmouth. Lorimer slashed, and the ball flew to

Jordan who, off-balance, hit it inside a post. With the players still unaware of Brazil's third goal, they fancied they were safe.

The heartbreaking news only dawned as they left the pitch. The electronic scoreboard flashed up Brazil's result from Gelsenkirchen. History had been repeated. In 1958, Scotland had drawn 1-1 with Yugoslavia and been eliminated while Yugoslavia prospered. The fact that Scotland were knocked out unbeaten – they were the first country ever to suffer that fate – prompted much misplaced pleading of bad luck. True, this was as good a team as Scotland had ever assembled. But equally true, the writing had been on the wall way back against Zaïre. The Africans' goals-against tally, fourteen, saddled them with the distinction of being the worst team ever to depreciate the finals of the World Cup.

YUGOSLAVIA   (0) 1   SCOTLAND   (0) 1
  Karasi 81   Jordan 88

YUGOSLAVIA: Maric, Buljan, Hadziabdic, Oblak, Katalinski, Bogicevic, Petkovic, Acimovic, Bajevic (Karasi), Surjak, Dzajic.
SCOTLAND: Harvey, Jardine, McGrain, Holton, Buchan, Bremner, Dalglish (Hutchison), Hay, Morgan, Jordan, Lorimer.

A proud, if crestfallen Scottish party flew into Abbotsinch airport to the rapturous acclaim of ten thousand well-wishers. There was a great sense of 'if'. If Scotland had made the second phase, how would they have fared? Although Scotland had found winning difficult, they had proved themselves hard to beat.

Yugoslavia fell at the next hurdle, bottom of their second phase group. Brazil, so different from the team revered in the past, kicked their way steadily onwards until even they had no answer to the Dutchmen, Cruyff and Neeskens. Brazil eventually finished an unloved fourth, while West Germany took the title, beating Holland 2-1 in the Final.

Final positions – Group 2

	P	W	D	L	F	A	Pts
YUGOSLAVIA	3	1	2	0	10	1	4
BRAZIL	3	1	2	0	3	0	4
Scotland	3	1	2	0	3	1	4
Zaïre	3	0	0	3	0	14	0

Scotland appearances and goalscorers (substitute appearances in brackets)
World Cup qualifying rounds and final competition 1974

	Apps	Goals		Apps	Goals
Dalglish K	6 (1)	1	Brownlie J	2	–
Bremner W *†	6	–	Colquhoun E	2	–
Morgan W	6	1	Graham G	2	–
Harvey D	5	–	Harper J	1 (1)	1
Hay D	5	–	Bone J	1	1
Jardine S	5	–	Clark R	1	–
Lorimer P *	5	2	Connelly G	1	–
McGrain D	5	–	Donachie W	1	–
Jordan J	4 (1)	3	Forsyth A	1	–
Buchan M	4	–	Forsyth T	1	–
Holton J	4	1	Hunter A	1	–
Law D *†‡	3	–	Macari L	1	1
Hutchison T	2 (2)	–	Carr W	– (1)	–
Blackley J	2	–	Ford D	– (1)	–

* Appeared in 1970 World Cup.   *84 apps   11 goals*
† Appeared in 1966 World Cup.   *35 Scottish League*
‡ Appeared in 1962 World Cup.   *49 English League*
                                       28 players used

8

THE 1978 WORLD CUP

Even allowing for the frustrating circumstances of their elimination, there was no doubting that Scotland's performances through the 1974 World Cup – both in qualifying rounds and finals – were the finest they had ever turned in. Whether or not by coincidence, the 1974 World Cup was the first in which Scotland fielded more Anglos than domiciles. In any case, optimism for the future was no longer misplaced or fanciful, and the international standing of the team and its unassuming manager was probably never higher. Docherty and Ormond – awarded the OBE for his efforts – had brought Scottish international football out of the shadows. With the World Cup and European Championship alternating every two years, Ormond was granted an early opportunity to gauge his team's progress in the European tournament.

Disappointment lay in store. Before 1974 was out, Scotland had been beaten at home by Spain, an insuperable setback to hopes of attaining the European finals. Though other results that season were satisfactory, a 1-5 thrashing at the hands of England dispersed any notions of grandiosity. Scotland had lost the two matches that mattered. By the time the next World Cup came round, Scotland had registered one win (Denmark), one loss (England), and four draws away from Hampden. Happily, that drubbing at Wembley spurred the team to a nine-match unbeaten run.

News that Scotland's opponents would be Wales and, would you believe, Czechoslovakia, invited accusations of incest. In the case of Scotland and Wales, British footballers already played each other every week. Now they were asked to commit fratricide, as they had in the 1950s. As for the Czechs, they were now paired with Scotland for the third time. In 1962, Czechoslovakia had had a fine side, too strong for Scotland's. In 1974 the Czechs were poor, and Scotland turned the tables. The Czechs had risen from the doldrums with a bang. In the 1976 European Championship they had knocked out England, swept past the Soviet Union and Holland on their way to the Final, and then taken the title in a penalty shoot-out with West Germany. Scotland had been the seeded nation when the World Cup draw was made, but there was little doubt that it was Czechoslovakia who rightfully belonged to the master class.

Qualifying Group 6

CZECHOSLOVAKIA v SCOTLAND

Wednesday, 13 October 1976   *Prague – 38,000*

Scotland were unable to test the temperature of Group 6 with their elbows: they were plunged in at the deep end. The match in Prague might hold the key to the group. Scotland had recently used Finland for shooting practice, hitting them for six, and extending their winning run to five. Three of these victories had been in the British Championship, which Scotland won outright for the first time in eleven years. Sober Scots were not carried away: all five wins had been at Hampden and would count for little in Prague in view of Scotland's time-honoured travel sickness.

The Czechs needed retentive memories to recall their own team's last defeat. It was at Wembley in 1974, since when they had chalked up twenty-three unbeaten matches. A handful of players remained from the 1973 clashes with Scotland. Indeed, Petras, Dobias and the balding Pollak were also still around, having played in Mexico '70. The strengths of the current side were said to include the centre-half and captain, Ondrus, and the lethal striking duo, Zdenek Nehoda and Marian Masny.

The Scottish team had evolved since 1974 and the creation a year later of the Premier League. Alan Rough, of part-timers Partick, had been introduced in goal at the start of the winning Hampden sequence. McGrain was maturing into a world-class full-back, now switching to the right where his overlaps were most effective. Willie Donachie partnered him on the left. The central stoppers were the Leeds giant Gordon McQueen, who returned after a year's absence, and Martin Buchan, who brought his reassuring presence to the back line.

All eyes were on the Scottish midfield. The fruitful combination in West Germany of Bremner and Hay was no more. Hay's international career was cut short by injury, and Bremner's indiscretions on and off the pitch had provoked the authorities once too often. This double loss had been softened by the unearthing of able replacements. Scotland now paraded a new, entirely Anglo midfield, comprising QPR's Don Masson plus the Derby pair Bruce Rioch and Archie Gemmill. Gemmill was Scottish captain. In attack, in the 4-3-3 format of the time, Joe Jordan teamed up with the English first division's top scorer, Andy Gray, and Celtic's captain, Kenny Dalglish, who was given a free role.

On the Tuesday, the Scottish Under-21s achieved a goalless draw against the Czechs. The conduct of the seniors the next day was much improved from that lacklustre, feeble defeat in· Bratislava three years earlier. The match was relentless and uncompromising. Throughout the first half one Scottish name after another – McQueen, Gemmill, Buchan – was jotted into referee Michelotti's notebook.

These transgressions did not suggest Scotland were up against it. Although Dobias' first-minute volley flew just inches wide, Scotland shaded the first half. Their rapid counter-attacks posed constant danger. Jordan's header from Rioch's cross forced a good save from Vencel, while Rioch's power shooting kept the Czechs on their toes.

Scotland were looking forward to the interval, the job half done, when Ondrus and Andy Gray waged a one-man war on the other. Mr Michelotti had little choice but to send them off.

If Ormond, shorn of a striker, was tempted to play safe, his plans were at once redundant. Czechoslovakia began the second half in a frenzy. From a quickly won corner Nehoda smashed goalwards, Rough blocked, and Panenka cracked the loose ball under the bar.

McQueen's thunderous challenge had been responsible for Goegh's early withdrawal. The fair-haired giant now made atonement to the Czechs. He fluffed a cross and the blond Petras flashed home a diving header. Two goals in two minutes.

Czechoslovakia then went on the rampage, the Scottish midfield brushed aside like gossamer. Birmingham's Kenny Burns brought his iron qualities to the fray, in place of Dalglish, and promptly scythed Dobias. Manchester City's Asa Hartford took over from Masson. The Czech full-backs continued to pour forward to support their forwards. The names of Donachie and Czech substitute Jurkemic were added to the referee's black book. The nearest Scotland came to scoring their first World Cup goal in Czechoslovakia was when Jordan's looping header brought a flying stop from Vencel. By the close, the European champions had soundly disposed of the tartan pretenders.

CZECHOSLOVAKIA (0) 2   SCOTLAND (0) 0
Panenka 46, Petras 48

CZECHOSLOVAKIA: Vencel, Biros, Ondrus, Capkovic (Jurkemic), Goegh (Kroupa), Dobias, Panenka, Pollak, Masny, Nehoda, Petras.
SCOTLAND: Rough (Partick), McGrain (Celtic), Donachie (Man C), Buchan (Man U), McQueen (Leeds), Rioch (Derby), Dalglish (Celtic) (*sub* Burns, Birmingham), Masson (QPR) (*sub* Hartford, Man C), Jordan (Leeds), Gray (Villa), Gemmill (Derby).

SCOTLAND v WALES

Wednesday, 17 November 1976   *Hampden – 63,233*

Defeat in Prague left Scotland hanging over the precipice. There could be no more slips. Czechoslovakia had staked a weighty advantage, and if Scotland should drop a home point to Wales it might scuttle Ormond's team's chances.

Dai Davies looks glum. Ian Evans, on the ground, has just scored an own goal. (v Wales)

Wales were no longer the Hampden bogey of the immediate post-war years. They hadn't won in Scotland in twelve attempts since 1951. They had been the only British team to reach the last eight of the 1976 European Championship, where they were put out by Yugoslavia. They had recently been sunk 1-3 at Hampden in the British Championship. Wales were clearly alive to the danger confronting them, for they introduced seven fresh players.

Ormond saw no need for panic changes, but Andy Gray was missing through suspension, Buchan through injury, and Masson likewise – the consequence of colliding with Welsh skipper Terry Yorath in a recent league match. Yorath denied dishonourable intent. Masson's shirt was claimed by the abrasive Kenny Burns, John Blackley stepped in for Buchan, and Eddie Gray – injured prior to the Prague game – deputised for his Villa namesake. There was no place for Scotland's leading scorer, Joe Harper of Aberdeen.

Welsh manager Mike Smith was frank about his instructions, which were to attempt to hold Scotland at bay for twenty minutes. By that time, he hoped, the Hampden crowd would have lost their rag. Wales were five minutes short of Smith's target when Scotland scored. Rioch sent the overlapping McGrain galloping down the right touchline. Dalglish took a swing at the full-back's low cross and Ian Evans did the rest. The Welsh stopper lunged to intercept but could only perform Dalglish's job for him. The ball lay snugly in the net.

In theory, the goal should have opened the game up, obliging Wales to tally-ho. Scotland were in no mood to grant titbits. All the visitors could offer by way of reply was a hopeful pot-shot by Evans – desperate to erase his earlier error – which sailed out of harm's way, and a Yorath shot that flew through a forest of limbs before being pounced upon by Alan Rough.

Otherwise, Scotland ran the match till the end. One or two players must have thought twice about mixing it. A second booking, on top of those meted out in Prague, carried automatic suspension. McGrain rendered poor Leighton James impotent, forcing the frustrated winger's early substitution. Early in the second half McGrain embarked on a sixty-yard run. The ball seemed tied by invisible elastic as half-challenges came and went. McGrain's enterprise was finally terminated by the intervention of Welsh keeper Dai Davies. McGrain landed upside down. 'Penalty' screamed Hampden. The chorus of boos told of the referee's opinion.

Burns was unpassable; Dalglish unstoppable. The gifted forward, so often maligned, was on top of his game. Jordan and McQueen won more than their share of aerial battles. For Wales, Ian Evans found himself in the referee's notebook twice – once as goalscorer, then as villain for yet another angry tackle on Jordan.

Dalglish set up Rioch, but the shot flew off a post to nestle in Davies' arms. Asa Hartford took over from Rioch, and Gemmill's shot shortly afterwards left the Welsh crossbar twanging.

This was Wales and Liverpool striker John Toshack's first exposure to Hampden. He almost made his mark with a firm header from Thomas's centre, but Rough was equal to it. Scottish hearts missed a beat, but soon recovered. Willie Pettigrew was given a run out and the final whistle sounded on an emphatic victory marred only by the nature of the goal. The win was all the sweeter because earlier that day England had gone down 0-2 in Rome and were staring elimination in the face. That night it was learned that Czechoslovakia had lost 0-2 in a friendly in West Germany, their first defeat in twenty-five matches. The Czechs had lacked incentive and had fielded a makeshift side. They were in any case not due to visit Hampden for ten months, but had their bubble burst?

SCOTLAND (1) 1   WALES (0) 0
  Evans 15 (o.g.)

SCOTLAND: Rough, McGrain, Donachie, Blackley, McQueen, Rioch (Hartford), Burns, Dalglish, Jordan, Gemmill, Gray (Pettigrew).
WALES: D Davies (Everton), Page (Birm'ham), J Jones (L'pool), L Phillips (Villa), I Evans (Palace), Griffiths (Wrexham), M Thomas (Wrexham), Flynn (Burnley), Yorath (Coventry), Toshack (Liverpool), L James (Derby) (sub Curtis, Swansea).

SCOTLAND v CZECHOSLOVAKIA

Wednesday, 21 September 1977   *Hampden – 85,000*

Guiding Scotland through the rest of the qualifiers was a new manager, someone who would prove to be the most controversial appointment ever made by the SFA. Willie Ormond had been engaged in long-standing contractual difficulties with his employers. These finally drove him back to the apparently more secure world of club management, with Hearts. Jock Stein was asked to take over, but he preferred to stay at Parkhead. The SFA turned instead to the man who had masterminded Aberdeen's 1976 League Cup Final triumph. Ormond's predecessor, Tommy Docherty, had been flamboyant: Ormond's successor was even more so. Defeat never entered Ally MacLeod's head. 'It's Argentina or Siberia,' he pledged.

MacLeod had taken office in time for the British Championship in the spring, which Scotland won for the second season running. He was wise to encourage cohesion, having no wish to dismantle Ormond's well-oiled team.

Since prospering from Ian Evans' own goal, Scotland had played eight internationals, defeat being reserved for the last two – Brazil in Rio (at the end of an acclimatising tour of South America) and East Germany in Berlin. Scotland had earned laudable victories, notably over England at Wembley and Chile in Santiago. No one could put much store by Scotland's form, which was never other than unpredictable, but Czechoslovakia had, it seemed, lost their way. Defeat in West Germany had not proved an isolated setback. In March, the Czechs had travelled to Wrexham and been whacked 0-3 – a godsend to the Scots. Czechoslovakia failed to score in three of their next four matches. Wales, however, were now very much alive and the group was wide open. Each team had won one and lost one.

History told that Czechoslovakia had never so much as drawn at Hampden. They could ill-afford to lose this time, and fearing themselves to be past their peak tore up the team that had sunk Scotland in Prague. Faith was retained in veterans Dobias and Pollak, as with strikers Masny and Nehoda. Crucially, centre-half Ondrus was suspended.

MacLeod's first World Cup eleven were all Ormond's men, other than Sandy Jardine and Willie Johnston, both recalled. The gifted but wayward Johnston seemed revitalised following a move from Rangers to WBA. He was now back on international duty for the first time in seven years. Johnston was not the only Scot to have changed clubs. Dalglish had succeeded Kevin Keegan at Liverpool while Rioch had gone to Goodison. Rioch had also added the captaincy of Scotland to his duties, the first player born in England to do so.

MacLeod's team was represented by nine different clubs. Old hands McGrain, Jardine, Dalglish and Jordan all savoured pleasant memories of that storming 1973 Hampden victory.

In view of the game's importance, the Czechs could be forgiven a few grumbles at their travel arrangements. An air strike obliged them to sit up overnight on a train from London to Glasgow. Sleeping accommodation was unavailable. FIFA refused a request for a twenty-four hour postponement. Yet come the match, any lingering effects of train-lag seemed to have dissipated. The Czechs looked sprightly enough, but Scotland, spurred on by Rioch, Masson and Hartford, refused to let their opponents settle. Scotland's high-ball tactics threatened to disconcert the more terrestrial Czechs.

Chances had been few when Scotland took the lead on nineteen minutes. Rioch won a corner. The ball was swung in by Johnston, and McQueen's decoy jump created space behind him. Jordan filled it, thumping a firm header inside the far post.

The Czechs had had their moments, and would continue to enjoy them. Goegh flashed at a corner but miscued, and Dvorak's header was off target. But ten minutes before half-time Scotland engineered a second, vital, goal. Johnston's cross had everyone in the Czech penalty area converging upon it. As Michalik came to intercept he was impeded by a colleague, and was further handicapped by colliding with Jordan. Another referee another day would have penalised the striker. This one did not, and when the ball fell kindly to Hartford the goal was allowed to stand.

Czechoslovakia brought on substitute Knapp at the start of the second half and Gallis later. Czech composure was long forgotten, and by the end two players apiece had been cautioned. Czech resistance was finally stilled in the fifty-fourth minute by the ubiquitous Dalglish. McQueen harassed Michalik at a corner. McQueen and Jardine played head tennis before Dalglish got the final, decisive nod. Aerial sorties had produced all three Scotland goals.

Hampden had been noisy from the start; now the 'roar' was unstoppable. Its volume slackened only fleetingly, when Gajdusek's thirty-yard trundler eluded Alan Rough. In these times of goal difference there was no longer any such thing as a 'consolation' goal. Rough's boob might prove costly. But at the end the crowd was happy. Cock-a-hoop in fact. 'We want Ally,' they sang. And well they might: the side had looked ominously strong. It was also, according to Czech manager Josef Venglos, a trifle too physical.

SCOTLAND   (2) 3   CZECHOSLOVAKIA   (0) 1
    Jordan 19, Hartford 35,   Gajdusek 80
    Dalglish 54

SCOTLAND: Rough, Jardine, McGrain, Forsyth, McQueen, Rioch, Dalglish, Masson, Jordan, Hartford, Johnston.
CZECHOSLOVAKIA: Michalik, Paurik, Capkovic, Dvorak, Goegh, Dobias (Gallis), Gajdusek, Moder (Knapp), Pollak, Masny, Nehoda.

WALES v SCOTLAND

Wednesday, 12 October 1977   *Anfield, Liverpool – 50,800*

When the draw for Group 6 was announced the Czechs doubtless shook their heads. This had to do with facing two British teams. Most Scots and Welsh internationals were well acquainted through the medium of the English League. In effect, there could be no such thing as an 'away' fixture inside the almost incestuous British context. Scotland and Wales, backed by armies of vociferous support, viewed a visit to the other as only marginally less homely than playing at home. In essence, the Czechs had to play two 'away' fixtures, one more than the Scots and Welsh.

Nothing less than a Welsh win would keep the Czechs alive. A draw would eliminate the east Europeans and leave Wales needing to win in Prague. Scotland had not lost in six visits to the principality. The Czechs were even more disgruntled when the Welsh FA transferred the fixture to Liverpool, to offset drastic crowd restrictions imposed on Ninian Park and Wrexham's Racecourse Ground. Most tickets fell into Scottish hands, allowing Scotland to enjoy an 'away' tie in an environment tantamount to playing at Hampden.

Wales could point to a six-match unbeaten run, conceding only one goal in the process. But having to field four players from the English lower reaches (including Mickey Thomas, plucked from Wrexham's reserves), encouraged pundits to plump for Scotland.

This was Ally MacLeod's ninth match, and his team had settled nicely. He had, however, lost two key players through injury. Bruce Rioch reported a calf strain and Danny McGrain had succumbed to a mysterious foot problem. Their replacements were Willie Donachie and Lou Macari. The eleven had earned a healthy 245 caps between them. Don Masson assumed the captaincy.

It was a night of unforgettable passion. Scotland seized the game by the throat, winning a profusion of early corners. They screamed for a penalty when Dai Davies brought down Dalglish, who had burst clear. The reprieved keeper then saw the ball squeeze like soap through his fingers, precipitating much flailing of legs before the danger passed.

As the game stabilised, Wales created chances of their own. One fell to Peter Sayer, still to play in a losing Welsh side in six appearances. He fastened on to Phillips' shrewd pass but shot wide.

By the break there was little to choose between the sides. The stalemate continued afterwards. Scotland could perhaps claim a moral advantage in goal attempts, but the Welsh midfield of Mahoney, Flynn and Yorath gave the 'home' team the edge in stability. Both sides brought on substitutes (Buchan for Jardine; Deacy for Sayer); both had players booked (Donachie and Yorath). John Toshack scripted one of the second half's two turning points. He was still on the comeback trail after sustaining a serious injury seven months previously, and had not yet forced his way back into Liverpool's first team. On the hour he was presented with a clear chance at his beloved Kop end – even though the 'Kop' happened to be wearing tammies. At an angle to the left, Toshack beat the offside trap. His lofted shot was dipping over Rough until the goalkeeper acrobatically touched it against the bar. Wales were as close as that.

Scotland struck back with verve. Davies did well to parry Dalglish's point-blank header, and Jordan drove wastefully high. But eleven minutes from time came the second decisive incident, which heralded one of the most outrageous goals ever to disfigure a football match. A high ball hurled into the Welsh penalty area was pushed away by a raised hand. French referee Wurtz had had a fine match up to that point, only to make a critical error. He (along with many others at the time) adjudged the guilty hand to belong to David Jones. In fact, it belonged to Joe Jordan. Television pointed the finger, but the referee had no TV. Masson scored from the spot to give his side a quite undeserved lead. Monsieur Wurtz's magic wand had conjured a goal from mid-air and waved Wales out of the World Cup.

Dalglish's fine scoring header three minutes from time, when almost the entire Welsh side were camped in the Scottish half, served only to lighten Scottish embarrassment. In truth, it was the penalty that took Scotland to Argentina. In truth, the result was a travesty.

'Que Sera Sera, we're going to Argentina,' chorused the Scottish throngs. If they appreciated their debt to Monsieur Wurtz they would have sung the Marseillaise. Yet in football, as in life, the celestial tribunal ensured the debt was rendered. Scotland would pay for their good fortune heavily, and with interest, the following summer.

WALES (0) 0   SCOTLAND (0) 2
                               Masson 79 pen, Dalglish 87

WALES: D Davies (Everton), R Thomas (Derby), J Jones (Liverpool), Mahoney (Midd'bro), D Jones (Norwich), Phillips (Villa), Flynn (Burnley), Sayer (Cardiff) (*sub* Deacy, PSV Eind), Yorath (Coventry), Toshack (L'pool), Thomas (Wrexham).
SCOTLAND: Rough, Jardine (Buchan), Donachie, Masson, McQueen, Forsyth, Dalglish, Hartford, Jordan, Macari, Johnston.

Qualifying Group 7

	P	W	D	L	F	A	Pts
SCOTLAND	4	3	0	1	6	3	6
Czechoslovakia	4	2	0	2	4	6	4
Wales	4	1	0	3	3	4	2

Other group results

Wales v Czechoslovakia	3-0	Czechoslovakia v Wales	1-0

World Cup finals – ARGENTINA   June 1978

Scotland's qualification provoked a ballyhoo unlike anything experienced in 1974 or, for that matter, at any other time. Taking their cue from the manager, large swathes of the Scottish nation seemed consumed by a kind of xenophobic optimism that caused considerable disquiet among more discerning Scots and, if truth be told, derision from outside. Referee Wurtz's gift goal had turned 'Mohammed Ally' into a self-appointed Scottish national messiah.

MacLeod's stridently anti-English, anti-world crusade was given impetus by England's later failure to qualify, enabling Scotland for the second successive World Cup to corner the media's attention outside Scotland and in. MacLeod's beaming face leered from billboards and TV screens.

MacLeod's managerial record was not exactly electrifying, ten years in the twilight world of part-timers Ayr United, followed by a mere eighteen months in the top flight at Pittodrie. But for Aberdeen lifting the Scottish League Cup prior to Willie Ormond's resignation, MacLeod probably would have remained on the margins of the Scottish football hierarchy. His early successes with Scotland produced the widespread feeling, 'cometh the hour, cometh the man'.

To be fair, the manager's excessive exuberance was not universally welcomed in Scotland. The fear that he generated more hot air than sense (coming close to predicting Scotland would win the World Cup) intensified during his final preparations for Argentina. Aside from a home friendly with Bulgaria, MacLeod did not seek warm-up matches against continental or South American opponents. Instead, Scotland flew out a few days after a strenuous schedule of Home Internationals, all played at Hampden within a week.

There were shrugs when Northern Ireland forced a draw, sighs when the Welsh followed suit. But when England triumphed 1-0 anyone would have thought – listening to MacLeod – that Scotland had won. It was, he insisted, only bad luck that was responsible for Scotland's downfall. To compound matters, his players embarked on a lap of honour to celebrate qualifying for Argentina. A lap of honour after losing – especially to England – was surely stretching credibility. One could sense many Scots wincing at the banality of it all, embarrassed players forcing a smile as they trotted around Hampden's vastness. Several would later admit their misgivings. Laps of honour were for victors, and Scotland had won nothing – yet.

The SFA also staged a send-off party at Hampden. Supporters could roll up to show their appreciation, and pay for the privilege! 25,000 did so. How could it be that a nation justly proud of itself and its football could stoop so low? One could almost anticipate the coming disaster.

MacLeod had named his World Cup squad before the Home Internationals. Brought up to date to include those fixtures, the list reads:

No	Name	Position	Club	Age	Caps	Goals
1	Alan Rough	Goalkeeper	Partick Thistle	26	18	–
2	Sandy Jardine	Full-back	Rangers	29	34	1
3	Willie Donachie	Full-back	Manchester C	26	30	–
4	Martin Buchan	Central defence	Manchester U	29	28	–
5	Gordon McQueen	Central defence	Manchester U	25	20	3
6	Bruce Rioch (c)	Midfield	Derby County	30	22	6
7	Don Masson	Midfield	Derby County	31	16	5
8	Kenny Dalglish	Forward	Liverpool	27	54	18
9	Joe Jordan	Forward	Manchester U	26	30	7
10	Asa Hartford	Midfield	Manchester C	27	24	3
11	Willie Johnston	Winger	WBA	31	21	–
12	Jim Blyth *	Goalkeeper	Coventry	23	2	–
13	Stuart Kennedy	Full-back	Aberdeen	24	3	–
14	Tom Forsyth	Central defence	Rangers	29	19	–
15	Archie Gemmill	Midfield	Nott'm Forest	31	26	2
16	Lou Macari	Midfield/Forward	Manchester U	28	22	5
17	Derek Johnstone	Forward	Rangers	24	13	3
18	Graeme Souness	Midfield	Liverpool	24	6	–
19	John Robertson	Winger	Nott'm Forest	25	2	–
20	Bobby Clark *	Goalkeeper	Aberdeen	32	17	–
21	Joe Harper	Forward	Aberdeen	30	3	2
22	Kenny Burns	Central defence	Nott'm Forest	24	11	–

* Would not play in the finals or in future.		*Averages*		27.3	19.1	

Reserves: (uncalled upon) Jim Stewart, Willie Miller, John Blackley, Andy Gray, Arthur Graham, Ian Wallace.

For all his prickliness on the subject of England, MacLeod was not above naming fifteen Anglos in his squad. Only two of the twenty-two names invited surprise; firstly, Joe Harper from MacLeod's old stomping ground, Aberdeen, to the exclusion of the free-scoring Andy Gray; and secondly, raw John Robertson on the wing in place of ex-Don Arthur Graham. Manchester United's latest recruit, Gordon McQueen, had crashed into a goalpost at Hampden and damaged knee ligaments. Though his prospects were bleak, McQueen was not withdrawn. Nor was another orthodox centre-half included as cover. With incomparable full-back Danny McGrain still incapacitated, and

Willie Donachie, booked at Anfield, suspended from the first match, MacLeod would have to send out an improvised back four behind a part-time goalkeeper. Group 4, in which Scotland were balloted, seemed a mite kinder than that in West Germany. MacLeod was certainly happy with it. In 1974 Scotland had been pooled with the world champions, Brazil; now they would face World Cup runners-up Holland. Instead of playing Zaïre, Scotland would face Iran. Much of a muchness, so far. What made 1978 appear more agreeable was the substitution of Yugoslavia by Peru. Yugoslavia had proved formidable. Peru, the sages insisted, were here to make up the numbers.

In 1974, shrewd judges among the footballing throngs advised being wary of Scotland as dark horses. Similar words were uttered in 1978, but with shakier foundations. MacLeod's boast about intending to win medals evidently made an impression on his fellow managers and coaches, many of whom were happy to ignore Scotland's failings in the British Championship and the critical unavailability of key defenders. 'Scotland are a team to watch,' spoke many wise football heads in Argentina. Strange to say, at one stage Scotland's odds on lifting the trophy shortened to 8-1.

Had those admirers peeped inside the Scottish camp at Alta Gracia, in the foothills of the High Sierras, their enthusiasm might have cooled. All was not well with Scottish morale. From the first night it was clear that the gutter press was determined to find smoke and turn it into fire. It located a whiff and transformed it into an inferno. Stories of players' brushes with armed guards, boozing, gambling and womanising were flashed around the globe, creating a lurid picture of rampant indiscipline and wantonness.

The Scottish players were already demoralised by failure, as in 1974, to exploit lucrative commercial bonuses. Their tarnished public image, which bore little resemblance to the fàcts, upset them further, as did their hotel and their inadequate training facilities. These threatened to exacerbate MacLeod's injury list. All boded ill – a state of affairs as yet unknown to the 500 or so Scottish supporters, tagging themselves 'Ally's Army', who had saved their pennies for the experience of a lifetime.

Ally's Army wouldn't enjoy the best views. The pitch at Córdoba, venue for Scotland's opening two matches, was remote from the spectators. First opponents were Peru. Had MacLeod watched them play? Of course not. 'Let them worry about us!' he blustered.

PERU v SCOTLAND
Saturday, 3 June 1978   *Córdoba – 45,000*

MacLeod's team selection for what was likely to prove Scotland's make or break match produced a hail of reproach. With the exception of Buchan, as stand-in full-back for Donachie, MacLeod nominated the team that had lost to

England. Derek Johnstone's forty-one goals for Rangers, not to mention both Scotland's goals in the British Championship, did not merit a call-up. His shirt went to bustling Joe Jordan, who had accumulated just two goals for his country in four years. MacLeod was nothing if not loyal, but that commendable quality could be taken to extremes. His selection in midfield ignored the inescapable reality that his captain and vice-captain, Rioch and Masson, were wretchedly out of form. They had recently come together at Derby County, only for the Rams' ex-Scotland manager Tommy Docherty to publicly declare them to be 'bad buys'. They were both slapped on the transfer list.

Competing against the 'bad buys' were the 'old men' of Peru. Hector Chumpitaz, Hugo Sotil and Teofilo Cubillas had all played in the exciting Peru team that in 1970 had reached the quarter-finals. They were now part of an ageing side that almost nobody seemed to take seriously. These were only Peru's second World Cup finals since the war, and they had clinched their place only by beating Chile in their final qualifier. Scotland, or so it appeared, had only to run on to the pitch to be assured of victory. It was overlooked that Rioch and Masson (and Gemmill on the bench) hardly constituted a youthful midfield. All three were in their thirties.

For fifteen minutes on a balmy evening everything proceeded to plan. Scotland, playing in navy shirts and shorts, had taken a grip and were a goal to the good. Quiroga, 'El Loco' – an eccentric keeper who liked to go walkabout – couldn't hold Rioch's powerful shot, and Jordan pounced. The scorer of Scotland's last goal in 1974 had opened his team's account in 1978.

From the restart anyone would have thought it was Peru who had scored. They immediately served notice that they were not the decrepit mugs they were taken to be. Cubillas might have played World Cup football all of eight years previously, but he had lost none of his pace and power, and quickly stamped himself as the game's most imposing presence. As for the wingers, Muñante and Oblítas, nobody had warned Scotland's callow – and in the case of stopgap Buchan, painfully slow – full-backs of their electrifying speed. The lesson, it seemed, had never sunk in: in Switzerland in 1954 the Uruguayans' pace had torn Scotland apart; ditto the Paraguayans in Sweden. In 1972 Peru had been defeated 0-2 at Hampden. Even so, Gemmill, Hartford and Donachie, survivors from that day, could vouch for their speed and control. Now, a goal behind, Peru, with their bright red sashes, proceeded to dissect the Scottish defence. Rough's goal led a charmed life. Cubillas ran free, with Rioch and Masson chasing shadows, unable to mark or contain him.

The only surprise was the time it took Peru to equalise. The interval was two minutes away when another sleek move involving Cubillas and Velásquez created a chance for Cueto to blast past Rough. The red sashes danced wildly.

Peru's Inca magic continued to mesmerise the Scots after the break. Around the hour mark the game threw up its decisive moment. Cubillas challenged

Tom Forsyth cannot prevent Cubillas putting Peru in front. (v Peru)

Rioch, the whistle blew, and Scotland were awarded a penalty. The decision looked harsh, but then Scotland specialised in enjoying harsh penalties.

In view of Masson's previous lack of accomplishment, he could consider himself fortunate not to have been substituted. He was, however, Scotland's customary penalty taker. Masson's self-doubt was manifest with his spot-kick, which sailed at catching height to Quiroga's right and was saved with contemptuous ease. Back home, the armchair millions must have sensed what lay in store. Muñante and Cueto scythed open the Scottish defence and Cubillas' blistering shot from twenty yards exonerated Rough from any blame.

At long last Rioch and Masson were whipped off, and one wondered when was the last occasion any team withdrew its captain and vice-captain together. The thankless task of plugging the gaps fell to Archie Gemmill and Lou Macari, who, with Peru in full flow, might have preferred the comforting anonymity of the bench. No sooner were the changes completed than Stuart Kennedy, rated a fast full-back in Scotland, was overwhelmed by Oblítas, whom he brought down just outside the box. Cubillas' free kick was full of insult, struck with the outside of his foot round wall and goalkeeper to put Scotland out of their misery. At the end both managers bared their souls: 'The end of the world,' sighed Ally MacLeod; 'I would like to congratulate Scotland and Mr MacLeod for the team they presented to us,' smiled Marcos Calderon.

PERU   (1) 3   SCOTLAND   (1) 1
  Cueto 42, Cubillas 70, 76   Jordan 15

PERU: Quiroga, Duarte, Manzo, Chumpitaz, Díaz, Velásquez, Cueto (P Rojas), Cubillas, Muñante, La Rosa (Sotíl), Oblítas.
SCOTLAND: Rough, Kennedy, Burns, Buchan, Forsyth, Rioch (Gemmill), Masson (Macari), Hartford, Dalglish, Jordan, Johnston.

IRAN v SCOTLAND
Wednesday, 7 June 1978   *Córdoba – 8,000*

The aftermath of the Peru defeat was yet more traumatic. At a press conference MacLeod appeared to disown his own players. Then it became known that Willie Johnston, one of two players chosen for mandatory dope testing, had tested positive. Johnston had – he insists unknowingly – taken 'stimulants', a cause for surprise only in view of his listless performance. Never mind the player, the whole team was now under threat of expulsion. Before the FIFA judiciary could convene, the SFA took swift steps to defuse the situation. 'Bud' was whisked out of Argentina, flown home, and had a life-ban slapped on him. He would never play for Scotland again. The severity of his punishment probably ensured that the team was not victimised – save for the jibes and taunts now accompanying the mention of the word 'Scotland'.

For Willie Johnston there was just one redeeming aspect of the tragedy. Had Scotland won, his offence would automatically have resulted in the game being awarded to Peru. As it was, he was allowed to slip back into Britain largely unnoticed. Had his actions caused Scotland to forfeit a match they had actually won, his reception does not bear thinking about.

Needless to say, MacLeod knew as little about Iran as he did Peru. For Scotland, victory was imperative, defeat unthinkable. Iran's first appearance in the World Cup finals – posting twelve unbeaten qualifiers in the Asia-Oceania section – had got off to an inauspicious start, losing 0-3 to the Dutch. In essence, Scotland needed to surpass that score, otherwise – at best – be faced with elimination on goal difference as in 1974. Yet Iran were unlikely to be pushovers. In their warm-ups they had drawn with Yugoslavia and Bulgaria, and lost only 0-1 to Wales. Holland had themselves needed two penalties to elevate their margin of victory. Iran were, furthermore, well versed in British ways. They had recently been coached by the former Manchester United boss, Frank O'Farrell.

Scottish morale was pitifully low. Representatives of the SFA intervened to calm ill-feeling over financial incentives; then it was learned that the team-sheet was shown to the press before the players. MacLeod had made sweeping changes, some incomprehensible. Irrespective of his splendid form in helping

Liverpool retain the European Cup, Graeme Souness was listed only among the substitutes. So was Derek Johnstone, with his potential goal supply. Rioch and Masson were both missing – the former through injury to body, the latter to soul. Their replacements against Peru, Gemmill and Macari, lined up from the start. Gemmill was captain.

In defence, Tom Forsyth stood down to accommodate the now-available Willie Donachie. The shell-shocked Stuart Kennedy gave way to Jardine. Kenny Burns and Martin Buchan had never played together, until now. Up front, John Robertson assumed Willie Johnston's responsibilities.

The match itself ranks as one of the worst ever to abuse the standards of play appropriate to the World Cup finals. Iran kept Scotland at bay with derisive ease. Any strategy behind Scotland's play was impossible to fathom. MacLeod retained four permanent defenders to police Iran's two nominal forwards, yet Iran might have stolen the lead after thirteen minutes. Rough had to move smartly to challenge Faraki. The ball bounced away and was hoisted clear by Buchan.

The interval was two minutes away when Scotland were credited with a goal no less valuable for its absurdity. Keeper Hejazi emerged to gather Hartford's through ball. Pressured by Jordan and his own centre-half, Eskandarian, the keeper could not prevent the ball breaking free. Eskandarian panicked, turned, and rolled it back fifteen yards into his own net. A few Scottish players expressed delight, the rest looked abashed. Somebody up there liked Scotland: two own-goals and two silly penalties had paved their route to Argentina. If only the players could take advantage of His favours.

In the second half the aggrieved Eskandarian was booked for extracting his revenge on Jordan. Buchan's participation ceased when he bumped into Donachie and gashed his head. MacLeod might have sent on a forward, but it was Tom Forsyth who pulled off his tracksuit.

At length Iran sensationally – and deservedly – equalised. Danaifar took the ball from Sadeghi, fended off Gemmill and Jardine, and shot past Rough from a narrow angle. Within seconds, a lightning Iranian raid ended with Ghasempour foiled by Rough's last-ditch intervention. The beating of Scottish hearts was audible.

Dalglish was substituted, not by Derek Johnstone, but by wee Joey Harper, who had not played international football for three years and would never do so again. Robertson's header, cleanly saved, marked Scotland's last aggressive gesture. At the end, furious Scottish supporters vented their wrath at manager and players: 'You only want the money.'

The performance lost none of its awfulness in retrospect. At one poignant moment MacLeod had been pictured on the bench, abjectly holding his head in his hands. *The Times* summed up the shambles brutally: 'Scotland came here to compare themselves with the best, and could not even run with the weakest.'

IRAN   (0) 1   SCOTLAND   (1) 1
   Danaifar 77   Eskandarian 43 (o.g.)

IRAN: Hejazi, Nazari, Kazerani, Abdolahi, Eskandarian, Parvin, Ghasempour, Sadeghi, Danaifar (Nayebagha), Faraki (Rowshan), Djahani.
SCOTLAND: Rough, Jardine, Burns, Donachie, Buchan (Forsyth), Gemmill, Macari, Hartford, Dalglish (Harper), Jordan, Robertson.

HOLLAND v SCOTLAND
Sunday, 11 June 1978   *Mendoza – 40,000*

All pretence at Scottish self-respect had vanished. Never in her proud sporting history had Scotland presented such an abject performance before the world. Back home, windows were smashed in the offices of the Scottish Football Association. Billboards equating Scottish footballers with a make of motor car – 'running rings round the opposition' – suddenly looked like a sick joke. To be tainted with Scottish football was now a leaden commercial liability. The day after the Iran humiliation was, for manager and players, akin to a wake.

While Scotland were suffering their latest agonies, the Dutch were going through the motions with a goalless draw against Peru. Scotland, to all intents, were now out: they would be packing their bags unless they beat Holland by three clear goals. Some wit was heard to ask: 'Where are we going to find three Dutchmen willing to score own-goals?' Such a score against the World Cup runners-up overstepped the bounds of probability. In any case, did the Scottish players have the stomach for the fight? Did they wish to endure their Argentine nightmare one second longer than necessary? Many must have wished to jump on the first plane.

If, however, Scotland were to climb the heights, Holland might unwittingly assist. Barring an unconscionably heavy defeat, they were already through to the second round. They had injuries to worry about, not least to their midfield architect Johan Neeskens. Evidently, the Dutch would not wish to exert themselves, unless they had to.

Moreover, the Dutch camp appeared even more unsettled than the Scots'. Money was the root of the evil. Having qualified for Argentina comfortably ahead of Belgium and Northern Ireland, the Dutch squad was now shorn of the services of Cruyff, van Hanegem, Peters, Kist and Geels, all of whom for personal reasons declined to travel. That left nine players from the 1974 finals still included. This time round, Holland recruited the managerial services of Austrian Ernst Happel, who had played against Scotland in 1954, and who was now seconded from his post at Bruges.

It would appear that MacLeod's senior players now muscled in on team selection and tactics. Souness was finally given an outing. Rioch also returned.

Kenny Dalglish hooks past Jongbloed to equalise. (v Holland)

In defence, Kennedy and Forsyth resumed their places. The players to stand down were Jardine, Burns, Macari and Robertson, which meant Scotland abandoned a winger in the attempt to counter Dutch strength in midfield.

In the small, cramped Mendoza stadium with its lush pitch, Scotland gave the powerful Dutch the fright of their lives. After just five minutes Rioch – given a free role – headed Souness's cross against the angle of post and bar. Neeskens shortly lunged at Rioch, inflicted further damage to his own ribs, and took no further part. Boskamp deputised. Then Dalglish 'scored', only to have the effort chalked off through Jordan's earlier foul.

Rough had seen little action. But in the thirty-fourth minute Scotland's enterprise rebounded in their faces. Kennedy lost out to Rep. The full-back chased back, the goalkeeper rushed out, and Rep was brought down within a tartan sandwich. Gemmill was booked for protesting against the penalty, before Rensenbrink slotted the 1,000th goal in World Cup finals.

Rensenbrink's penalty effectively ended lingering Scottish dreams. They now needed four. But in the seconds before half-time they pulled back to all-square. The Dutch goal had been living under siege when Souness's centre was headed back by Jordan for Dalglish to hook past Jongbloed.

The equaliser did wonders for Scottish confidence. They came out for the second half to discover Holland had brought on Wildschut for Rijsbergen, injured through an earlier Jordan challenge. Within two minutes Scotland were in front. Souness, the inspiration behind his team's resurgence, chested down Dalglish's centre and was bundled off the ball by Willy van de Kerkhof. Gemmill converted the penalty, and now Scotland scented a sensation.

The Dutch retaliated: Rough saved from Rep. But soon the traffic was again bearing down on Jongbloed. Dalglish headed over, Jordan headed wide, before the stadium and the watching millions rose to their feet to acclaim a goal of genius. Out on the right Archie Gemmill embarked on a slalom worthy of any Olympic skier. He wriggled past man after man, changing direction this way and that. The ball was poked through Krol's legs and now Gemmill had only Jongbloed to beat. The goalkeeper sprawled, the ball was flicked round him, and Scotland led 3-1.

Scotland had twenty-two minutes to find the fourth and – could it happen? – stay in the competition. But the ecstasy was short-lived. Steaming through the middle, Rep unleashed another snorter. Rough was beaten high to his right from twenty-five yards to put paid to Scottish dreams. The Dutch had been stung into action: as soon as they needed to score they did. They might well have equalised, too, as Scotland tailed away. At the death, René van de Kerkhof streaked away down the left. His shot beat Rough but squeaked past the far post. For Scotland it was goodbye as expected, but the players' heads were high as they left the pitch.

HOLLAND   (1) 2   SCOTLAND   (1) 3
   Rensenbrink 34 pen, Rep 71   Dalglish 43, Gemmill 47 pen, 68

HOLLAND: Jongbloed, Suurbier, Krol, Rijsbergen (Wildschut), Poortvliet, Nees-kens (Boskamp), W van de Kerkhof, Jansen, Rep, R van de Kerkof, Rensenbrink.
SCOTLAND: Rough, Kennedy, Buchan, Donachie, Forsyth, Rioch, Gemmill, Hartford, Souness, Dalglish, Jordan.

Holland showed their mettle as the competition progressed, winning the second phase group (completed by Italy, West Germany and Austria) before losing to Argentina in the Final. The host nation's ultimate triumph was perhaps the most farcical in the history of the World Cup. Outrageous refereeing decisions favoured them from start to finish. Each match they won swung on an incident that turned in their favour. Required to beat Peru by four goals to reach the Final, they managed six – but only after Peru had hit the post at 0-0. In the Final, Holland, handicapped by yet more refereeing connivance, struck wood in the dying seconds. They were three inches from the World Cup, which eventually went to Argentina, arguably the worst team ever to lift the trophy.

The fact that Scotland beat the World Cup runners-up gave rise to endless distortion. In reality, beating a side for whom a two-goal defeat was a 'victory'

The goal of the tournament. Archie Gemmill in full flow. (v Holland)

is a hollow triumph. Holland's ability to strike back when danger threatened emphasised the emptiness of Scotland's victory as a propaganda coup.

This is not to say that Scotland in their final match did not play the best football seen under Ally MacLeod. If anything, such a belated showing further angered the Scottish public, for it underlined the earlier failings. But such is the self-destruct quality so often apparent in Scottish football: the team they had to beat was the one in the mirror.

Poor Ally MacLeod's short reign was inevitably over. He was not so much a team manager as a cheerleader. There was talk of the emptiest vessels making the loudest noises. MacLeod's manifest failings in Argentina were not, of course, ultimately his fault, but that of the Scottish FA which appointed him. At a stroke, all the good work of Tommy Docherty and Willie Ormond, which had made Scottish international football something to be reckoned with, had been cast to the winds. The next Scotland manager would have to pick up the pieces and start all over again.

Final positions – Group 4

	P	W	D	L	F	A	Pts
PERU	3	2	1	0	7	2	5
HOLLAND	3	1	1	1	5	3	3
Scotland	3	1	1	1	5	6	3
Iran	3	0	1	2	2	8	1

Scotland appearances and goalscorers (substitute appearances in brackets)
World Cup qualifying rounds and final competition 1978

	Apps	Goals		Apps	Goals
Dalglish K *	7	3	Jardine S *	3	–
Jordan J *	7	2	Johnston W	3	–
Rough A	7	–	McGrain D *	3	–
Hartford A	5 (2)	1	Macari L *	2 (1)	–
Donachie W *	5	–	Kennedy S	2	–
Rioch B	5	–	Blackley J *	1	–
Buchan M *	4 (1)	–	Gray A	1	–
Forsyth T *	4 (1)	–	Gray E †	1	–
Gemmill A	4 (1)	2	Robertson J	1	–
Masson D	4	1	Souness G	1	–
McQueen G	4	–	Harper J *	– (1)	–
Burns K	3 (1)	–	Pettigrew W	– (1)	–
			(own-goals)		2

* Appeared in 1974 World Cup.

† Appeared in 1970 World Cup.

86 apps   11 goals
25 Scottish League
61 English League
24 players used

9

THE 1982 WORLD CUP

The task of restoring Scottish self-respect in the wake of the Argentine fiasco fell to Jock Stein. Irony of ironies, the job had been his a year earlier had he wanted it. But he was then still convalescing after a horrendous car accident, and was understandably averse to leaving Celtic when a lucrative testimonial was in the offing.

In the lead-up to the 1978 World Cup the merry-go-round of Scottish club managers threatened to spin out of control. Jock Wallace quit champions Rangers, who elevated John Greig from the playing staff to the hot seat. Celtic had had a comparatively poor season. The time was right to bring in a younger face to keep in tune with developments at Ibrox. That face belonged to Billy McNeill, hero of Celtic's halcyon days, who vacated his post at Aberdeen just one year after succeeding Ally MacLeod. The Pittodrie club duly recruited Alex Ferguson, freed by St Mirren.

Stein, the most successful and esteemed manager in Scotland, thereby turned his back on his new appointment with Leeds United to take charge of the Scottish national team. It was his second stint: he had, of course, guided their fortunes on a caretaker basis back in 1965. Now his job was to uplift Scottish football from the deepest depression in memory.

His players did not have long to wait for competitive experience. The preliminary rounds of the 1980 European Championship were already upon them, and a defeat already lodged in Vienna. The closing of the MacLeod book spelled the end for those players inextricably associated with him – Rioch, Masson, Macari, Tom Forsyth, Joe Harper, not to mention Willie Johnston. Masson and Macari were banned for airing their views to the press.

Success for Jock Stein took its time. His team finished fourth out of five in the European Championship, trailing behind Belgium, Austria and Portugal. In the spring of 1979 Scotland were beaten by Wales, England, and at Hampden by world champions Argentina, eighteen-year-old Diego Maradona included. Peru were invited to the national stadium, ostensibly to put the record straight. Even with home advantage Scotland could not turn the tables, requiring an own-goal to draw.

1980 was little better. In the Home Internationals Scotland again lost two out of three, including a Hampden defeat by England. This was followed by defeats in Poland and Hungary. By the time the 1982 World Cup qualifiers came round Stein's record was played eighteen; won five; lost eleven. Rumblings of discontent hung in the air.

As part of the FIFA revolution, which could be traced back to Brazilian João Havelange ousting Sir Stanley Rous as president in 1974, the quota of finalists in 1982 would be increased from sixteen to twenty-four. In essence, this was to accommodate more participants from the Third World, but it also meant more places available to Europe. Scotland needed to overcome Portugal, Sweden, Israel and Northern Ireland, with two to qualify. Jock Stein must have fancied his chances.

Qualifying Group 6

SWEDEN v SCOTLAND

Wednesday, 10 September 1980   *Stockholm – 39,831*

Scotland opened their inflated eight-match programme in front of a near-40,000 crowd in Stockholm's Solna Stadium. For a country not completely rid of the part-time ethos, Sweden had thrown their share of World Cup punches. They had qualified for seven of the past eleven finals, finishing fourth in 1938, third in 1950, second in 1958, and adjudged fifth in 1974. That was a fine record for a country with a population as small as Sweden's. They had not lost a home eliminator for fifteen years and not failed to qualify since 1966.

These accomplishments in the cup of cups were something of a mystery. Sweden had no pedigree in the European Championship and their recent form was wretched. They had mustered just one win from their last six, and even been held by tiny Luxembourg. In Group 6 they had already drawn 1-1 at home to unfancied Israel. Scotland's Swedish file made for poor inspection: Scotland's 1977 win, at Hampden, was their first win in four attempts. Clearly, this was a match between teams more accustomed to defeat than victory. Whichever won would have little to brag about.

Swedish coach Lars Arnesson would call up one vastly experienced player. Goalkeeper Ronnie Hellstroem was lining up for the seventy-sixth time, having featured in the World Cup finals of 1970, 1974, and 1978. Hellstroem earned his wages in West Germany with Kaiserslautern. With the exception of Hasse Borg of Eintracht Brunswick, the rest of the Swedish team comprised home based part-timers.

Swedish club football rarely captured headlines, but in 1979 Malmö had reached the Final of the European Cup, losing to Nottingham Forest. Malmö's Erlandsson and Forest's John Robertson now renewed their acquaintance.

Kenny Burns was another of that triumphal Forest side, though he was for the moment out of international favour. In recent games Stein had tried several central defensive pairings. In Stockholm it was the turn of Liverpool's Alan Hansen and Aberdeen's Alex McLeish. McLeish's Pittodrie captain, Willie Miller, was pushed into midfield, and there was room for a third member of Aberdeen's title-winning side, Gordon Strachan, winning his sixth cap. Frank Gray – brother of Eddie, not Andy – had already won eight caps at left-back.

The team showed a welcome streak of experience. Six players were veterans of the 1978 campaign – Rough, McGrain, Dalglish, Andy Gray, Robertson and Archie Gemmill, now with Birmingham City and Scottish captain. Rough was now Scotland's most capped goalkeeper, a position notoriously hard to keep, and the butt of countless English jokes. Though continuity was welcome, Rough, laid back and unflustered, was not everyone's choice.

Since the 1978 World Cup, Scotland had played six times on the continent (Austria, Portugal, Norway, Belgium, Poland, Hungary). Scotland had lost the lot – bar Norway. Stein would, therefore, presumably settle for a share of the points in Stockholm. To this end he focused on the virtues of hard work rather than flair. Robertson dropped deep, leaving Andy Gray (a £1½ million buy for Wolves) and Kenny Dalglish as lone front runners.

Dalglish found space for an early shot, but most of the first-half excitement was generated by the Swedes. One flowing intricate move climaxed with a Sjoberg header that brushed an upright. Shortly before half-time Willie Miller's clearance was struck back viciously by Nilsson against Rough's post. The ball cannoned off the goalkeeper and was belted away by McLeish.

It was already likely that one goal would settle the match. The Swedes had thus far come closer, and Andy Gray popped up to clear Gustavsson's menacing free kick. Both sides had muted claims for a penalty. But the goal that broke the deadlock was more worthy. It fell to Scotland, was unexpected inasmuch as it was their first golden opportunity, but was sufficiently noble as to raise many a Scottish roof. The tiny Strachan dispossessed Erlandsson, switched passes on the left with the tinier Gemmill, and fired along the ground inside the far post. Scottish patience had been worthwhile, for it was a textbook goal, Strachan's first for Scotland.

With Tottenham's Steve Archibald on for Dalglish, Scotland held out to record a rare away victory. 'Professional' and 'disciplined' were the appropriate adjectives to describe the performance, with a moment of Strachan magic worthy of the winning side. An away win for starters was just what the doctor ordered. It turned out to be a bleak evening for Scandinavia, Norway going down 0-4 at Wembley.

SWEDEN   (0) 0   SCOTLAND   (0) 1
                                      Strachan 72

SWEDEN: Hellstroem, Gustavsson, Borg, Bild, Arvidsson, Erlandsson (P Nilsson), Ramberg, Nordgren, T Nilsson, Sjoberg, Ohlsson.

SCOTLAND: Rough (Partick), McGrain (Celtic), F Gray (Forest), Miller (Aberdeen), McLeish (Aberdeen), Hansen (Liverpool), Dalglish (Liverpool) (*sub* Archibald, Spurs), Strachan (Aberdeen), A Gray (Wolves), Gemmill (Birmingham), Robertson (Forest).

SCOTLAND v PORTUGAL

Wednesday, 15 October 1980   *Hampden – 60,765*

Sweden had let slip three points from two home games. They would struggle to make up the deficit. If Scotland could now overcome Portugal, they would open up a psychologically imposing gap. Unlike Sweden, Portugal had no tradition in the World Cup. They had reached the finals just once, in 1966, when they staged a memorable semi-final with England. Nor had Portugal ever graced the later stages of the European Championship. Portugal's footballing fortunes were club-oriented. Benfica had been five times European Cup finalists in the 1960s. With the 1982 World Cup to be staged in neighbouring Spain, and vast travelling support guaranteed, Portugal were as desperate to qualify as Scotland had been in 1966.

Portugal were no strangers to Scotland. This was the ninth clash since the war. Scotland had won three and lost one at Hampden, the last of which was in the recent European Championship. Scotland had won 4-1, though with both teams already eliminated that match had lacked spice.

The Portuguese, for whom this was their opening World Cup fixture, prepared thoroughly. New coach Julio Cernadas Pereira cancelled the domestic programme so as to concentrate minds and resources. In contrast, there were no postponements to the Scottish or English Leagues, despite England's own World Cup trip to Romania.

Portugal were captained by Manuel Bento from Benfica. He had not impressed on his last visit to Hampden, nor against Liverpool in the 1978 European Cup. Without key players – sweeper Humberto, Alves in midfield, and Alberto, who scored Portugal's winner against Scotland in Lisbon in 1978 – Portugal were expected to pursue a goalless draw.

Stein retained virtually the same eleven victorious in Stockholm. The sole change was necessitated by Alex McLeish's knee ligament trouble. Miller fell back to partner Hansen, and Graeme Souness returned to midfield.

Scotland enjoyed enough possession to invite accusations of gluttony. So idle was he, Alan Rough might easily have brought his sandwiches with him. But Bento and his countrymen were in no mood to be brushed aside. In the first half Scotland found no chink in the Portuguese armour. A Dalglish swivel and shot, ably smothered by Bento, and a Souness long-range effort that flew high was all Scotland mustered. Their opponents contrived just one chance, but it would be the best of the match. Costa worked the ball down the left and cut it back to Fernandes. With the goal yawning, Fernandes brushed the cobwebs from Scotland's left-hand post. Fernandes looked mortified.

In the second period Portugal abandoned all pretence at attack and were quite content for Bento to make a hero of himself. This he was eager to do, brushing himself down from a collision with Miller to become the most unpopular man in Scotland. Bento plunged to divert Dalglish's shot-on-the-turn. Dalglish then tumbled twice without winning a penalty.

The Portuguese hauled off their notional strikers, Chalana and Jordao, but Stein kept his own subs on the bench. Souness challenged Bento with a mighty shot through a ruck of players, but the keeper clung on. Robertson, playing deep, rarely escaped the attentions of Gabriel, and only McGrain's sorties down the right hinted at the unexpected. Four minutes from time a Strachan drive was deflected into Bento's waiting arms and that was that. Portugal had achieved what they had come for, but Scotland still had three points to show from two matches. Jock Stein would have settled for that beforehand, and besides, he had more cause to smile than Ron Greenwood. England lost in Bucharest.

SCOTLAND (0) 0   PORTUGAL (0) 0

SCOTLAND: Rough, McGrain, F Gray, Souness, Hansen, Miller, Strachan, Dalglish, A Gray, Gemmill, Robertson.
PORTUGAL: Bento, Gabriel, Pietra, Simoes, Larangeira, Fernandes, Eurico, Costa, Chalana (Sheu), Dos Santos, Jordao (Nene).

ISRAEL v SCOTLAND
Wednesday, 25 February 1981   *Tel Aviv – 35,000*

Scotland were not in the habit of playing internationals in the freezing month of February. That they did so now was due to the fact that their hosts were Israel, basking in the comparative warmth of the eastern Mediterranean. The inclusion of Israel in a European World Cup section owed its illogicality to politics. Geographically, Israel belonged to Asia but was not welcome among FIFA's Asian confederation and in 1976 had been expelled. Israel sought affiliation with Central and South America, but eventually found refuge as an honorary constituent of Europe.

Group 6 was taking shape. Portugal were in front with five points. Israel had proved resilient, losing only one of their opening four games and forcing goalless draws at home to Northern Ireland and Sweden. They had beaten Austria in a friendly and been preparing for Scotland's visit in monastic seclusion. Scotland would receive no presents in the Ramat Gan Stadium.

Israeli football was heavily shaped by English football, which was televised every week. The Israel manager – Jack Mansell – was English, and the country's most gifted player, Avi Cohen, had played a dozen matches for Liverpool. His Anfield colleagues, Souness and Dalglish, knew his worth.

Other Israelis to look out for included Ytszak Shum, veteran central defender from the 1970 World Cup finals, and two speedy front runners, Damti and Sinai. Damti had sixty-two internationals behind him, Sinai none. Levi was another making his debut.

Stein made changes. Willie Miller had recently served a suspension and was lacking match sharpness. McLeish and the reinstated Kenny Burns teamed up for the first time. With Strachan out with a serious stomach injury, Ipswich's goal-bagging midfielder John Wark made a comeback. Andy Gray dropped down among the substitutes, allowing Steve Archibald to play centre-forward. Archibald and Wark were the English first division's leading scorers.

Sporting red shirts and navy shorts, Scotland tried to seduce the rain-soaked crowd before kick-off by distributing flowers. But lest anyone interpret this as a Scottish peace-offering, once play began Burns promptly savaged Damti.

Discerning Scots appreciated that this might be a tricky fixture, and they were proved correct. After forty-five minutes Israel had everything but a goal to show for their superiority. Playing to a methodical 4-4-2, in white shirts with blue sleeves, the home side appeared much the more cohesive. With Avi Cohen orchestrating from the sweeper position, it had needed the admirable Rough to foil whatever Israel threw at him. Tabak had raced into the box to be frustrated by Rough's plunge. Damti then carelessly shot into the sky. Rough blocked Tabak's shot with his legs. Souness's abortive effort, sailing wide, was Scotland's only serious reply. In midfield, Wark and Gemmill had been in danger of being swept into the West Bank. 'A shambles' was how Jock Stein described his team during that worrisome three-quarters of an hour.

The Scottish manager must have delivered inflammatory words in the dressing room, for there was a perceptible uplift in performance. John Wark, uncomfortable without the Ipswich support of Franz Thijssen and Arnold Muhren, stayed behind. Burns pushed forward and Miller lined up to partner McLeish in defence. Robertson switched to the right. Within nine minutes Scotland were ahead. Robertson swung over a corner and McLeish nodded it back, where it fell to Dalglish loitering with intent on the six-yard line. Dalglish had suffered a mild concussion earlier in the match and had contemplated coming off. He would be glad he didn't, for his ferocious volley – almost decapitating a defender on the line – marked his twenty-fourth goal in his seventy-eighth international.

The goal worked wonders for Scottish confidence, but did not prevent the Israelis looking perfectly capable of equalising. Rough was busy till the end, and Frank Gray once belted clear with the Scottish goal under siege. Andy

Gray replaced Dalglish and might have scored with an instant volley, yet the final whistle could not come quickly enough for Scotland. Dalglish had scored from one of only two real chances coming their way. Stein was not fooled. Scotland's play had not been pretty, but they had won away again.

ISRAEL (0) 0   SCOTLAND (0) 1
                                        Dalglish 54

ISRAEL: Mizrahi, Mahness, J Cohen, Ekhois, A Cohen, Barr, Shum, N Cohen, Sinai, Damti, Tabak.
SCOTLAND: Rough, McGrain, F Gray, Souness, McLeish, Burns, Wark (Miller), Dalglish (A Gray), Archibald, Gemmill, Robertson.

SCOTLAND v NORTHERN IRELAND
Wednesday, 25 March 1981   *Hampden – 78,444*

Scotland's record to date – two away wins; no goals conceded in three games – was most un-Scottish, a sign of Stein's determination to instil functionalism and consistency dispensing with the fancy stuff. Alan Rough's 270-minute shut-out equalled the record established by Jim Cruickshank back in 1970.

Whether Northern Ireland might end that sequence would depend on whether they presented themselves like lambs to the slaughter, as so often in the past, or played to their new-found potential as cultivated by manager Billy Bingham. Northern Ireland were defending British champions, the first time they had won the championship outright. They had beaten Scotland in Belfast in 1980. In the 1970s the 'troubles' had necessitated Scotland-Ireland matches being played at Hampden – Scotland winning five, Ireland three.

In Group 6, the Irish had three points to show from three matches, having lost a mite sadly by the only goal in Portugal. The Irish welcomed back Pat Jennings in goal after an eight-match absence. He had first played for his country in 1964: this was his eighty-fourth cap. Ireland had to omit the injured Martin O'Neill. Sammy McIlroy needed a late test on his knee.

The balance of his team was not to Stein's liking. He found himself with an abundance of defenders and strikers, but a dearth of talent in midfield where Scotland had been strongest in 1974 and 1978. This weakness was underlined by Stein playing surplus defenders, Burns and Miller, as makeshift midfielders.

Injuries to Souness and Dalglish did not lift Stein's spirits. Dalglish had enjoyed a run of forty-three consecutive appearances. John Wark, deputising for Souness, had recently been voted English 'Player of the Year'. Stein kept faith with Andy Gray and Steve Archibald, bypassing all the leading scorers in Scotland – McGarvey and Nicholas (Celtic); Sturrock and Dodds (Dundee Utd); McGhee and McCall (Aberdeen); McAdam and McDonald (Rangers).

The early play was scrappy and tense, and McLeish's nudge on Sammy McIlroy provoked Irish howls for a penalty. Archibald's response was to spin on McGrain's pass to crash the ball against the base of Jennings' post. McIlroy raced clear, to fall victim of Miller's professional foul. The Aberdeen captain was booked. Scotland saw more of the ball in the wet conditions but made limited use of it. Burns and Wark carved into the Irish defence, but Archibald's shot was repulsed by Chris Nicholl's diving clearance. All Northern Ireland had to show for their first-half puff was a McCreery shot that soared high.

If Scotland shaded the first half they were inferior for much of the second. Almost at once, Sammy McIlroy's centre was nodded goalwards by Billy Hamilton, playing with Burnley in the English third division. Alan Rough flung himself to turn the header against a post. McLeish cleared up the mess. Rough shortly hurt himself disputing possession with Hamilton.

Scotland's difficulties stemmed from midfield, where Gemmill, Wark, Burns and Robertson were unable to plug the gaps. Sammy McIlroy looked the best player afield. In desperation, Miller and Burns switched positions, and Scotland relied ever more heavily on McGrain's forward surges. Sammy Nelson was yellow-carded for a crude challenge on Wark, but with twenty minutes left Ireland opened the scoring. McClelland was fouled by Burns on the touchline. From McIlroy's free kick Hamilton stole in to plant an emphatic header inside Rough's left-hand post. It was Scotland's first lost goal of the campaign.

Scotland were stung into action, squaring the match with its most incisive move. Miller's inch-perfect pass to Wark cleaved open the Irish defence. The Ipswich player slotted the ball wide of Jennings. The Hampden jeers of 'What a load of rubbish' switched in mid-breath to 'We'll support you evermore'.

Scotland now pressed for the winner. Asa Hartford came on for Kenny Burns; Derek Spence for Billy Hamilton. Rough had struggled since his earlier knock, and with the play now concentrated at the other end, St Mirren's Billy Thomson deputised for the closing minutes. Scotland created just one more chance, Gray set it up and Archibald blazed over.

Having played each of their opponents once, Scotland had harvested six points. A further six from the return fixtures would see them through.

SCOTLAND (0) 1	NORTHERN IRELAND (0) 1
Wark 75	Hamilton 70

SCOTLAND: Rough (Thomson), McGrain, F Gray, Burns (Hartford), McLeish, Miller, Wark, Archibald, A Gray, Gemmill, Robertson.

N IRELAND: Jennings (Arsenal), J Nicholl (Man U), C Nicholl (Southampton), J O'Neill (Leicester), Nelson (Arsenal), McCreery (Tulsa R), McIlroy (Man U), McClelland (Mansfield), Cochrane (Middlesbrough), Armstrong (Watford), Hamilton (Burnley) (*sub* Spence, Southend).

SCOTLAND v ISRAEL

Tuesday, 28 April 1981   *Hampden – 61,489*

Six points from four matches was healthy enough; but Scotland had scored just three goals. Stein rang the changes for the task of running up a score against Israel, sending out an adventurous formation. His midfield was reconstructed. Miller, Burns, Wark and Gemmill stood down, along with unfit Andy Gray. Alex McLeish partnered Alan Hansen for the first time since their encouraging display in Stockholm. Souness and Hartford were brought together in midfield, and Celtic's Davie Provan brought in to balance John Robertson on the flanks. It was Provan's fifth cap, the previous four having been as substitute. Andy Gray was replaced by Jordan, recalled for the first time in a year. Gemmill's international career was over, the captaincy passing to Danny McGrain.

With only five goals conceded from five games, Israel were having a profound influence on Group 6. They made one change from the side that deserved better than defeat in Tel Aviv, and at Hampden almost caused an early sensation. Mahness found Tabak with only Alan Rough to beat; Tabak shot hurriedly and wildly. Tabak then manufactured a second golden opportunity. Rough – the Scottish Football Writers' 'Player of the Year' – plunged to parry, then blocked Damti's follow-up.

At the other end, keeper Mizrahi thwarted Andy Gray, but a goal was not long delayed. Archibald and Robertson exchanged passes, and the winger was hauled down by Mahness. Robertson's penalty went in off a post.

With the tension eased, Scotland piled men forward. Archibald raced on to Hartford's glided pass and was felled by Shum. Robertson struck his second penalty as he had the first, this time not requiring the assistance of the upright. Scotland might even have had a third, but McLeish's thumping header crashed against the bar and bounced down and out. Archibald tried to force the ball in, but Mizrahi saved.

There was no satisfying Scotland. Israel were made to look like the pretenders they were. Eight minutes into the second half Jordan, enjoying a distinguished return, touched the ball to Souness who spread it wide to Provan. The Celtic winger cracked a fine goal.

Israel redeemed themselves by pulling a goal back. Rough intercepted Tabak's drive, but Sinai swept home the rebound. It was Israel's second goal from six matches, but failed to dampen Scottish ardour. Robertson hammered a Frank Gray clearance against a post and Jordan's header was whacked away.

Chances were now falling to Scotland with abandon. Souness had a shot saved; Archibald a goal disallowed. Mizrahi performed valorously till the end.

Scotland's win put them clear of the pack. The following evening Northern Ireland defeated Portugal 1-0, heatedly, at Windsor Park. The Irish were now second to the Scots, and Portugal's threat began to recede.

SCOTLAND   (2) 3   ISRAEL   (0) 1
   Robertson 21 pen, 30 pen,   Sinai 58
   Provan 53

SCOTLAND: Rough, McGrain, F Gray, Souness, McLeish, Hansen, Provan, Archibald, Jordan, Hartford, Robertson.
ISRAEL: Mizrahi, Mahness, J Cohen, Ekhois, A Cohen, Barr, Shum, Zeituni, Sinai, Damti, Tabak.

SCOTLAND v SWEDEN
Wednesday, 9 September 1981   *Hampden – 81,511*

Scotland hung up their boots for the summer with the hardest part of their task already accomplished. Five matches had been played, eight points garnered. The visit of Sweden in September was Scotland's final home tie. A win might secure qualification. There remained uninviting trips to Belfast and Lisbon, where points might not be so easy to come by.

In June Sweden had done themselves a power of good with home wins over Northern Ireland and Portugal. From being potential wooden spoonists, they could yet qualify if they won in Glasgow and Lisbon. Only two of the Swedish team beaten in the first match were retained for the second, Lars Arnesson axing his ageing 'stars' and packing the side with younger, hungrier players.

The wits on the terraces poked fun at England, earlier in the day beaten, unaccountably, in Norway. Wales also lost in Czechoslovakia, and as things stood Scotland seemed poised to qualify, unburdened by British rivals, for the third successive time.

Of the team that sank Israel, only Souness and Archibald were missing, both injured. Wark and Dalglish were the natural replacements. John Wark had yet to settle in a Scotland shirt, despite bagging over fifty league goals for his club. That was a handsome tally for a forward; a phenomenal one for a midfield player. A month into the new season he had already mustered eight. Strachan was not back into international reckoning, which did not displease the Swedes.

Much debate, as ever, attended the inclusion of Joe Jordan. His robustness inflamed passions and irritated the purists. He was now playing in Italy, where he had netted seven goals in nine matches for Milan. This burst was worthy of acclaim, for whatever Jordan's plusses, scoring goals was not among them. It also said much for his timing: although his headed goals against the Czechs had taken Scotland to the 1974 and 1978 finals, his overall record was eight goals in forty-seven internationals – a paltry return. Hence the value of Wark.

Scotland began with panache. Wark's header from Robertson's free kick rolled infuriatingly along the goal-line. When the Swiss referee blew for a questionable foul on Jordan, Robertson flipped the ball to the near post, where

Jordan flashed a diving header wide of Ravelli. It was the kind of goal only he could score, and the arguments over his inclusion were temporarily adjourned.

For Scotland, passion and patience were mixed into an irresistible force. Hartford was always in the action. Jordan outjumped Borgesson at will, while the Swedes tried to hide behind an offside trap. Even that was impotent against McGrain's surges down the right. A Hartford 'goal' came to nothing, offside.

The interval fired up the Swedes. With nothing to lose, they came out with guns blazing. Within seconds Rough was summoned into action for the first time. The keeper shortly misjudged a swirling centre, Bjornlund fired towards goal, and McGrain somehow kept it out.

Scottish cohesion was now a memory, passes went astray. Swedish substitute Hallen toppled Dalglish in full flight and was booked. Dalglish was pulled off yet again, this time in favour of Andy Gray, while the Swedes brought on a fresh winger, Nilsson for Svensson. Jordan was cautioned for time-wasting. With the Swedes enjoying their best spell of the match, Borgesson tackled Gray. The forward went down, the referee pointed to that small, white circle, and Robertson despatched the penalty. Gray's televised confession that he had conned the ref by taking a dive did not amuse the Swedes; nor Jock Stein, who would rather he had kept his mouth shut. Over ninety minutes there was no doubting Scottish supremacy, apart from the referee's complicity in both goals. It would now take a freakish series of results to prevent Scotland reaching the World Cup finals in Spain.

SCOTLAND (1) 2   SWEDEN (0) 0
  Jordan 20, Robertson 83 pen

SCOTLAND: Rough, McGrain, F Gray, Wark, McLeish, Hansen, Provan, Dalglish (A Gray), Jordan, Hartford, Robertson.
SWEDEN: T Ravelli, Erlandsson, Hysén, Borgesson, Fredericksson (Hallen), Borg, A Ravelli, Bjornlund, Larsson, Sjoberg, Svensson (Nilsson).

NORTHERN IRELAND v SCOTLAND
Wednesday, 14 October 1981   *Belfast – 35,000*

Scotland had to wait five weeks for the opportunity to clinch a place in Spain. One point from the trip to Windsor Park would put the issue beyond doubt. As for the Irish, victory alone, it seemed, would suffice. Portugal were entertaining Sweden the same evening.

The Scots harboured vivid memories of their 1980 Belfast defeat. No British love would be wasted on the other. Stein may not have instructed his players to play defensively, but it did not take a wise man to realise that Scotland might need to defend, and that the team would be picked accordingly. Sadly, those redoubtable defenders, McGrain and McLeish were unfit, as was Jordan. West Ham's Ray Stewart filled in at right-back for his fourth cap, while Willie Miller deputised for McLeish. Archibald resumed the target man's duties from Jordan.

In the 1-1 Hampden draw, the Scottish midfield had comprised Wark, Burns and Gemmill. Two of these, Burns and Gemmill, had reached the end of the international road, and Wark was dropped. The replacements were Souness, Strachan (playing his first international for a year) and Hartford – who had returned to Manchester City from Everton, and who was now handed the captaincy of his country. With their Irish counterparts – McIlroy, O'Neill and McCreery – equally uncompromising, the game had the makings of a midfield war. The Irish were building one of their finest teams. Of their last thirteen fixtures they had lost but three, and in fifteen matches in Belfast since 1975 only Holland and England (thrice) had triumphed.

The game spelled high excitement from start to finish. Scotland began well. Souness's shot was too high, and a marauding burst by Strachan brought a smart save from Pat Jennings. For Ireland, the balding Noel Brotherston was pivotal to their attacks. On one occasion he cut inside to hook O'Neill's centre over the top. McIlroy's drive was too close for comfort.

The half-time breather provided pause for reflection. Scotland hadn't looked like scoring. Now the priority was to avoid losing. Not that they had much choice about second-half tactics. Ireland resumed as if demented, seizing the game by the scruff of the neck and shaking it until Scotland threatened to fall apart. Hartford and Co. looked like being swept away.

Ireland's forward momentum left inevitable gaps. Chris Nicholl's misplaced back-pass rolled wide of his own post when it could easily have rolled in. The omnipresent Strachan set up Archibald, whose effort curled tantalisingly over the bar. But these fleeting Scottish opportunities were eclipsed by the activity at the other end. Chris Nicholl's attempt at the correct goal passed even closer than that at his own. A corner carelessly conceded by Strachan produced further Scottish palpitations. In the ensuing melee Rough parried, Gerry Armstrong powered back the rebound, and the ball was hacked off the line by Hartford.

As the game entered its final ten minutes, Scotland were hanging on any way they could. Andy Gray replaced the exhausted Strachan, Dalglish dropped back into midfield, and on the final whistle Hamilton's firm header was juggled on the goal-line by Alan Rough. Would he or wouldn't he drop it? He didn't, and Northern Ireland had been denied.

Scotland were euphoric at qualifying, not inclined to dwell on probably their least impressive ninety minutes of the whole campaign. But Irish dejection turned to cheers an hour or so later when news from Lisbon told of a Swedish victory. Scotland, it turned out, could have lost but still qualified, and Northern Ireland had only to beat Israel to join the Scots in sunny Spain.

NORTHERN IRELAND (0) 0   SCOTLAND (0) 0

N IRELAND: Jennings (Arsenal), J Nicholl (Man U), C Nicholl (So'ton), J O'Neill (Leicester), Donaghy (Luton), M O'Neill (Man C), McIlroy (Man U), McCreery (Tulsa R), Brotherston (Blackburn), Armstrong (Watford), Hamilton (Burnley). SCOTLAND: Rough, Stewart, Hansen, Miller, F Gray, Strachan (A Gray), Souness, Hartford, Robertson, Dalglish, Archibald.

PORTUGAL v SCOTLAND
Wednesday, 18 November 1981   *Lisbon – 25,000*

It was time to take stock. Scotland's achievement could be interpreted two ways. They had won their group with a match to spare. They were unbeaten after seven matches and Alan Rough had conceded a miserly two goals. These statistics were not the kind commonly associated with Scotland. Jock Stein deserved every credit for them. Few Scots would welcome the comparison, but their team's dour outlook was more in keeping with that expected of England over the years, at a cost of sacrificing much of the flair though to be a Scottish prerogative. Qualifying for World Cup finals required damned hard work.

Realist that he was, Stein would also have appreciated that, match-by-match, Scotland's performances were shakier than the overall record suggested. Three of their eight goals had been penalties – at least one awarded in error. Away from home, five points from the visits to Stockholm, Tel Aviv and Belfast was a proud achievement, but the ball had rolled kindly. Had Scotland lost one or two of those matches, they could have had no complaint. Indeed, in most of Scotland's games the tide might have turned against them at a critical juncture. Jock Stein appeared to have two things going for him: the shrewdest of football brains, and that priceless knack of having his teams make their own luck.

Portugal's team was in crisis, having lost four matches in a row, the most recent being a 1-4 drubbing in Israel. The Portuguese nation mourned their team's absence from the finals in Spain. It was as well Scotland had matters sewn up, for Lisbon was no happy hunting ground. They had lost on their past three visits and failed to score.

Scotland's trip to the Stadium of Light could now be regarded as something of a luxury. Only Frank Gray remained of the team that played there in 1978. Of Stein's regulars, McGrain and McLeish were still unfit, and a late training injury to Alan Rough presented Billy Thomson with a rare cap. Davie Provan was reinstated and a fourth cap granted to Paul Sturrock, scorer of thirteen goals already this season for Dundee United. John Robertson (a yellow card hanging over him) and Kenny Dalglish were the players who made way.

Playing with the freedom to which they were entitled, Scotland took a brisk lead. Ray Stewart tossed back Bento's misdirected clearance. The keeper was stranded as Sturrock coolly clipped the ball over his head. It was his first goal for his country, and the buoyant scorer raced into the net to cuddle the ball.

Souness and Strachan had been instrumental to Scotland's fine start, but Portugal hit back with verve. Hansen's last-ditch tackle thwarted the menacing Oliveira. The same forward's next effort was beaten out by Thomson, but the equaliser was only delayed. Romeu unleashed a long range shot that Thomson couldn't hold. Manuel Fernandes was handily placed to convert the loose ball.

After the break Scotland switched their full-backs. Stewart moved over to the left to accommodate Stuart Kennedy, who had come on before the interval to replace Frank Gray, the victim of shoulder injury. The readjustment did not inspire confidence, and before long Portugal were in front. Miller failed to dispossess Fernandes, who strode on to shoot past Thomson. Pleased as the scorer was with his double, he would probably have swapped both for the one he missed at Hampden.

Scotland continued to live dangerously. Up front, Sturrock posed whatever threat Scotland presented. Archibald had now failed to score in six outings, and he made way for Dalglish. Thereafter Scotland brightened. Provan tried his luck but saw his shot parried by Bento; and Dalglish was only just wide.

The defeat spoiled Scotland's unbeaten record, but theirs was the proud distinction of heading Group 6. For good measure, the same evening, Northern Ireland beat Israel to qualify, while down at Wembley England secured the necessary result against an apathetic Hungary to bring the British contingent in Spain up to three. Not since 1958, when all four home countries reached the finals, would the British nations be so generously represented in the world's premier football championship.

PORTUGAL   (1) 2   SCOTLAND   (1) 1
Fernandes 39, 56   Sturrock 9

PORTUGAL: Bento, Frixo, Simoes, Teixeira, Eurico, Dito, Jaime, Romeu, Fernandes, Oliveira, Costa.
SCOTLAND: Thomson, Stewart, F Gray (Kennedy), Souness, Hansen, Miller, Provan, Strachan, Archibald (Dalglish), Hartford, Sturrock.

Qualifying Group 6

		Home				Away						
	P	W	D	L	F	A	W	D	L	F	A	Pts
SCOTLAND	8	2	2	0	6	2	2	1	1	3	2	11
N IRELAND	8	3	1	0	5	0	0	2	2	1	3	9
Sweden	8	2	1	1	5	2	1	1	2	2	6	8
Portugal	8	3	0	1	7	3	0	1	3	1	8	7
Israel	8	1	2	1	4	2	0	1	3	2	8	5

Other group results

Israel v N Ireland	0-0	N Ireland v Portugal	1-0
Sweden v Israel	1-1	Sweden v N Ireland	1-0
N Ireland v Sweden	3-0	Sweden v Portugal	3-0
Israel v Sweden	0-0	Portugal v Sweden	1-2
Portugal v N Ireland	1-0	Israel v Portugal	4-1
Portugal v Israel	3-0	N Ireland v Israel	1-0

World Cup finals – SPAIN   **June-July 1982**

Jock Stein had two friendlies, plus the Home Internationals, to serve as target practice before the Big Event. The first of these was in Valencia against World Cup hosts Spain, Scotland trailing away to a disappointing 0-3 defeat. Holland, having astonishingly failed to qualify, were beaten 1-2 at Hampden.

Before the British Championship got under way, events in the South Atlantic threatened to wreck the World Cup. The Argentine invasion of the Falkland Islands and the subsequent build-up of hostilities provoked intense speculation that the British teams would withdraw. The British public, or so it appeared, would not stomach their footballers basking in the glamour of a World Cup while their armed forces were fighting for their lives. Certain Scottish players were forthright in their belief that Scotland should pull out.

Should Argentina have to play a British team there seemed little hope of the fixture going ahead. But such a scenario was improbable. The draw dictated that Argentina could not meet England or Northern Ireland except in the World Cup Final itself. Even for Argentina to face Scotland required some conspiracy on the part of the gods.

As the weeks passed, the near-certainty that Britain would withdraw faded, before the whole question died in its own silence. This, despite the mounting casualties in the war. The Scottish press changed its tune: one day clamouring for withdrawal; the next, hoping nobody had listened to them.

The draw itself had been made back in January and was the stuff of farce. Miniature footballs containing miniature national flags held the key to each nation's fortunes. The balls were juggled in whirling lobster pots. Some balls – including Scotland's – were allocated wrongly, so the whole procedure had to restart from scratch. Then one of the balls broke and choked its lobster pot.

When all was settled, six groups of four teams were neatly arranged. There had been nothing to prevent Scotland, England and Northern Ireland all landing up together, but thankfully that dreary prospect did not materialise. England, ludicrously, had even been seeded in their group, despite their laughable record in the World Cups of 1974 onwards.

The Scotland manager and players could not conceal their disappointment at the composition of their own section, which threw up a near replica of 1974. It was bad news to have to face the expected weaklings first, in this instance New Zealand. The second game, as in 1974, would be against Brazil. The concluding fixture was again likely to prove decisive. Eastern Europe provided the opponents: Yugoslavia then, the Soviet Union now.

Even at the blueprint stage, Scotland looked like having their fate settled by goal difference – at best. Ill-conceived mutterings were heard to the effect that Scotland had drawn the toughest group of all. As it turned out, this was not the case, but Scotland's insistence that they had drawn a bad hand seemed to prey on their minds. Their confidence was not boosted by losing to England at Hampden for the third successive time, whereupon Stein announced his chosen pool. The World Cup was just three weeks away.

No	Name	Position	Club	Age	Caps	Goals
1	Alan Rough	Goalkeeper	Partick Thistle	30	48	–
2	Danny McGrain (c)	Full-back	Celtic	32	60	–
3	Frank Gray	Full-back	Leeds	27	22	1
4	Graeme Souness	Midfield	Liverpool	29	24	–
5	Alan Hansen	Central defence	Liverpool	26	14	–
6	Willie Miller	Central defence	Aberdeen	27	17	1
7	Gordon Strachan	Midfield	Aberdeen	25	11	1
8	Kenny Dalglish	Forward	Liverpool	31	86	25
9	Alan Brazil	Forward	Ipswich	23	7	–
10	John Wark	Midfield	Ipswich	24	15	3
11	John Robertson	Winger	Nott'm Forest	29	21	6
12	George Wood *	Goalkeeper	Arsenal	29	4	–
13	Alex McLeish	Central defence	Aberdeen	23	15	–
14	David Narey	Defence/Midfield	Dundee United	25	13	–
15	Joe Jordan	Forward	AC Milan	30	51	10
16	Asa Hartford	Midfield	Manchester C	31	49	4
17	Allan Evans	Central defence	Aston Villa	25	3	–
18	Steve Archibald	Forward	Tottenham	25	14	3
19	Paul Sturrock	Forward	Dundee United	25	17	1
20	Davie Provan	Winger	Celtic	26	9	1
21	George Burley	Full-back	Ipswich	25	11	–
22	Jim Leighton	Goalkeeper	Aberdeen	23	–	–

* Would not play in the finals or in future.   *Averages*   26.8 23.1

Jock Stein had continued to instil that most vital commodity – experience – into his squad. Long gone were those days when players could be asked to make their international debuts in the finals of the World Cup. Stein, that master of pragmatism and man-management, apologised to no one for following Ally MacLeod's example and packing his squad with Anglos.

West Ham's Ray Stewart and Celtic's Tommy Burns were omitted at the last moment. The twenty-two showed just one surprising inclusion. Stein was clearly unhappy with his central defenders. In his final warm-up matches he suddenly introduced Allan Evans – a big, hard, orthodox stopper from Aston Villa – and indulged in a belated experiment with a sweeper that came a mighty cropper against England. Otherwise, the squad was filled by those players who had booked Scotland's ticket. For Joe Jordan and Kenny Dalglish, it would be their third World Cup finals. Dalglish had long been talked about as Scotland's greatest ever footballer. Expert at shielding the ball and making space, lethal in the goalmouth, Dalglish was far and away Scotland's most capped player. His two previous World Cup finals had not seen the best in him. At thirty-one, this would surely be his last chance.

The party based themselves at Sotogrande on the Costa del Sol, within sight of Gibraltar. Stein was cautious when questioned about his team's chances. His understatement carried far more conviction, and threat, than the bluster of Ally MacLeod four years earlier. Scotland were once again tipped as possible dark horses. All they needed, it seemed, was to lose to England at Hampden to have everyone raving about them.

Group 6 commenced with the much-heralded clash of Brazil and the Soviet Union. With 1974 in mind, Scotland did not want a draw. The Scottish camp was heartened when Brazil won 2-1. Now the pressure was on the Soviets.

NEW ZEALAND v SCOTLAND
Tuesday, 15 June 1982   *Malaga – 36,000*

Having New Zealand appear in a world soccer, as opposed to rugby, championship was an oddity. They had qualified by the longest route, claiming the second Asia-Oceania place, behind Kuwait, after a play-off with China in Singapore. *En route* they had set a new record score in a World Cup qualifier when overwhelming Fiji 13-0. Having played fifteen matches and travelled distances commensurate with a voyage to the moon, New Zealand felt they had earned their passport to Spain.

This match had the makings of an old-fashioned British cup-tie. Kiwis manager John Adshead had weaned his players on British methods. Three of them had been born in Scotland; others had played in the English League.

Jock Stein stuck with those players introduced in Scotland's warm-up fixtures. Allan Evans – now the proud possessor of a European Cup medal with Villa – lined up for his fourth cap alongside Alan Hansen, to the exclusion of the tried and tested pairing of Miller and McLeish. In attack, Stein continued with Alan Brazil, unused in the eliminators, but looking sharp for Ipswich. Brazil was preferred to the more conventional front runners, Jordan and Archibald. Brazil had not scored in any of his seven internationals, but it was his twenty-third birthday and he would be looking for a double celebration.

The British were in festive spirits: the Argentine garrison at Port Stanley had surrendered. Now Scotland must learn from the mistakes against Zaïre and Iran, and deliver New Zealand a good hiding.

Though the pitch at Malaga's La Rosaleda Stadium delighted footballers, the heat and the humidity did not. New Zealand wore white, perhaps to con people into thinking they were Real Madrid. Scotland felt at home. Their supporters were numerous and noisy. One banner proclaimed 'Don't worry lads, Ally MacLeod is in Blackpool'. The Tanoy screeched 'Scotland the Brave', and battle began.

New Zealand must have been encouraged by their early possession, though Rough was untroubled and John Robertson looked in the mood. So did Strachan. It was Strachan's run that loaded the gun for Scotland's first goal. Jinking his way from his own half into the Kiwi penalty area, he threaded the ball to Dalglish, who wheeled to clip it past van Hattum. The tension lifted, then returned as Hansen passed back to an AWOL goalkeeper. Rough had to scamper back to claim the ball under his crossbar.

On the half-hour Scotland went two up. McGrain fed Strachan, who tee'd up a chance for Alan Brazil that van Hattum couldn't hold. There, vulturing on the remains, was John Wark. Three minutes later it was Strachan again, projecting a delicate cross onto Wark's head. The ball glanced inside van Hattum's right post and Scotland led 3-0. The watching Brazilians and Soviets must have sat dry-mouthed at the spectacle of a Scottish team for once doing everything right. Until the interval Scotland were queuing up to score, winning a rash of corners and keeping van Hattum on his toes. The nearest New Zealand came was a Steve Wooddin drive that squirmed out of Rough's clutches.

One can imagine Stein's interval comments: 'keep it steady, and more of the same.' Upon the resumption, Evans nodded Robertson's cross narrowly past. Boath almost put through his own goal and Brazil blazed wastefully over the top from Dalglish's pull-back. The birthday boy was substituted by Archibald and within seconds it was 3-1. McGrain was pressurised by Kiwi captain Steve Sumner – once of Preston North End. McGrain's pass back was suicidally short and Sumner nipped in to tuck the ball into goal off Rough's body.

Was this an isolated setback or a presage of disaster? It might have been the former had Archibald not hooked the ball over the top: it threatened the latter when Hill's deep, speculative pass found ex-Tranmere Rovers' Wooddin all alone to power the ball past Alan Rough. 3-2, and all Scotland's habitual self-destruct buttons had been activated. Sensing a sensation, New Zealand whipped off their sweeper for a forward and urged themselves to new heights.

The Scotland team line-up to face New Zealand.

It was now a case of holding out. It came, therefore, almost as a surprise when Scotland scored to make the game safe. Scottish players feigned to argue as they prepared for a free kick, leaving Robertson to flip the ball exquisitely into the top corner. The scorer stood motionless, arms raised, as if he'd fathered quintuplets. Ten minutes from time Strachan's corner fell squarely onto Archibald's head for the fifth. The brilliant Strachan – architect of four goals and indubitably Man of the Match – looked drained. Narey took his place. Frank Gray was denied a sixth by van Hattum, but afterwards attention did not dwell on Scotland's five loaves, but on New Zealand's two fishes, which now threatened to lodge painfully in Scotland's gullet.

NEW ZEALAND (0) 2   SCOTLAND (3) 5
   Sumner 55, Wooddin 65   Dalglish 18, Wark 29, 32,
                                  Robertson 73, Archibald 80

NEW ZEALAND: van Hattum, Hill, Malcolmson (Cole), Elrick, Almond (Herbert), Sumner, McKay, Cresswell, Boath, Rufer, Wooddin.
SCOTLAND: Rough, McGrain, Hansen, Evans, F Gray, Souness, Strachan (Narey), Dalglish, Wark, Brazil (Archibald), Robertson.

BRAZIL v SCOTLAND
Friday, 18 June 1982   *Benito Villamarín Stadium, Seville – 47,379*

For a country that hadn't won the World Cup for twelve years, Brazilian mystique in 1982 was undimmed. They had qualified with maximum points against Bolivia and Venezuela and galloped through a European tour, inflicting defeats on England, France and West Germany. In Spain, Brazil's very presence seemed to induce reverence in the press, public and opposition. In beating the Soviet Union 2-1, Brazil had looked magical at times, vulnerable at others. In midfield, coach Tele Santana was almost overburdened with speed, grace and power. For one team to include in its ranks Socrates, Zico, Falcão and Cerezo (missing against the Soviets) was simply unfair to its opponents.

Brazil's problems lay elsewhere. Their goalkeeper, Waldir Peres, like others before him, was – in a word – fallible. The left-back, Junior, supreme venturing forward, was less assured when defending. The attack contained no Garrincha, no Pelé, no Tostão, no Jairzinho. It relied instead on an erratic winger, Eder, and a sub-standard centre-forward, Serginho. Such was the brilliance of the Brazilian midfield that deficiencies elsewhere were apt to be overlooked – by the public if not by the professionals. It was to be hoped that Stein would not overlook them. Scotland would welcome a repeat of the goalless draw achieved in West Germany eight years to the day previously. Scotland had faced Brazil once since, going down 0-2 in Rio in 1977. All told, Scotland had just one goal to show from five matches against the triple World Cup winners.

The Scottish manager had some juggling to do. Some of his players had not recovered from their exertions in Malaga. In Seville, 150 miles inland, it would be even hotter. Adding to Stein's calculations was the realisation that, though a good result was now *desirable*, it was not *imperative*. The Soviet match would still hold the key to Scotland's fortunes. Put simply, it was preferable that Scotland lose heavily, but remain fresh, than drain themselves in an attacking frenzy that left them exhausted without time to recover for their crunch game.

Weighing his options, Stein made four changes. In defence, the Tannadice utility player, David Narey, switched for McGrain (Souness assuming the captaincy). Willie Miller took over from Allan Evans, whose international star fell as swiftly as it had risen. In midfield, Stein opted to counter the Brazilian quartet with his own quintet. This required Dalglish and the still-dehydrated Alan Brazil to step aside. Commentators were happy: they didn't fancy Brazil playing Brazil. Asa Hartford came back, plus a lone Scottish striker, Steve Archibald. The game provided a personal landmark for Alan Rough. It would be his fiftieth international, a total reached by only six previous Scotsmen.

In the Benito Villamarín Stadium a lone Scottish piper did his best to be heard above the drumming rhythm of the samba. On the pitch, Scotland were content to play patiently, and with Brazil operating at walking pace there were

1-0! David Narey smashes his shot past Falcão, No. 15. (v Brazil)

few early scares. Rough was periodically employed gathering back-passes, but was stranded when the loping Socrates headed carelessly into the side-netting.

Scotland had fully held their own when their treasured moment arrived. Souness, coordinating his team's every breath, swung the ball over from left to right, where Wark headed back to Narey. The Dundee United player had taken time off from policing Eder and Junior to stride into the enemy's nerve centre. Escaping Luizinho's challenge, Narey unleashed a sizzler with the outside of his right foot, that screamed high to Waldir Peres' left. It was a peach of a goal.

With Miller winning all the tackles expected of him and some that weren't, Scotland looked comfortable – other than when Eder's angled chip landed on top of the net. Brazil required the assistance of scarlet-clad Costa Rican referee Luis Calderon to equalise. Hansen's challenge on Cerezo was scarcely illegal, but Brazil were awarded a free kick twenty paces in front of Rough. To Brazil such a prize was tantamount to a penalty kick. Zico aimed for a tiny gap inside Rough's left-hand post. And found it.

Shortly afterwards Serginho, under pressure, headed Eder's swinging centre a shade too high, and Scotland were beginning to reel. When Waldir Peres saved at Archibald's feet, Scotland's last chance of taking the game had gone.

Scottish legs looked increasingly heavy. Three minutes into the second half Socrates bewildered Narey, and Hansen conceded a corner. Junior swung it towards the near post, where centre-back Oscar, with not a ghost of a challenge, thumped a close-range header past Rough. It was, to coin a phrase, a 'British' type of goal, and a criminal one to give away. Scotland were now on the ropes: Zico went close, then closer still.

Brazil now manufactured a dazzling goal. A silky move, in which Narey was 'nutmegged', saw the ball splayed wide to Eder. As Rough came out, Eder floated the ball over his head for a goal beyond Scottish compass.

Stein sent on Dalglish and McLeish for the spent Strachan and Hartford. They made little impact, though Robertson did cut in to shoot over. Brazil were now cruising, happy to turn on the exhibition stuff. Near the end they worked an exhibition goal. An entrancing build-up climaxed with a square pass to Falcão, who crashed the ball through a shadow-chasing Scottish defence and in off the far post. Scotland had been taught an almighty lesson.

BRAZIL   (1) 4   SCOTLAND   (1) 1
  Zico 33, Oscar 48, Eder 64,   Narey 18
  Falcão 86

BRAZIL: Waldir Peres, Leandro, Oscar, Luizinho, Junior, Falcão, Cerezo, Zico, Socrates, Eder, Serginho (Paulo Isidoro).
SCOTLAND: Rough, Narey, Miller, Hansen, F Gray, Wark, Souness, Strachan (Dalglish), Hartford (McLeish), Archibald, Robertson.

SOVIET UNION v SCOTLAND
Tuesday, 22nd June 1982   *Malaga – 45,000*

It was with a sense of *déjà vu* that Scotland prepared for their showdown with the Soviet Union. Eight years earlier Scotland had been in an identical position against Yugoslavia. Their opponents needed only to draw. For both states of affairs the Scots had only themselves to blame. In 1974 they rued their failure to turn the screw against Zaïre. Now, their inability to emulate the Soviets in restricting Brazil to a one-goal victory put Scotland at a disadvantage. Had Scotland not tossed away a couple of goals to New Zealand, the Soviets would have taken the field against the Kiwis seeking a minimum of four. Needing only two, they ticked them off – plus a third – without ever playing well. Jock Stein tried to turn the situation to his players' advantage, suggesting they were better equipped to fight for a win than hang on for a draw. It was scatterbrained logic, for it hardly flattered his side, but a sensible morale-booster.

Scotland had lost both their previous matches with the Soviet Union – 0-2 at Hampden in 1967, 0-1 in Moscow in 1971. The managers of Brazil and New Zealand – who were in the best position to judge – were united in predicting a Soviet victory. Eder's late winner had inflicted on the Soviet Union their first

Scotland fans salute Joe Jordan's goal. (v USSR)

defeat in twenty-three games. Dasaev, the goalkeeper, and Chivadze the
sweeper and captain were widely canvassed as the best at their positions in the
tournament. Coach Constantin Beskov would rely up front on the Soviet Player
of the Year, Ramaz Shengelia, and the fitfully brilliant left-winger, Oleg
Blokhin, European Footballer of the Year as far back as 1975.

There was much speculation about the team Stein would send out. Alan
Rough – not for the first time in his life – was receiving adverse comment. In
the event, Stein made just one change, shedding one of his surfeit of midfield
players – Asa Hartford – for target man Joe Jordan. With Jordan and Archibald
spearheading the attack, there was little doubt about Scotland's aerial tactics.

It is not often that Scottish sides are described as predictable or consistent.
But for the third match running they began in a manner to draw praise from all-
comers. The Soviets looked put out by Scotland's virile opening. Souness
looked even sharper than he had against the Brazilians. Scotland almost took
the lead when Jordan launched himself at Robertson's cross and watched
Dasaev make the save of the night in touching the header away.

On the quarter hour Scotland sensationally scored. Archibald won the ball
off Chivadze and stroked it into the path of Jordan. It was one against one,
Jordan versus one of the world's top keepers. One wondered whether Jordan
had the composure, never mind the skill, to score. The sceptics were shamed as

he slotted the ball between keeper and near post. Jordan had now scored in three successive World Cup finals, the only British player to post such a feat.

For the third successive match Scotland were in front, a luxury denied them in 1974 and 1978. Surely they could hang on this time. The Soviets emerged from their shell but Miller looked unpassable, Strachan inexhaustible, Robertson unstoppable. Souness was not particular how the enemy were softened up, and some of his tackles on Shengelia were not for the squeamish.

Before half-time Jordan headed wide, and Strachan's impudent burst obliged Dasaev to turn his cross-shot away from the lurking Wark. The keeper then leapt to keep out Jordan's hook. At the other end, Chivadze's run and interchange with Shengelia was unceremoniously interrupted by Souness.

Scotland could have made the game safe shortly after the interval, Archibald, Wark and Robertson taking turns to pepper the Soviet goal. The Soviets showed few signs of an equaliser when, after an hour, they found it. Gavrilov carried the ball into the Scottish area, whence it flew around as if on a pinball table. Chivadze's miscued shot would have carried no danger had Rough been in his goal. But he had needlessly strayed from his line and the ball bounced insultingly over his shoulder and into the net.

If the score stayed at 1-1 Scotland were out. Demianenko lashed a shot wide and Scotland were becoming desperate. Danny McGrain and Alan Brazil came on for the fatigued Strachan and Jordan, with Narey pushed forward into midfield.

Six minutes from time Scotland committed their second act of kamikaze. Out on the touchline Miller and Hansen – always an ill-fitting double act – both converged on the ball, which broke free in the confusion for Shengelia to home in on the unprotected Rough. Shengelia scored as coolly as had Jordan earlier. Scotland were now well and truly dead. Souness's cleverly worked goal at the death (shades of Jordan in 1974), which went in off the post, restored pride but not hope.

SOVIET UNION (0) 2   SCOTLAND (1) 2
  Chivadze 60, Shengelia 84   Jordan 15, Souness 88

USSR: Dasaev, Sulakvelidze, Chivadze, Baltacha, Demianenko, Shengelia (Andreyev), Bessonov, Bal, Borovsky, Gavrilov, Blokhin.
SCOTLAND: Rough, F Gray, Hansen, Miller, Strachan (McGrain), Narey, Souness, Jordan (Brazil), Wark, Robertson, Archibald.

The statistics tell the tale that for three World Cups in a row Scotland had been eliminated on goal difference. It is sequences like that which give statistics a bad name, for they obscure the fact that Scotland were always chasing the improbable in their third matches. In each, their opponents were in the driving seat. They – Yugoslavia, Holland, and now the Soviet Union – were unwilling to be budged and Scotland were ill-equipped to budge them. Scotland never did more than flirt with success, as if it was some beautiful woman tantalisingly out of reach. Last-gasp equalisers might restore self-respect but they should not distort the harsh truth that Scotland never quite deserved to progress. Their elimination was always their own fault, nobody else's. In 1974 they were knocked out because they couldn't score goals; in 1982 because they couldn't prevent them.

In many ways Scotland emerged with much credit from the 1982 World Cup, measured by the dignified conduct of manager and players off the pitch, and their positive, adventurous, and – at times – effective football on it. It was Gordon Strachan, not one of the Brazilians, who was voted by the Spanish press the outstanding player of Group 6. He was also voted into a world team. Set against these credits was the lengthy debit column. The team's tactical naïveté and technical limitations had been ruthlessly exposed. Scotland took a much-coveted early lead in each match, only to capsize under the weight of eight goals. Of these, seven were in the second half as Scotland's discipline and composure wilted. At least five of the eight (both New Zealand's, both the Soviet Union's, and Oscar's header for Brazil) owed nothing to attacking virtuosity and everything to fragile defending. An eight-goal debit column could hardly commend success.

In 1958, the last occasion Britain had mustered a broad-fronted assault on the World Cup, it was Scotland who were first to return home. Likewise in Spain, where England and Northern Ireland remained to do battle in the second round, though they progressed no further.

It was oft-heard that Scotland had found themselves in the toughest of all groups, and that had they been allocated elsewhere they would doubtless have survived. This unwarranted notion should have been exorcised by the demise of Brazil and the Soviet Union in the second phase. Poland comfortably disposed of the Soviets. As for Brazil, this is what Stein had to say: 'We lost to a rather special team in Brazil. Barring some catastrophe they will win the World Cup for sure.'

In fact, it did not take a catastrophe to beat Brazil, merely their own shortcomings. There came a time when the magic of their midfield could no longer paper up the cracks in front of, and behind, it. Italy – whose form in the first round had been wretched – capitalised on defensive lapses to show Scotland how to bring the over-confident Brazilians down to size. They were beatable after all. Verily, the most attractive side in the world was not the best.

So, neither Brazil nor the Soviet Union reached even the semi-finals, never mind the Final. Their conquerors, Italy and Poland, had both emerged from Group 1, which on paper did not seem as star-studded as Group 6. But paper, as Jock Stein should have known, burns easily.

West Germany's route to the Final was littered with good fortune and chicanery. They had lost to the no-hopers of Algeria, connived with the Austrians so that both might go through, watched helpless as England failed to beat Spain, and overcame the French in a penalty shoot-out after trailing by two goals and after their goalkeeper, Schumacher, had almost killed Battiston with a forearm smash.

To the cheers of football lovers everywhere, the Germans met their come-uppance in the Final. Italy were indubitably worthy winners of the 1982 World Cup.

Final positions – Group 6

	P	W	D	L	F	A	Pts
BRAZIL	3	3	0	0	10	2	6
SOVIET UNION	3	1	1	1	6	4	3
Scotland	3	1	1	1	8	8	3
New Zealand	3	0	0	3	2	12	0

Scotland appearances and goalscorers (substitute appearances in brackets)
World Cup qualifying rounds and final competition 1982

	Apps	Goals		Apps	Goals
Gray F	11	–	Gemmill A *	4	–
Robertson J *	10	4	Gray A *	3 (3)	–
Rough A *	10	–	Jordan J *†	3	2
Hansen A	9	–	Provan D	3	1
Souness G *	8	1	Narey D	2 (1)	1
Archibald S	7 (2)	1	Burns K *	2	–
McGrain D *†	7 (1)	–	Stewart R	2	–
Miller W	7 (1)	–	Brazil A	1 (1)	–
Strachan G	7	1	Thomson W	1 (1)	–
Dalglish K *†	6 (2)	2	Evans A	1	–
Wark J	6	3	Sturrock P	1	1
Hartford A *	5 (1)	–	Kennedy S *	– (1)	–
McLeish A	5 (1)	–			

* Appeared in 1978 World Cup.   *136 apps   17 goals*
† Appeared in 1974 World Cup.   *49 Scottish League*
                                 85 English League
                                 2 Italian League
                                 25 players used

10

THE 1986 WORLD CUP

The modern international footballer faces a daunting schedule. No sooner have the echoes of one competition faded away than the noises of the next begin. Straight after the Spain World Cup came the qualifying rounds for the 1984 European Championship. If Scotland could claim modest success from their efforts in global tournaments, they were more embarrassed by the continental stage. Jock Stein led his Spanish veterans into Europe only to watch them sink to the bottom of a mediocre group completed by Belgium, East Germany and Switzerland. In view of Scotland's chronic travel sickness it came as little surprise that their three away fixtures yielded no points whatsoever.

On the domestic front, a Scottish club was making headlines. Only twice had a European trophy adorned a Scottish boardroom – Celtic and Rangers taking the honours in 1967 and 1972. Such was the stranglehold imposed by those two titans that it was cause for raised eyebrows if another club lifted a Scottish trophy, never mind a European one. Yet this was Aberdeen's achievement in May 1983, returning from Gothenburg clutching the European Cup-Winners' Cup. Dons' manager Alex Ferguson had shrewdly invited Jock Stein along to Gothenburg to lend his massive experience to a Scottish cause. In the early- and mid-'eighties Aberdeen players hogged the international limelight to an extent paralleled only by the Old Firm in years gone by. Against Northern Ireland in 1983, there were six Pittodrie players on the pitch, one of whom was a substitute.

There seemed little sign that the robust health of Scottish club football would spill over onto the national side. The British Championship was wound up in 1983-84, with Scotland propping up the table. A wooden spoon in Europe had been followed by another at home, and an emphatic defeat in France by the European champions-elect rubbed salt into festering wounds.

But fate now intervened. Wales and Northern Ireland were still smarting at the insult of Scotland and England turning their backs on them. FIFA stepped in to refurbish their empty coffers. The qualifiers for the 1986 World Cup, the finals to be staged in Mexico, pitched the Irish into the same group as England, and paired Wales with Scotland. Spain and Iceland would complete the quartet.

With each successive World Cup the qualifying arrangements became more tortuous and complex. The entry list for 1986 extended to 121 nations. Half the European groups comprised five teams with the top two to qualify. The other three sections, including Scotland's, had just four teams. Only the winners were sure to progress.

FIFA's original intention was that the three runners-up should combine with qualifiers from Asia or the Antipodes in a worldwide free-for-all for a second bite at the cherry. Swamped with protests, FIFA backed down. In the case of Scotland and Wales, the revised plan was warmly welcomed. To finish second in Group 7 would herald a two-way play-off with the Oceania winners.

By the time the eliminators were under way, Scotland's fortunes were showing an upturn. A touchline ban on assistant manager Jim McLean had sparked a search for a replacement. The job went to Aberdeen's Alex Ferguson, who insisted on the title 'coach', not 'assistant manager'. The Stein-Ferguson ticket inspired the Scots (wearing red!) to wallop the powerful Yugoslavs 6-1 at Hampden, just the tonic for the visit of Iceland a month away.

Qualifying Group 7

SCOTLAND v ICELAND
Wednesday, 17 October 1984   *Hampden – 52,829*

An opener against the school dunces is designed to yield two points, head the table from the start, and heap all the pressure on your rivals. A setback here could wreck Scotland's entire programme. Already, Iceland's unexpected 1-0 home victory over Wales looked like casting a blight on Wales' hopes.

Jock Stein's team was unrecognisable to that which partook of the 1982 World Cup. Only four players remained: Miller and McLeish; skipper Graeme Souness, now in Italy with Sampdoria; and the evergreen Kenny Dalglish. The Liverpool legend, though recently dropped from the Anfield first team, stepped out for his fourth World Cup as a sprightly thirty-three year old.

Aberdeen's bandy-legged keeper, Jim Leighton, taken to Spain as a virginal second understudy to Alan Rough, was promoted to first-team duty thereafter. Protected by Miller and McLeish, Leighton completed the Pittodrie-dominated backbone of the national side. Completing the defence were full-backs Steve Nicol and Arthur Albiston, of Liverpool and Manchester United. Nicol's was a versatile talent, not employed in defence at Anfield. Ex-Ranger Jim Bett, exiled to Lokeren of Belgium, played left-side midfield. The twinkling toes of Davie Cooper earned an international recall after five long years, the reward for the extra motivation instilled by Jock Wallace's messianic return to Ibrox.

Public interest focused on two Celtic babes. Fair-haired Maurice 'Mo' Johnston had been a Watford player the previous week. Coming north to the club of his dreams for the princely fee of £400,000, he now pulled on Scottish navy for the fifth time. His team-mate Paul McStay, although short of his twentieth birthday, was a Celtic prodigy. His recall to colours was the only change from the slayers of Yugoslavia.

As for the Icelanders, who knew what to expect? They had never faced Scotland and never come close to qualifying for a World Cup. Their players performed for prestige – no fee being paid for international appearances – though seven earned their living in the bright lights of West Germany, Holland and Belgium. Sigurvinsson had helped Stuttgart lift the German title. One of Iceland's home-based stars, the Akranes midfielder Sigi Jonsson, was reportedly attracting the spies of Rangers and Aberdeen.

The first scare was Scotland's. Gudjohnsson powered his way towards Leighton, producing a scrambling save at the keeper's right post. Iceland played 'catch us if you can'. Their defenders were tough and blond, fitting descendants of their warrior Berserker forbears. McStay, Bett, and Cooper all tried their luck, and when Souness's free kick cannoned off the defensive wall the ball broke to McLeish on the blind side. The effort was cleared.

Scotland squealed for a penalty when Atli Edvaldsson – brother of an ex-Celtic player – elbowed the ball. But the goal which separated the teams after twenty-two minutes was more satisfying. Dalglish's short corner enabled Cooper to skip past an Icelandic obstruction and flight the ball beyond the far post to McStay. The youngster's downward header reared up and flew inside Bjarni Sigurdsson's near upright. It was McStay's baptismal Scottish goal.

Scotland blossomed. Dalglish's wriggling slalom and chip deserved better than to brush wood, before McStay crowned the match with a goal to savour. Dalglish turned the ball to him forty yards out. Touching it ahead, McStay powered his shot inside the top corner as if the ball was wired to an invisible hoist. The boy-wonder threw back his head to milk heaven's applause.

Stung into action, Iceland surged forward on the reflex. Leighton clung on to Edvaldsson's close-range flick to protect his team's two-goal interval margin. Upon the resumption Souness, twice, might have made the game safe. Both efforts were thwarted, and Hampden sucked in its breath when Leighton plunged at Petursson's feet to frustrate an Icelandic attack.

Midway through the half, Dalglish, his job done, gave way to Charlie Nicholas – a precociously gifted player with Celtic, now a wayward one with Arsenal. The switch soon showed its reward. Miller journeyed down the right and chipped a floating centre parallel with the goal-line. The ball dropped beyond Sigurdsson and onto the head of the in-rushing Nicholas, who could hardly miss. Who would believe that Nicholas's first World Cup goal for Scotland would also be his last.

McStay's hat-trick aspirations were foiled by the crossbar, but Jock Stein was a contented man. One down: five to go.

SCOTLAND   (2) 3   ICELAND   (0) 0
McStay 22, 40, Nicholas 70

SCOTLAND: Leighton (Aberdeen), Nicol (Liverpool), Albiston (Man U), Souness (Samp'), McLeish (Aberdeen), Miller (Aberdeen), Dalglish (Liverp'l) (*sub* Nicholas, Arsenal), McStay (Celtic), Johnston (Celtic), Bett (Lokeren), Cooper (Rangers).
ICELAND: Sigurdsson, Thrainsson, Edvaldsson, Bergs, Margeirsson, Jonsson, Gudlaugsson, Gudjohnsson, Petursson, Sigurvinsson, Sveinsson.

SCOTLAND v SPAIN
Wednesday, 14 November 1984   *Hampden – 74,299*

The *hors d'oeuvre* had been tasty: now the main course was dished up to a packed banqueting hall. Hampden was crammed to the rafters with 74,299 all-ticket customers. Spain travelled to Glasgow as runners-up in that summer's European Championship, having lost with distinction to France. Scotland was all a-buzz, even though Spain had no pedigree on the global stage. Since 1950 they had four times failed to qualify for the finals, and in 1982, as hosts, had managed just one win in five starts.

Spain were infrequent visitors to Scotland, this being only the fourth occasion. On the first, in 1957, Scotland had triumphed dazzlingly in a World Cup eliminator. But a draw in 1965 and a defeat in 1974 meant that it was now twenty-seven years since Hampden had sunk a Spanish armada. A few personal skirmishes were about to be resumed. Liverpool's Souness, Dalglish and Nicol had been bruised by Urquiaga, Urtabi and Goicoechia of Athletic Bilbao in the European Cup. Goicoechia was tagged 'the Butcher of Bilbao' following a grotesque foul, seen around the world on TV, on Diego Maradona.

Jock Stein enjoyed an embarrassment of riches. Several of his stars wouldn't even find a place on the bench. Spanish coach Miguel Muñoz expressed his surprise, and relief, at the omission of Gordon Strachan, now revitalised at Old Trafford. Muñoz had fond memories of Hampden, having managed the Real Madrid team that thrilled the world in the 1960 European Cup Final.

In case Scotland became too cocky, their Under-21s were roundly beaten, 2-0, by Spain's on the Tuesday. Weighing up the odds on the seniors, the *Guardian* condescendingly decreed: 'Taking the opposition into account, the Scots should not regard a draw as a disaster.'

The popular pundits predicted a stultifying approach by Spain. They were wrong. Having scored in all but one of their previous dozen away matches, Spain were brave enough to attack. Gordillo's easy escape from Nicol, and Victor's threatening shot, caused early flutters among Scottish commentators.

But the pundits equally misjudged, and underplayed, Scottish ingenuity. Spain's red shirts and blue shorts were soon inexorably back-peddling, not by choice, but in the face of relentless tartan attacks. Kenny Dalglish – winning his ninety-sixth cap despite a secret knee injury – was in the mood. One moment he was wrong-footing his shadow, Camacho; the next, spearing a shot wide.

Souness and Bett were no less incisive. Bett sent over a cross that seemed sure to herald a goal. But the closely shackled Davie Cooper, better at juggling the ball than heading it, connected badly and it bounced back off an upright.

Cooper was distracted by his miss for just four minutes before contributing to a spectacular goal. His corner was flicked on by McLeish for Nicol to rake a blistering volley. Arconada, the veteran Spanish keeper and captain, was a player much revered by undiscerning sports writers. In truth he was a tension-racked performer whose international career was littered with banana skins. Now he plunged to parry, threw himself out of the firing line, and left the ball bobbling on the goal-line. Mo Johnston dived to nod it into the net.

Before long, Scotland contrived a second, yet better goal. Bett collected Miller's pass on the right and retained his balance in the face of an elephantine Spanish challenge. His centre was headed irresistibly home by Johnston, unimpeded by two defenders positioned between him and the goal.

After the break Emilio Butragueno replaced Rincon as Spain committed themselves to attack. Gordillo took the eye and Urtabi took liberties, wasting one chance. Camacho was booked for his umpteenth assault on Dalglish before despatching the free kick that gave Spain hope. Central defender Goicoechia's header was firm, but directed down in front of Leighton. The keeper was caught, literally, on the hop. An eminently saveable header bounced up over his shoulder, leaving Leighton with mud on his knees and egg on his face.

Scottish confidence plummeted, then soared with a stunning third goal. Dalglish shimmied his way across the face of the goal, drawing three defenders in turn. When it seemed he had run out of options he swivelled to strike a murderous shot across Arconada and up into the far junction. The scorer threw his arms wide as if to embrace the universe. He had just equalled Denis Law's all-time record of thirty goals for Scotland.

Afterwards a crestfallen Muñoz conceded that this was the best Scottish team he had ever seen. 'It was a masterpiece of technique,' he admitted, and he spoke nothing short of the truth. Scotland's finest all-round performance in years seemed to have prised open the door to Mexico.

SCOTLAND (2) 3	SPAIN (0) 1
Johnston 33, 42, Dalglish 75	Goicoechia 68

SCOTLAND: Leighton, Nicol, Albiston, Souness, McLeish, Miller, Dalglish, McStay, Johnston, Bett, Cooper.
SPAIN: Arconada, Urquiaga, Maceda, Goicoechia, Camacho, Señor, Urtabi (Carrasco), Victor, Gordillo, Santillana, Rincon (Butragueno).

SPAIN v SCOTLAND

Wednesday, 27 February 1985   Sánchez Pizjuán Stadium, Seville – 70,000

The winter of Scottish contentment lasted long. The media occasionally did a MacLeod and went overboard. One commentator suggested that the current eleven constituted the best Scottish team in history. But Scotland had flattered at home before, and often. A trip to Spain was, in the vernacular, a whole new ball game. It was five long years since Scotland had avoided defeat on opponents' turf on the continent. Scottish confidence, in other words, was a vastly inflated commodity.

Preparations for the big match were far from amicable. The Spanish authorities procrastinated over the choice of venue, before opting for Seville's Sánchez Pizjuán Stadium, an arena renowned for its patriotic fervour in times of need. The crowd were separated from the pitch by no more than the width of a matador's cape. Spain had not lost in fifteen internationals played in the stadium, and though Scotland had faced Brazil in 1982 in Seville, that had been in the city's other, Benito Villamarín Stadium. To compound the aggravation, Scottish training sessions were disrupted by unruly local gate-crashers.

On account of a match which Spain dare not lose, Spanish league engagements were postponed. Not so in Scotland, where half the national team featured in a bruising top-of-the-table clash involving Celtic and Aberdeen. Spanish eyebrows were raised at this manifest disregard for players' welfare, not to mention Scotland's strange sense of priorities.

Miguel Muñoz axed five players – including the entire strike force – from the team humbled at Hampden. Jock Stein hoped to field his magic eleven, until a virus laid low Steve Nicol and Kenny Dalglish. It was not till an hour before kick-off that these misfortunes were made public.

Nicol's shirt was reliably filled by the equally versatile Richard Gough of Dundee United. Dalglish was somewhat harder to replace, the job going to Steve Archibald, more of a target man who, since transferring to Barcelona, could double as a 'fifth columnist'. Archibald ('Archee' to the Catalonians) topped the Spanish League's goalscoring charts. Sadly, he had scored in only four of his twenty-three matches for Scotland. Stein's reshuffled team included just one token Anglo, Arthur Albiston of Manchester United.

The partisan Seville crowd pelted Leighton with oranges, toilet rolls and other sundries before and during the match. No sooner had play begun than Gough was booked for bisecting Gordillo near the halfway line, but fortunately the game never lived up to its violent potential.

A draw was all Scotland needed. In the first half they saw plenty of the ball, but were as creative as a dead bull. Spain shaded the honours in that dreary half. Only a coat of paint denied them a goal after seven minutes. Goicoechia's drive caught Leighton in a tizzy. He could only repulse the ball whence it came. Clos headed it back beyond the mortified keeper and past the upright.

Scotland, for their part, could boast no such near misses. The players were performing in direct proportion to their distance from Arconada. The defence looked solid enough; the midfield, so fired up at Hampden, was lacklustre; while the attacking duo of Johnston and Archibald were an irrelevance. The evidence of the first half told that Scotland would be unlikely to score in the second, but could they keep Spain at bay?

Scotland learned the answer before Stein's cautionary words had faded. Butragueno's intelligent burst from his own half sent Señor clear on the right. His cross was tailor-made for Miller or McLeish to repel. Alas, they were inexplicably absent and debutant Francisco Clos, having come so near in the first half, headed beyond Leighton.

One sensed the inevitable. There looked no way back for Scotland. McStay and Archibald were pulled off for Strachan and Nicholas. In his eight-minute stint Nicholas alone looked likely to prise gaps in the Spanish rearguard. Yet Arconada remained a virtual spectator to the end, and it was Spain who came nearer to scoring as Scotland slid miserably from the match. Souness, culpably casual throughout, climaxed his indiscretions with a crass professional foul.

Afterwards the Scottish press charged to the rescue. The Spaniards were cheats, criminals. The intimidating crowd had, would you believe, unnerved seasoned professionals accustomed to the hatreds generated by soccer at home and abroad. In truth, Scotland were as disappointing as they had been inspired at Hampden. The press tried to twist a one-goal defeat into a good result. It wasn't.

SPAIN   (0) 1   SCOTLAND   (0) 0
Clos 50

SPAIN: Arconada, Gerardo, Camacho, Maceda, Goicoechia, Gordillo, Señor, Roberto, Butragueno, Gallego, Clos.
SCOTLAND: Leighton, Gough, Albiston, Souness, McLeish, Miller, Archibald (Nicholas), McStay (Strachan), Johnston, Bett, Cooper.

SCOTLAND v WALES
Wednesday, 27 March 1985   *Hampden – 62,444*

The defeat in Seville could be quickly rectified. No lasting damage had been done. Wales' own chances appeared dashed by losses in Iceland and, heavily, in Spain.

Scotland were well accustomed to slaying the Welsh dragon at Hampden, not having lost since 1951. For Wales even to score there was an achievement, and not since 1967 had they breached the Scottish rearguard more than once. In their last visit, in 1984, Wales went down 1-2. With Dalglish and Nicol restored to full health, Jock Stein reverted to the line-up that had served him well.

Wales were widely written off in this, the 100th meeting between the two nations. Only an outright win could keep their hopes flickering. But how could a team beaten in Iceland and fielding one full-back, Slatter, playing in the English third division reserves, and another, Joey Jones, as a makeshift centre-half, hope to contain Scotland's aristocrats? Wales' slender chances seemed to rest on a vital trio. In goal, Neville Southall was performing with the consistent excellence that would shortly help Everton to the English title and earn Southall the sports writers' 'Footballer of the Year' award. In attack, the threat posed by Ian Rush was well known, but his side-kick was quickly becoming the revelation of British soccer. Manchester United's muscular Mark Hughes completed one of Europe's most lethal strike forces.

Scottish commentators, nevertheless, seemed unperturbed. John Greig, for one, said the result was a foregone conclusion. Scotland simply had to sever the lines to Rush and Hughes, and goodbye Wales. The tabloids, searching for titbits to stoke up the pre-match atmosphere, latched onto Graeme Souness's ghosted autobiography, which offered unflattering appraisals of Scottish team-mates. But all was smiles and handshakes, before the cameras at least.

Those sports correspondents keen to gloss over the failure in Seville could find no scapegoats this time, as Scotland slumped miserably. There were no illnesses to blame; no orange-hurling Spaniards to accuse of intimidation. Stein's favoured eleven were knocked out of their stride with embarrassing ease by a Welsh team equipped for a physical battle.

The midfield of Souness, McStay and Bett, only recently compared with the heroes of yesteryear, were ragged beyond belief. They failed to sustain the supply to the front runners, and failed to prevent Rush and Hughes enjoying more of the ball than they could have bargained for. The terrible twins buffeted Miller and McLeish with the attrition that reduces battlements to rubble.

The first half was British football at its worst. Huff and puff, bags of energy, with not a touch of class. No worthwhile opportunities had been manufactured at either end when, in the thirty-third minute, Wales scored a stunning goal. Mike England, the Welsh manager, had warned beforehand that Ian Rush needed only a split second's freedom, and would need to be policed constantly.

England was right. McLeish was set to head clear when he was clattered by the muscular frame of Mark Hughes. The Welshman had little hope of winning the ball, but every hope of disconcerting the centre-half. The ball bounced from McLeish's chest and into the path of the one player who could exploit the half-chance. Rush smashed the half-volley in a blur inside Leighton's near post. According to the letter of the law, Hughes' challenge was questionable. In a match with no quarter asked, few Scots were going to quibble. Rush's first-ever goal against Scotland was a gem.

After half-time Johnston missed a gaping goal when rounding Southall but shooting wide. It was Scotland's first genuine chance. The temperature of battle rose, climaxing with Souness's horrendous two-footed thrust at Peter Nicholas's throat. A judge might have sent Souness to prison: the Belgian referee, Ponnet, did not even send him from the pitch.

Changes were needed. Hansen replaced Albiston, pushing Nicol forward and leaving only three defenders. Then the inert McStay was substituted by Charlie Nicholas, who miskicked horribly. At the death, Johnston's angled shot was easily saved – it was Southall's one and only save – and the final whistle sounded. Scotland had lost at home in the World Cup for only the fourth time, and the first in twenty years. The refrain of 'What a load of rubbish' announced the first occasion in Group 7 that the home side had failed to win.

SCOTLAND (0) 0   WALES (1) 1
                                   Rush 37

SCOTLAND: Leighton, Nicol, Albiston (Hansen), Souness, McLeish, Miller, Dalglish, McStay (C Nicholas), Johnston, Bett, Cooper.
WALES: Southall (Everton), Slatter (Bristol R), J Jones (Chelsea), Ratcliffe (Everton), Jackett (Watford), D Phillips (Man C), R James (QPR), P Nicholas (Luton), M Thomas (Chelsea), Hughes (Man U), Rush (Liverpool).

ICELAND v SCOTLAND
Tuesday, 28 May 1985   *Reykjavik – 15,000*

Wales' effrontery in overturning the laws of history was a devastating blow to Scotland. In the space of ninety minutes the Scots had tumbled from being favourites to reach Mexico to being outsiders. Both remaining matches were away, and three points were still needed. The Welsh, having knocked Group 7 off its feet at Hampden, then proceeded to stand it on its head when crushing Spain 3-0 in Wrexham. With the finishing line in sight, Wales led the pack.

Scotland travelled to the Laugardalsvollur Stadium in Reykjavik with a bagful of woes unimaginable during the heady autumn. The team was in tatters and needed surgery. The Scottish cause was further hampered by a regrettable clash of fixtures. On the Saturday, Scotland entertained England for the Rous Cup, short-lived successor to the Home Internationals. In any ordered sense of priorities Scotland's players would have held something back for the more pressing task in Iceland, but that was alien to the Scottish psyche. In the event all went well: England were beaten and Scotland sustained no injuries.

More damaging to Jock Stein's plans was Liverpool's march to the ill-fated 1985 European Cup Final. The Anfield contingent – Dalglish, Nicol and Hansen – would therefore be fighting for club not country. As a final indignity the Everton pair, Graeme Sharp and Andy Gray, were held back for a rearranged league fixture and flown out at the last moment, fitness permitting. Through no fault of his own, Stein's team selection was thrown to the winds.

Only Leighton, McLeish, Miller, Bett, and Souness remained of the eleven that had captured the plaudits earlier in the season. The Dundee United pairing of Gough and Malpas filled the full-back berths, Gordon Strachan and Celtic's Roy Aitken buttressed the midfield, leaving Sharp and Gray to do for Scotland what they had done all season for Everton, for whom they had shared forty-four goals. It was Sharp's first cap, Gray's twentieth.

Despite the short hop across the north Atlantic, Icelandic football inhabited another world. Their manager, Tony Knapp, an ex-pro with Leicester and Southampton, insisted on Iceland's capacity to cause an upset. If they could beat Wales without the assistance of Iceland's expatriate players, why couldn't they dispose of Scotland with them? To underline Knapp's bullishness, Iceland's Under-21s duly beat Scotland's 2-0.

No sooner had a helpful parachutist descended into the centre circle bearing the match ball, than the game commenced. Scotland's players, unrecognisable in their performance against Wales, were now unrecognisable in their new strip. Lemon shirts invited fruity insults, while the blue shorts sported a hideous yellow hoop as if the entire team had squatted in a freshly 'lined' kerb.

Jim Leighton was in grey, but that was his only drab aspect as he turned in the most sparkling performance of his three-year international career. Within four minutes he clung on to Iceland's first goal attempt, the first of many.

The play was fast and furious, with more chances created than in any of Group 7's fixtures to date. Gray was set up by Strachan and Bett, but his effort flew at Gudmundsson. Sharp and Souness were the next to try their luck.

The game would be remembered for several incidents, any of which could have turned the outcome. The first arrived midway through the first half when Sigi Jonsson (having signed for Sheffield Wednesday) was laid out by Souness. Jonsson was stretchered off and Soviet referee Milchenko took the name of the Scottish captain. Souness was booed loudly thereafter, and Scotland never recaptured their earlier promise.

They ought shortly to have fallen behind. A neat pass reached Petursson, who was toppled by Aitken six yards from goal. Doubling the range, from the penalty spot, proved too much for Icelandic captain Thordarsson. Leighton flung himself to his left to pull off a save beyond the call of duty. When the ensuing corner bounced back off the near post, one sensed the warrior Norse gods were losing the battle for divine intervention. Christian prayers seemed to be having greater effect.

After the turnaround Gudmundsson wafted at a Souness cross, allowing Bett a muscular volley that left the crossbar with a mighty headache. Iceland, however, continued to call the shots. McLeish hooked off the line from

Edvaldsson and Leighton tipped over a thirty-yarder from Gudlaugsson. The midfield seemed to have been abandoned as time without number Iceland broke through to bear down on Miller and McLeish. The out-of-touch Gray trudged off to be replaced by Archibald.

Then, in an extraordinary climax, Strachan's centre was swept home by Bett at the far post. Only four minutes remained, but within seconds Gudlaugsson controlled a cross on his chest, found himself in the clear and shot criminally wide of Leighton's right post. The Iceland team clutched their heads, and well they might. Scotland greeted their victory with joy and embarrassment in equal measure. 'We stole it,' admitted Denis Law, while Rod Stewart – Scotland's self-proclaimed No. 1 fan agreed: 'We were a wee bit lucky,' he chuckled.

ICELAND (0) 0   SCOTLAND (0) 1
                                      Bett 86

ICELAND: Gudmundsson, Thrainsson, Sigi Jonsson (Torfason), Bergs, Petursson, Saevar Jonsson, Gudlaugsson, Edvaldsson, Thordarsson (Gretarsson), Thorbjornsson, Sveinsson.
SCOTLAND: Leighton, Gough, Malpas, Aitken, McLeish, Miller, Strachan, Souness, Gray (Archibald), Bett, Sharp.

WALES v SCOTLAND
Tuesday, 10 September 1985   *Cardiff – 39,500*

The Welsh were the principle victims of Scotland's poached win in Iceland, for the Scots had leapfrogged above them on goal difference. In June, Spain came from behind to win in Reykjavik, leaving all three countries locked on six points with one match to play. Scotland needed only to draw in Wales to secure second place and a play-off. A win would, in all likelihood, bring qualification, for Spain would then need to thrash the Norsemen by five goals to finish top.

The summer was spent counting the cost of the tragedies of Bradford and Brussels. Heightened security considerations ruled out Wales' 'lucky' ground, Wrexham, and the Arms Park rugby stadium, leaving the shoot-out to be staged at Ninian Park.

The media harped on the revenge factor, Wales' urge to repay Joe Jordan's infamous handball at Anfield in 1977. The Welsh line-up, Mike England's strongest, contained two survivors from that luckless night – Mickey Thomas and Joey Jones. Jock Stein's preparations were again disrupted by absentees. Dalglish was ruled out with a septic knee, and Hansen, Archibald and Johnston also withdrew. Souness was suspended, the result of cautions against Wales and Iceland. Miller assumed the captaincy. With Jim Bett now on Aberdeen's payroll, the four-man Dons contingent would be Scotland's only ever-presents.

Jock Stein made two changes. Nicol came in for Souness, while in place of the hammer of Andy Gray, Stein opted for the whiplash of Chelsea's David Speedie. The possessor of quick legs and an even quicker temper, Speedie had already earned one early bath in the new season.

Comedians joked about Scotland's new strike-force: how could it fail with names like Sharp and Speedie? Critics bemoaned the duo's inexperience. They had one cap apiece, had never played together, and Sharp had just returned to the Everton first team.

In terms of experience, the Scots outfit fared badly, having an aggregate of 181 caps against Wales' 302. The Welsh line-up boasted a stock of thirty international goals, eleven to Ian Rush. Scotland's tally was six. With a nose to the wind, the bookies fancied Wales.

Twelve thousand tickets were allocated to Scottish fans, a ludicrous underestimate of those inside the ground. 'Hoolivans' toured the streets. Wales kicked off to a tumultuous reception, and immediately Mark Hughes began laying all about him, battering McLeish, twice, and Miller. McLeish exacted revenge on Rush and was booked by Dutch referee Keizer.

Scotland's tactics were for Miller to sweep behind McLeish and Gough, who were marking Rush and Hughes. Sharp sped into the six-yard box but shot into the side-netting. Scotland might have been a goal up; two minutes later they were a goal down. On the left touchline Peter Nicholas collected a throw and veered into the theoretically unbreachable wall of Aitken and Nicol. But the wall crumbled, the tackles made of straw. Nicholas was clear, and his low cross was hammered by Mark Hughes through Miller's legs and into goal. Ninian Park blew steam.

Scotland sagged, the wind knocked out of them. On twenty minutes Wales nearly scored a second, but Robbie James' header floated tantalisingly wide. The Scottish goalkeeper, robust in Reykjavik, was more fragile in Cardiff. Twice he should have punched clear, but twice he failed to make decisive contact. On the stroke of half-time he allowed a harmless punt to bounce away off his shins. Leighton rescued the situation by plunging at Hughes' feet.

Leighton stayed behind after the interval, having displaced a contact lens. Alan Rough deputised, an apparition from a bygone age. Rush was booked, his victim, Strachan, was subbed by Davie Cooper (the fans wanted Andy Gray), and Rush might have scored had he connected with a deflection off Hughes.

Cooper's brief was to penetrate Wales' suspect right flank. His first touch produced a corner, and it was not long before his audacious waltz along the by-line was whacked clear of the goalmouth. Cooper's virtuosity symbolised his team's revival, but the Welsh goal remained largely unthreatened.

With nine minutes left, the fates intervened. Wheeling on Sharp's downward header, Speedie hooked the ball hard against David Phillips' arm. The referee, to Welsh dismay, awarded a penalty and Cooper, admirably cool, struck the ball home off Southall's left hand. Lightning had struck Wales twice. The best that could be said of the penalty award was that it was a Welsh arm and not a Scottish one. But it was still misjudged, for Phillips was so close to Speedie as to rule out evasive action. Be that as it may, Scotland were level, and Speedie might even have sealed a late win when thwarted by Southall. Scotland greeted the final whistle with delirium. A blushing Miller told a TV camera: 'Sure it was a penalty.' But then he would, wouldn't he? But what if it was *his* arm?

Unbeknown to all, Scottish fortune would pay a fearful price. An agitated Jock Stein, harassed by over-zealous photographers, collapsed at the game's end and within half an hour was dead. Celebrations turned to numbing grief.

WALES (1) 1	SCOTLAND (0) 1
Hughes 13	Cooper 81 pen

WALES: Southall (Everton), J Jones (Huddersfield), Van den Hauwe (Everton), Ratcliffe (Everton), Jackett (Watford), James (QPR) (*sub* Lovell, Millwall), Phillips (Man C), Nicholas (Luton), Thomas (Chelsea) (*sub* Blackmore, Man U), Rush (Liverpool), Hughes (Man U).
SCOTLAND: Leighton (Rough), Gough, Malpas, Aitken, McLeish, Miller, Nicol, Strachan (Cooper), Sharp, Bett, Speedie.

SCOTLAND v AUSTRALIA
Wednesday, 20 November 1985   *Hampden – 63,500*

The death of Jock Stein hung like a pall over the Scottish nation. The mind searched for men of comparable stature in the history of Scottish football – and drew a blank. But the show must go on: Scotland were not yet in Mexico.

The SFA were in no rush to appoint a successor, knowing that to act in haste would doubtless lead them to repent at leisure. Yet all along there was only one candidate. Alex Ferguson had been Stein's right-hand man for the past year. At Pittodrie he had manufactured the most potent force in Scottish football. He was the obvious man, though his commitments to Aberdeen meant he would combine both jobs for the duration of Scotland's interest in the World Cup.

Having a part-time manager in this day and age did not go down well in some quarters. Nor in Aberdeen. Going for a third successive league title, the Dons slumped from first – when Ferguson took up Scotland's reins – to fourth.

Spain, meanwhile, had squeezed past Iceland to qualify. Scotland thereby faced one final hurdle, a two-edged play-off against the winners of the Oceania group. Whether that would be Israel, Australia, New Zealand or Taiwan was not settled until November. The pundits favoured Israel; the results, Australia.

Although they had graced the 1974 World Cup finals, Australia were hardly a front-line soccer power. Cricket, tennis, rugby and Australian Rules football still provided their staple sporting diet. For the past three years Australia's footballers had been managed by Yugoslav-born Frank Arok. Arok was caricatured as a 'mad dog'. His players bore the affectionate, if patronising, tag of 'socceroos'. They were a motley assortment of part-timers and foreign imports. Included in their line-up were three Scots – Ken Murphy, Joe Watson, and David Mitchell (who had played for Rangers). These were collectively dubbed the 'Jockeroos', players who had failed to make the grade in Scottish football and gone to find their ray of sunshine elsewhere. For good measure Australia's assistant manager was also a Scot, Eddie Thomson, once of Hearts.

Arok had fostered his players' strengths – brawn, brawn and more brawn – to assemble an outfit strong on defensive resilience if short on attacking flair. He had yet to see his team dance in defeat to the tune of more than two goals. The only pointer to the Hampden result was a visit by Australia to Rangers a year earlier, when – according to Arok – he had anticipated the World Cup encounter to come. Rangers had won 2-1. Now that the gloves were off, Arok put his hopes on a draw, preferably, in the light of the away goals rule, a scoring draw. Depending on the degree of inebriation, Scottish supporters set their sights anywhere between a two-goal victory and infinity.

Ferguson had a new name on his teamsheet. During his years with St Mirren, Frank McAvennie had been a promising striker in a modest team. Since transferring to West Ham he had successfully auditioned as the reincarnation of Denis Law, scoring frequently and with style. Scotland's chief failing had been their miserable scoring rate. Ferguson looked to McAvennie and the recalled Dalglish (now manager of Liverpool, winning his ninety-ninth cap) to do the business. With both Cooper and Strachan included, Ferguson instructed his players to stretch their opponents wide.

Any sober thoughts of a double-digit victory disappeared once Australia erected their yellow-shirted blockades. The outcome might have been different had not Miller, free to advance at will, shot wide as the ball broke to him. It was, as they say, a defender's shot. Scotland wove pretty patterns, but seldom created any chances. The battle was waged in the Aussies' half, but suddenly Mitchell was through, bearing down on Leighton. The keeper raced to clear.

The visitors conceded corners, free kicks and bookings in abundance. When school-teacher Terry Greedy clutched Souness's pile-driver, it was his first and only save of an anti-climactic first half. As the interval approached, shots were bouncing off the socceroos as if on a frantic game of pinball.

From the restart Aitken miskicked, and Strachan's shot wouldn't have troubled his grandma. There grew nagging doubts – Mexico seemed more distant than Mars. But after almost an hour of profitless endeavour, McAvennie appeared to be clipped as he chased a through ball. The free kick was central, twenty yards out. Greedy positioned his wall to guard one half of the goal, yet left the other exposed as Cooper powered the ball inside the vacant post.

Two minutes later Mexico looked nearer than Manchester. McLeish returned Greedy's clearance, Dalglish nodded sideways, and the quicksilver McAvennie sprang the offside trap, flicking the ball over the advancing keeper's head. The ecstatic scorer punched the air in the manner of a certain Denis Law.

Scotland ought to have landed the k.o. Greedy smothered Dalglish's close-range effort before the exhausted striker was subbed by Graeme Sharp. Obliged to attack, Australia forced two unproductive corners, but were left sighing with relief as McAvennie misread the ball in front of an unprotected net. At half-time, 2-0 would have seemed a priceless result, but McAvennie's anguished expression told of his inner torment. He could have sealed Scotland's place in Mexico. Now they would have to live through the fires of Melbourne.

SCOTLAND (0) 2   AUSTRALIA (0) 0
    Cooper 58, McAvennie 60

SCOTLAND: Leighton, Nicol, Malpas, Souness, McLeish, Miller, Dalglish (Sharp), Strachan (Bett), McAvennie, Aitken, Cooper.
AUSTRALIA: Greedy, Davidson, Jennings, Yankos, Ratcliffe, O'Connor (Dunn), Watson (Patikas), Mitchell, Kosmina, Murphy, Crino.

AUSTRALIA v SCOTLAND
Wednesday, 4 December 1985   *Melbourne – 32,000*

By early December Scotland and Australia were vying for the twenty-fourth and final vacancy in Mexico. The football world – outside Britain – was rooting for Australia. Sympathy with the underdog had less to do with this than the fact that Australia should prove less troublesome to the other competing nations, one of whom would drop down the seedings to join the 'minnows', should Scotland deprive Australia of that privilege.

The Scotland squad embarked on the furthest journey of any European team in the cause of World Cup qualification. The bill, around £100,000, would be peanuts if Scotland survived. The real worry was not the money but the attitude of certain English clubs who, as ever, reasoned that league points were more important than the World Cup dreams of a sister nation. Jet-lag might rule out players for two Saturdays. There was talk of five-figure sums being demanded to compensate English clubs for borrowed players. Had Scotland tucked a four-goal lead under their belts at Hampden, the loss of key Anglos might have been shrugged off. As it was, only Dalglish and Strachan stayed behind, with Souness flying out from Sampdoria with a day to spare.

For two weeks the Scottish press milked Frank Arok's use of the 'verbals'. He wouldn't be accommodating, scheming to play the match on a rubbish-tip at noon, when the heat would reduce Scotland to jelly. Poor Arok was overruled.

The match went ahead at 8 pm in Melbourne's Olympic Stadium. The pitch was perfect, the weather sublime, and Scotland enjoyed the noisy backing of thousands of Scottish emigrants. It was, said Ferguson, just like Wembley.

His three changes were enforced. Gough's extra height ensured his inclusion in place of Nicol; Paul McStay took over from Strachan; and David Speedie's natural aggression was asked to compensate for Dalglish's natural skill.

Erudite man that he is, Ferguson probably turned to Shakespeare in his pre-match ruminations: whether 'twas nobler in the mind to chase an away goal and qualify with style, or hang on and hope for some outrageous fortune. The Aussies had no recourse to slings and arrows, but they had guts, and Scotland found themselves experiencing early blows to their self-esteem. Patikas, an anonymous substitute at Hampden, quickly established himself as the niftiest player on view. His pace, allied to Murphy's calm authority, gave Australia an ascendancy in midfield they maintained throughout.

Forty-yard back-passes to Leighton did not endear the visitors to the ex-colony. Crowd disturbances and a flare tossed onto the pitch sadly confirmed that loutishness ranked high among Britain's invisible exports.

In retrospect, the game was memorable for a mere handful of incidents. Midway through the first half Leighton twice took his life in his hands, plunging into a melee of flying bodies like a bouncer breaking up a pub brawl. The trainer who arrived to minister to his wounds doubtless poured warm words into his ear. Scotland were living dangerously, and never more so than when Mitchell dummied McLeish and streaked away from his marker for the one and only time. The cross fell to John Kosmina, six yards out, all alone. He should have scored, but his header flew straight at Leighton, whose alert reflexes enabled him to palm it out. It was a costly miss.

A goal at that stage would have put Scotland on the tightrope. McStay restored their dignity with a surging run and swirling shot that was touched over by Terry Greedy. Souness, looking bleary-eyed and performing as if on an early breakfast, mistook Oscar Crino for a fried egg and was booked.

Leighton opened the second half by parrying Patikas's angled volley. When Cooper was knocked sideways without gaining a penalty, an outraged Scottish bench rose to its feet in disbelief. That same bench then held its breath when Patikas's grass-trimming centre eluded everyone.

McLeish headed across the box where either McAvennie or Speedie might have scored but for the hindrance of the other. The ball bobbled along the bar.

Scotland were not yet safe, and substitute Odzakov fired narrowly over. Encouraged, Odzakov brushed aside two gossamer Scottish tackles to put himself clear. Leighton duly spread himself and the shot rolled wide. Australia knew they were destined to fail and the game slumbered to a close. Scotland had competed from the Arctic Circle to the Antipodes. Next stop, Mexico. One hopes Jock was watching.

AUSTRALIA (0) 0   SCOTLAND (0) 0

AUSTRALIA: Greedy, Davidson, Jennings, Yankos, Ratcliffe, Crino (Odzakov), Dunn (Farina), Murphy, Patikas, Kosmina, Mitchell.
SCOTLAND: Leighton, Gough, Malpas, Souness, McLeish, Miller, Speedie (Sharp), McStay, McAvennie, Aitken, Cooper.

Qualifying Group 7

		Home				Away				
	P	W	D	L	F	A	W	D	L	F	A	Pts
SPAIN	6	3	0	0	6	1	1	0	2	3	7	8
SCOTLAND *	6	2	0	1	6	2	1	1	1	2	2	7
Wales	6	2	1	0	6	2	1	0	2	1	4	7
Iceland	6	1	0	2	2	3	0	0	3	2	7	2

* Scotland qualified after play-off with Australia.

Other group results

Iceland v Wales	1-0		Wales v Spain	3-0
Spain v Wales	3-0		Iceland v Spain	1-2
Wales v Iceland	2-1		Spain v Iceland	2-1

The World Cup finals – MEXICO   **May-June 1986**

Scotland were set for their fourth successive World Cup finals, each under different management. Willie Ormond's team returned in frustration in 1974, Ally MacLeod's in disgrace in 1978, Jock Stein's battered by Brazil in 1982. But for his untimely heart attack, Stein would now be leading from the front, the first Scottish manager to marshal his troops in two World Cup finals. Alex Ferguson had taken the helm, and few doubted that the Scottish effort would lack direction. Not for Alex Ferguson the hollow euphoria of Ally MacLeod.

The indelible hand of Jock Stein was imprinted on the qualifying campaigns of both the 1982 and 1986 World Cups. The records are almost identical, few goals scored, fewer conceded. Scotland's chronic scoring headache, in other words, was balanced by a defence as mean as anything in Scottish history.

The performances in Spain, however, had led to much head-scratching. The team that qualified with a miserly goal-record threw open the vaults. Especially worrying was Scotland's failure to prosper despite leading in each match.

Scotland, it must be said, had also acquired the invaluable knack of winning without playing well. They might easily have lost in Reykjavik, in Cardiff, in Melbourne. It was a refreshing change to observe a 'lucky' Scottish team, not prone to shooting itself in the foot.

Ferguson's deeper problem was to inject weight into an attack that had spluttered ineffectually since the vivid victory over Spain in November 1984. He also had to confront the psychological hurdle faced by all Scotland managers: when had Scotland ever done themselves justice away from their beloved Hampden?

For a mid-ranking nation like Scotland, the draw for the finals of a World Cup can be crucial. Fate had not smiled in 1982, and this time she was positively hostile. Out of the hat came West Germany and Uruguay, between them winners of the World Cup four times, and both among the front runners this time. Balance might have been redressed had the allocated minnow been Iraq or Canada. But Scotland's eleventh hour elimination of Australia meant that a sixth tiddler had to be found to make up the quota. To their chagrin, Denmark were downgraded, on the grounds that this was their first World Cup, despite the opinion of good judges – Alex Ferguson among them – that the Danes were the best team in Europe. It was Denmark who landed in Scotland's group, dubbed by locals the 'Group of Death'. The opposition was so strong, suggested Tommy Docherty, that Scotland would do well to finish fourth.

On reflection, Scotland's draw might have been turned to advantage. Only Uruguay would be unflustered by the heat, and the high altitude of Scotland's venues, Querétaro and Nezahualcoyotl (a suburb of Mexico City), would distribute its hazards without favour. Scotland should have been grateful that there were no Zaïres or Irans to foul up against.

The 1986 World Cup followed its predecessor in inviting twenty-four finalists, but departed from it in other respects. In 1982, the traditional four-team groups with two to qualify still operated, but that left the conundrum of twelve teams having to be whittled down to two finalists. In 1986, it was decided that sixteen teams would progress from the first round, simplifying the latter stages while confusing the earlier ones. Those four extra, lucky teams would come from those who finished third in their groups.

On the face of it, these extra places were good news for Scotland and everyone else. But with no appetising minnow of their own, the teams in Group E would be denied the chance of easy pickings, theoretically putting its third-placed team at a disadvantage. One small mercy was that Group E would be the last to run its course, when the waterline would be known to all.

Alex Ferguson used the first half of 1986 to fine-tune his side with the help of four fixtures. Wins over Israel in Tel Aviv and Romania at Hampden were followed in April by a Wembley defeat by England. Final practice came in Eindhoven, where Scotland forced a pleasing goalless draw with the Dutch, who hadn't qualified, before flying to Santa Fe for final preparations. Scotland, the last team to qualify, were the first to arrive in Mexico, on 1 June. The squad based themselves an hour's drive from Mexico City in a hotel among the Aztec pyramids. The hotel grounds were patrolled by a hundred armed police.

No	Name	Position	Club	Age	Caps	Goals
1	Jim Leighton	Goalkeeper	Aberdeen	27	26	–
2	Richard Gough	Defence/Midfield	Dundee United	24	23	3
3	Maurice Malpas	Full-back	Dundee United	23	10	–
4	Graeme Souness (c)	Midfield	Rangers	33	53	4
5	Alex McLeish	Central defence	Aberdeen	27	43	–
6	Willie Miller	Central defence	Aberdeen	31	48	1
7	Gordon Strachan	Midfield	Manchester U	29	34	3
8	Roy Aitken	Defence/Midfield	Celtic	27	20	1
9	Eamonn Bannon	Midfield	Dundee United	28	9	1
10	Jim Bett	Midfield	Aberdeen	26	17	1
11	Paul McStay	Midfield	Celtic	21	15	3
12	Andy Goram	Goalkeeper	Oldham	22	3	–
13	Steve Nicol	Full-back/Midfield	Liverpool	24	8	–
14	David Narey	Central defence	Dundee United	29	28	1
15	Arthur Albiston	Full-back	Manchester U	28	13	–
16	Frank McAvennie	Forward	West Ham	26	2	1
17	Steve Archibald	Forward	Barcelona	29	26	4
18	Graeme Sharp	Forward	Everton	25	6	–
19	Charlie Nicholas	Forward	Arsenal	24	15	5
20	Paul Sturrock	Forward	Dundee United	29	16	3
21	Davie Cooper	Winger	Rangers	30	14	4
22	Alan Rough *	Goalkeeper	Hibernian	34	53	–

* Would not play in the finals or in future.	*Averages*		27.1	21.9	

When Ferguson announced his chosen twenty-two, he included nine players from the squad in 1982 – Leighton, McLeish, Miller; Rough, Narey, Strachan; Souness, Sturrock, Archibald. It might have been ten but for an eleventh-hour omission that provoked howls of rage. The World Cup was tailor-made for Liverpool's elegant, serene captain, Alan Hansen. But Ferguson left him out, not just out of the team, but out of the squad, arguing that Hansen was a one-position player who could not fill in elsewhere. David Narey, on the other hand, could double at full-back or in midfield if necessary. The furore was surprising to the extent that Hansen had hardly featured in the qualifiers, taking the field just once, as a substitute in the home defeat by Wales. Alex McLeish had been ever-present at centre-half and, surely, if either Stein or Ferguson had taken a shine to Hansen they would have played him. Both managers favoured the Pittodrie Triangle of Leighton, Miller and McLeish. The trio had played together for Scotland eleven times, losing just five goals. Now, the only worry was that Leighton's dislocated finger – which had caused him to miss three internationals – would mend in time.

The squad was captained by Graeme Souness, a fine passer and ferocious competitor; 'hard' to his admirers, 'dirty' to his critics. Now player-manager at Ibrox, he was embarking on his third World Cup, though his age was against him. At thirty-three he was uncertain to stand the heat of Mexico. Willie Miller and Kenny Dalglish were the usual standby captains. Miller had been described by Ferguson as the best penalty-box defender he had ever seen, but Dalglish (now player-manager at Anfield), having led Liverpool to the English league and cup double, had succumbed to knee trouble and was ruled out of his fourth World Cup. At thirty-five, one wonders what that once-great player had to offer a tournament that would sap younger men. Dalglish had failed before to impose himself in World Cups, even when in his prime. Maurice Johnston was another contributor to the qualifiers who didn't make it. Also left out was David Speedie, whose quick-fire temper probably could not be risked. In the light of the Anglo-centric squads of Ally MacLeod and Jock Stein, it is curious that Ferguson now went the other way. The absence of Hansen and Speedie gave weight to the view that he was plumping for a Scottish based squad, preferring players he knew to reputations he did not. One wonders, hypothetically, after his years at Old Trafford, whether Ferguson would again favour Scots based players to Anglos. One Anglo survivor was Arsenal's Charlie Nicholas, though even he was in doubt after a tired showing against England at Wembley.

Scotland's final run-out was in Los Angeles, against a local side called LA Heat, where Ferguson adopted a 3-5-2 formation, without wingers and with both full-backs pushing up. Denmark duly took notice.

DENMARK v SCOTLAND
Wednesday, 4 June 1986   *Nezahualcoyotl – 18,000*

It was England's fault that the Danes wore the badge of 'minnows'. Had Bobby Robson's team averted a last-gasp equaliser in Copenhagen in the European Championship qualifiers, or Phil Neal not conceded a penalty at Wembley in the return, Denmark would not have qualified or proceeded to make hay. They were penalty kicks away from the European Final itself. With their all-action, attacking style, Denmark were poised to emulate the Dutch, who rose from nowhere to storm the World Cups of the 1970s.

Sören Lerby (Bayern München), Jan Mölby (Liverpool) and Frank Arnesen (PSV Eindhoven) in midfield; Jesper Olsen (Manchester United), Michael Laudrup (Juventus) and Preben Elkjaer (Verona) in attack, were the mainstays of a side overflowing with mercenary talent. Most of the squad attended the best finishing schools in Italy, Germany, Holland, England. Laudrup showed

All-action Preben Elkjaer scores the only goal. (v Denmark)

astonishing maturity for someone of just twenty-one. He had blossomed early, whereas his striking partner, Elkjaer, blossomed late, overcoming a head-down, awkward gait to become a master dribbler with searing pace.

Elkjaer, scorer of thirty-seven goals in fifty-eight internationals and dubbed 'Golkjaer' by supporters of Verona, described the Danish style as 'playing by memory, football mixed like a cocktail, counter-attacking at full speed.'

Denmark had qualified impressively, topping a group that included the Soviet Union, Switzerland, the Republic of Ireland, and Norway. Their final qualifier, in Dublin, saw them crush a pre-Jack Charlton Irish Republic 4-1.

Sponsored by the brewery, Carlsberg, and coached since 1979 by the former West German international, Sepp Piontek, the side had metamorphosed, aided by funds to entice Denmark's legionnaires home for internationals, coupled with a philosophy of all-out attack. Several Danes were past their sell-by date and one sensed that they would need to strike while the iron was hot. They would fail to qualify both for Italia '90 and the 1992 European Championship. Profiting from a wild card entry, following the withdrawal of disintegrating Yugoslavia, Denmark shocked the footballing world by lifting the European title. But who is to say that another gate-crasher might not have done likewise?

Scotland would face Denmark in a new stadium, built incongruously amid the slums and wastelands of Nezahualcoyotl, abbreviated to Neza. It was less a town than a sprawling suburb of the most populated city on earth, many of whose three million inhabitants struggled into the city each day searching for work. Not a place for foreigners to venture at night. A neat stadium wrapped by poverty, like a diamond on a wart. No less eye-catching were Denmark's fans, who were determined to enjoy themselves. It was they who began the fashion of painting their faces in their team's colours.

Ferguson thought his line-up was under wraps, only to be told by Sepp Piontek after the match that someone had rung and told him. Evidently, Mexican walls had ears. Not that it was much of a surprise, for Ferguson asked Miller to sweep behind McLeish and Aitken, who would mark Laudrup and Elkjaer. The tactic so nearly worked. Scotland played their part in an absorbing match. For half an hour Denmark struggled to find their feet in their elevated surroundings. Contrary to predictions, they played walking football. Nicholas was a fraction late with one golden chance; Gough too hasty with another.

Having lulled the Scots into a false sense of security, Denmark turned up the heat in the second-half. Laudrup and Elkjaer began to slice open the Scottish defence. Miller's timely intervention impeded one rapier attack, but just before the hour Miller contributed to a Danish goal. The splendid Arnesen freed Elkjaer on the left. Elkjaer dragged the ball past Miller via a handsome ricochet off the defender's legs and scored off a post.

On what had passed before, the goal was harsh on Scotland, though it had hardly come out of the blue. Nor need it have cost them the match. An Aitken 'equaliser' was ruled out for offside. Though Strachan was hardly seen, and was substituted by Eamonn Bannon, Nicholas looked sprightly and inventive, now beating three Danes before setting up Souness who shot wide.

Scotland had seven minutes to claw their way back when they were thwarted by a gross foul that scarred the nice-guy image of Danish football. Nicholas sped past Pisa's Klaus Berggren, who lunged disgracefully, tearing Nicholas's ankle ligaments and threatening to put him in a wheelchair. Berggren had been booked just twice in four years in Italian football. He should have been shown a red card by Hungarian referee Lajos Nemeth; he was not even shown a yellow. Nicholas later described it as the worst tackle he had ever known. Berggren defended himself, saying: 'I did what I had to do.' It was that sort of World Cup, and Scotland hadn't seen anything yet.

DENMARK (0) 1   SCOTLAND (0) 0
  Elkjaer 58

DENMARK: Rasmussen, Busk, M Olsen, Nielsen, Lerby, J Olsen (Mölby), Berggren, Bertelsen, Arnesen (Sivebaek), Laudrup, Elkjaer.
SCOTLAND: Leighton, Gough, Malpas, McLeish, Miller, Souness, Aitken, Nicol, Nicholas, Strachan (Bannon), Sturrock (McAvennie).

WEST GERMANY v SCOTLAND
Sunday, 8 June 1986   *Querétaro – 30,000*

Believe it or not, West Germany were third favourites; not to win the World Cup, but just to win Group E! Such was the mountain of expectation heaped upon Denmark and Uruguay. Not that the Germans had anything to prove, having won the World Cup in 1954 and 1974 and been runners-up in 1966 and 1982. They had qualified ahead of Portugal, Sweden, Czechoslovakia and Malta, and were bidding for that rarest of feats. They had won the World Cup with Franz Beckenbauer as player, now they were aiming to do so with Beckenbauer as manager. This 'double' had been achieved only once, by Mario Zagalo of Brazil. The reason the bookies didn't fancy them was that the Germans had ended 1985 with six games without a win, a sequence of epic proportions for such a footballing power. They had even lost their undefeated-at-home World Cup record, to Portugal, and as the scent of victory grew fainter so the angst mounted. Classy Bernd Schuster had refused Beckenbauer's entreaties to assist the national cause, preferring to sulk in Barcelona.

Harald Schumacher might be an exceptional goalkeeper, but he would always be remembered for his assault on France's Patrick Battiston in 1982. Lothar Matthäus was reckoned one of the world's great midfield players. He would be even greater in 1990 as Germany's captain, and was a player to put even the redoubtable Souness in the shadow. Skipper Karl-Heinz Rummenigge looked more like a concert pianist than a footballer. Now thirty-one, he had been handicapped by a thigh-strain in Spain '82 and was cursing his luck in being semi-fit again. He had scored three goals in Argentina '78, five in Spain '82. Voted European 'Footballer of the Year' in 1980 and 1981, he had joined Internazionale in 1984 for £2.5 million, making him Germany's most pricey footballer. He would eventually retire with ninety-five caps – nineteen in World Cup finals – and forty-five goals. He already possessed a European Cup medal (with Bayern München) and a European Championship medal with West Germany (in 1980). If Rummenigge couldn't find the net in Mexico, then much rested with Rudi Völler, the latest in Germany's goal-grabbing production line that had unearthed Uwe Seeler, Müller, and Rummenigge himself.

Ferguson put his thinking cap on. Nicholas was obviously out, probably for the duration, but his striking partner against Denmark, Paul Sturrock, also failed to recover. In came Steve Archibald to perform his lonely vigil. Ferguson preferred to rely on the Scottish midfield to create openings and to cut out balls to Völler and Allofs. The manager also withstood a press campaign for the inclusion of Davie Cooper. This meant a formation approximating to 1-3-5-1. When Alex McLeish succumbed to the dreaded Montezuma's Revenge, David Narey was drafted in. Ferguson insisted he was happier playing the Germans, whose tactics, unlike the Danes', he knew.

Strachan lets fly to give Scotland the lead. (v W Germany)

Querétaro's La Corregidora Stadium was another of Mexico's specially built venues, 140 miles west of Mexico City. Querétaro means 'a place for ball games' and is a spruce, colonial city of some charm. It had already staged West Germany's match with Uruguay, who had scored early. Germany had not equalised until after Rummenigge's arrival, when Klaus Allofs netted.

In blazing midday heat, which must have turned Scotland's navy shirts into cloaks of fire, Germany found themselves yet again trailing to an early goal. Strachan would be as prominent against the Germans as he had been invisible against the Danes. Aitken rolled Nicol's cross sweetly into his path, near the corner of the six-yard box. Schumacher was well-positioned for the shot, but not for the deflection, that carried the ball inside his near post and left him hopping on the wrong foot. Though the build-up was well-conceived, deflected goals were surely the sign of a Scotland team that should ride its luck.

We might have known. Scotland had demonstrated in 1982 that they were soft touches at holding on to leads. Scotland's advantage lasted five minutes. Pierre Littbarski sent Allofs away, past Gough, down the left. Allofs chipped the ball over the covering Leighton leaving Völler – who had already struck a post – to stab the ball over the line with no Scottish defender within five yards.

One sensed Scotland's spirit draining away, for after that there was only going to be one winner. Five minutes into the second half Miller missed a

Willie Miller's legs are not long enough and Klaus Allofs scores. (v W Germany)

tackle on Völler who, repaying favours, set up Allofs to score from close in. Ferguson sent on Davie Cooper and Frank McAvennie. Half-chances fell to McAvennie, who was smothered on the six-yard line, and Richard Gough, who might have done better than head Cooper's cross over the top.

So Scotland had lost two out of two. Even though their football had been enterprising, their goal-shyness had, as feared, cost them dear.

WEST GERMANY (1) 2   SCOTLAND (1) 1
  Völler 22, Allofs 50   Strachan 17

W GERMANY: Schumacher, Berthold, Förster, Augenthaler, Briegel (Jakobs), Matthäus, Magath, Eder, Littbarski (Rummenigge), Völler, Allofs.
SCOTLAND: Leighton, Gough, Narey, Miller, Malpas, Nicol (McAvennie), Bannon (Cooper), Souness, Strachan, Aitken, Archibald.

URUGUAY v SCOTLAND
Friday, 13 June 1986   *Nezahualcoyotl – 20,000*

It was tough on Scotland, having to face three of the favourites to lift the World Cup. Uruguay were the shortest-priced of the three. They were, in fact, third favourites for the title, behind neighbours Brazil and Argentina. That ranking was not harmed by Uruguay's draw with West Germany, but was savaged by a 1-6 mauling by Denmark. That result – Uruguay's worst in half a century of World Cup football – proved the Danes to be genuine contenders, underlined the courage of Scotland's performance, and raised unexpected questions about the Uruguayans. True, they were reduced to ten men for most of the match – Bossio being ordered off at 0-1 for a grotesque foul after he had been booked for another – but that was the price of Uruguay's routine skulduggery.

What made Uruguay's dirty tricks all the more noisome was that the players had the talent to win on skill. Enzo Francescoli, midfield creator of sublime touch, was as good as any player in the world, Maradona, perhaps, excepted, and Jorge da Silva's close control had helped him head Atletico Madrid's goal-charts. Francescoli played for River Plate in Argentina, da Silva in Spain. Like Denmark's, most Uruguayan players were foreign exiles, a circumstance that hindered the fortunes of neither country. Indeed, their accomplishments briefly silenced Scotland's unceasing claim to have achieved much for a small nation. Denmark and Uruguay had populations even smaller than Scotland's.

Uruguay's last appearance in the finals was in 1974. This deprived them of the honour of being among the top-seeds in Mexico, and they only qualified this time by beating Chile 2-1 at home in their final match. Nevertheless, Uruguay's pedigree was astonishing. Winners in 1930 and 1950, they had not tasted defeat in the World Cup finals until Hungary undid them 4-2 in 1954. Earlier in that tournament, of course, they had humiliated Scotland 7-0 and gone on to beat England 4-2 in the quarter-finals.

Coached now by Omar Borras, Uruguay were defending South American champions, and their patient possession game, interspersed with bursts of lightning speed, was ideally suited to Mexican conditions. But here they were, reeling from a Danish drubbing, and with Omar Borras' family receiving death threats from irate Uruguayan fans back home. In previous World Cup set-ups, Uruguay and Scotland would now be contesting a dead match, for the positions of both teams were irretrievable. What breathed life into the fixture was FIFA's novelty in allowing four third-placed teams to progress. All other groups had been completed. Hungary and Northern Ireland were the two third-placed sides headed for home. Either Uruguay or Scotland would go through, Uruguay with a draw, Scotland with a win. Hooray for FIFA. It was now business as usual for the Scots in the World Cup, needing to win against the odds to survive.

So much for the reprieve. In reality, a match Uruguay needed only to draw played into their hands. Scotland did not, on the face of it, appear to have the firepower necessary to beat these of all opponents. Revenge for 1954 looked a long shot, notwithstanding the Danish demolition. Ferguson was quick to instruct his players to put that result out of their heads: if anything, it meant the Uruguayans would be even tougher now, when they would be at their most

Steve Nicol contests a ball with Acevedo. (v Uruguay)

defensively cynical. It had been, after all, Uruguay's first defeat in fourteen games. Either way, Ferguson needed to shake up his formation. He had studied Uruguay's goalless draw against Wales in Wrexham during the warm-ups for the finals and knew their strengths.

For the third World Cup in a row, Scotland's skippers paid the price for collective failure. In 1978, Rioch and Masson, captain and vice-captain, had been hauled off and substituted against Peru. In 1982, Jock Stein dropped Danny McGrain from the team to play Brazil. Now, Alex Ferguson dispensed with the listless Souness, who admitted that the searing heat of Querétaro had drained him more than any other match in his life. In came Celtic's Paul McStay. Ferguson's club captain, Willie Miller, wore the black armband.

Ferguson was thankful that Charlie Nicholas and his other injured players had made a speedy recovery, for he could select from a full squad. At left-back he replaced Maurice Malpas with Arthur Albiston. Ferguson left out Eamonn Bannon and lone striker Archibald, and pencilled in Graeme Sharp and Paul Sturrock. Nicholas would, for the time being, keep the bench warm.

The match had clocked up forty-five seconds when José Batista launched himself at Strachan. It was the game's first tackle, but was so reckless that French referee Joel Quiniou instantly flourished a red card. Playing in white instead of their traditional pale blue, Uruguay's talented thugs looked anything but angelic as they swarmed angrily around the official. Considering Uruguay's appalling disciplinary record, Quiniou was surely acting under FIFA instruction to clamp down. The Uruguayans seethed for the rest of the match, haranguing the referee at half- and full-time.

Initial Scottish delight at their opponents' depletion soon gave way to regret. As Ferguson was later to point out, playing with ten men was so natural for Uruguay they were used to it. Scotland were unused to playing ten men. Anyway, it was Friday the 13th!

Indeed, the longer the match wore on the more it became apparent that the Uruguayans might have had a couple more players dismissed and still outplayed Scotland. Though defending for most of the time, and wasting time by means obvious and not so obvious, they protected their goal so effortlessly and attacked so imaginatively that they might have won. Francescoli – allegedly headed for Racing Club de Paris for a prodigious fee – was permitted endless scope to run at, and through, the Scottish rearguard. At times, seven Scottish defenders were pinned down by three Uruguayan forwards.

The one moment of Scottish dismay came midway through the opening half, when Aitken's low cross found Steve Nicol unmarked at the far post. All it needed was a firm strike of the ball, but Nicol's was flaccid and Alvez had time to save. The wail of anguish that bellowed from Scottish bars and armchairs could be heard on the moon. But Nicol was wearing No. 13.

Scotland carved out little else. In the second half Leighton parried Cabrera's close-range header. Narey and Nicol were booked and Acevedo might have been sent off. Narey blazed a thirty-yarder over the top and the game ended with Scotland whistled from the pitch. That was less than fair, though there is no doubt that the team and manager had frittered away much of their hard-earned reservoir of sympathy. Ferguson was taken to task for leaving out wily Archibald in favour of workhorse Graeme Sharp, who had looked out of his depth. And this, surely, had been a match suited to Alan Hansen. Paul McStay had been unable to rise to the occasion, and the sauntering pace at which Uruguay played might even have suited Souness.

Funny game, football. Two defeats bring cheers, a draw brings jeers. The squad flew home to be greeted by silence. Uruguay would not be welcome visitors for many a year.

URUGUAY   (0) 0   SCOTLAND   (0) 0

URUGUAY: Alvez, Batista, Gutiérrez, Diogo, Acevedo, Pereya, Barrios, Santin, Francescoli (Alzamendi), Ramos (Saralegui), Cabrera.
SCOTLAND: Leighton, Gough, Miller, Narey, Albiston, Strachan, Aitken, McStay, Nicol (Cooper), Sharp, Sturrock (Nicholas).

The combined group matches of Scotland, England and Northern Ireland had produced one win, three draws, and five defeats. British football appeared once again to inhabit an isolated pocket of wretchedness. At least that solitary British victory, by England, kept them afloat, and another awaited, against Paraguay in the second round, before Maradona's Hand of God intervened. Argentina eventually went all the way, squeezing past Uruguay in the second round (when Spain dumped the cocky Danes 5-1) and West Germany in the Final.

Final positions – Group E

	P	W	D	L	F	A	Pts
DENMARK	3	3	0	0	9	1	6
WEST GERMANY	3	1	1	1	3	4	3
URUGUAY	3	0	2	1	2	7	2
Scotland	3	0	1	2	1	3	1

Scotland appearances and goalscorers (substitute appearances in brackets)
World Cup qualifying rounds and final competition 1986

	Apps	Goals		Apps	Goals
Leighton J	11	–	Dalglish K *†‡	4	1
Miller W *	11	–	Johnston M	4	2
McLeish A *	9	–	Sharp G	3 (2)	–
Souness G *†	9	–	McAvennie F	2 (2)	1
Nicol S	8	–	Archibald S *	2 (1)	–
Aitken R	7	–	Narey D *	2	–
Gough R	7	–	Speedie D	2	–
Cooper D	6 (3)	2	Sturrock P *	2	–
McStay P	6	2	Nicholas C	1 (4)	1
Bett J	6 (1)	1	Bannon E	1 (1)	–
Strachan G *	6 (1)	1	Gray A *†	1	–
Malpas M	6	–	Hansen A *	– (1)	–
Albiston A	5	–	Rough A *†	– (1)	–

* Appeared in 1982 World Cup.
† Appeared in 1978 World Cup.
‡ Appeared in 1974 World Cup.

138 apps   11 goals
79 Scottish League
42 English League
9 Italian League
5 Belgian League
3 Spanish League
26 players used

11

THE 1990 WORLD CUP

The sad performance against Uruguay was Scotland's one blip in Mexico. Alex Ferguson was in big demand even before inheriting control of the national side. Relinquishing the reins upon his return to Pittodrie, it wasn't long before a managerial offer arrived to which he could not say no. A year or two earlier he had been able to refuse Ibrox; he could not now refuse Old Trafford. By the end of the year, Scotland and Aberdeen had bid him farewell.

The pundits' short-list for the new Scotland manager threw up the predictable crop of club managers north and south of the border. Billy McNeill, at Manchester City, was red-hot favourite. Jim McLean of Dundee United was also in the frame. The list did not include Andrew Roxburgh, for ten years full-time director of coaching with the Scottish Football Association and one-time team-mate of Alex Ferguson at Falkirk. Ernie Walker, secretary of the SFA, spoke of Roxburgh as 'the best coach in the world'. Roxburgh's reputation, such as it was, was forged on the continent, where he was regarded as an enlightened innovator. Continental experts applauded his appointment, if the mainstream of Scots did not, for few had even heard of him. He was Scotland's fourth manager in a decade never to have played at full international level. Nor had he ever managed at club level. This was thought to be resented by certain high profile professionals. A dapper, engaging man, Roxburgh could assure his players proper schooling. To assist him, Craig Brown was appointed from Clyde, mainly to cater for Scotland's Under-21s.

Roxburgh's first task was to scale the qualifiers of the European Championship, something beyond all his predecessors. Scotland's prospects were doomed by defeat at home by a Republic of Ireland side fashioned by Jack Charlton. It was Scotland who then threw the door open to Irish qualification by beating Bulgaria in Sofia. As Charlton remarked afterwards: 'You can never trust the Scots – and I mean that in the nicest possible way.'

Encouraged by a goalless draw with Spain in Madrid in April 1988, Roxburgh embarked on moulding a side capable of reaching the World Cup finals for a fifth successive time. As in 1982, Scotland were drawn in a five-team section with two to go through. The opposition was stiff. Scotland should be able to beat Cyprus, they might beat Norway, but could they overcome Yugoslavia and France, the two favourites?

Qualifying Group 5

NORWAY v SCOTLAND
Wednesday, 14 September 1988   *Oslo – 22,769*

Playing Norway in Oslo was hardly a gentle reintroduction to the stresses and strains of a World Cup. If Norway were unlikely to be kings themselves, they had every capacity to be king-makers. In 1981 they had astonishingly beaten England in Oslo, though this had been a flash in the pan – Norway finished bottom of their zone, and again four years later. Come 1994, they would have fashioned a useful side, capable of humiliating both England and Holland, but in 1988, under coach Ingmar Stadheim, there were few signs of this coming emergence. Norway had shed the days when all her players were home based amateurs. Defenders Johnsen, Bratseth and Giske were hardened pros exported to the West German Bundesliga. Goalkeeper Erik Thorstvedt would shortly transfer from Gothenburg to Tottenham and open up a Norwegian exodus to English football. Others treading the same path would include Henning Berg, to Blackburn, and Jan Fjortoft, to Swindon. Scotland's past record with Norway showed six wins, one draw and one defeat (3-4 in Bergen, 1963). Scotland had triumphed 4-0 on their previous visit to Oslo, in 1979.

Looking at the eleven Scottish names chosen to face Norway, one is struck by an Ibrox void, though Ally McCoist might have been picked if fit, and Iain Durrant was still recovering from an injury sustained against Katowice in the UEFA Cup. Under the enlightened if iron-fisted generalship of Graeme Souness, Rangers were fashioning a side that would soon eclipse all opposition in a manner reminiscent of Celtic's glory days in the 1960s and 'seventies. By opening the door to non-whites, English, and even Catholics, Souness swept away the parochialism that so incensed critics of the Ibrox regime. Champions in 1986-87, Rangers would reclaim the title in 1988-89 and hang on to it.

It may have included no Ranger, but Roxburgh's first World Cup team was in other respects backward looking. Eight of the starting line-up were veterans of Mexico, the exceptions being Gary Gillespie, a spindly central defender from Liverpool, Kevin Gallacher, a whippet from Tannadice, and Brian McClair, gone to Old Trafford from Parkhead. Others to have changed clubs in the interim were goalkeeper Jim Leighton, swapping the red of Aberdeen for that of Manchester United, and Maurice Johnston, improving his French with Nantes. Roxburgh plumped for Celtic's Roy Aitken as his World Cup captain.

In Oslo's Ullevål Stadium, Miller and McLeish took a tight grip on strikers Sorloth and Fjortoft. When Nicol 'collided' with Sundby, the Norwegian found himself unable to continue. Henning Berg came off the bench and before Norway could rejig Scotland scored. Johnston reached Miller's cross, the ball broke to McStay, and he swept it left-footed into goal.

Scotland hoped to carry their advantage to half-time, but then Nicol elbowed Henriksen off the ball. Osvold (ex-Nottingham Forest) took the free kick, which was headed down at the far post by Sorloth for Fjortoft to score.

Just after the hour Gillespie exhibited neat close-control on the edge of the box. McClair set up Gallacher but Johnston swooped to stab past Thorstvedt. Aitken had been booked for a first-half contretemps with Berg, and when he took issue with Osvold he might have found himself dismissed. Taking no chances, Roxburgh whipped off his captain and sent on Rangers' brightest starlet, Iain Durrant. Norway seldom threatened to come back a second time, their best chance falling to Jakobsen, who ballooned his shot.

Scotland had set the standard. Now Yugoslavia and France had to match it.

NORWAY (1) 1   SCOTLAND (1) 2
Fjortoft 44   McStay 14, Johnston 62

NORWAY: Thorstvedt, Henriksen, Johnsen, Bratseth, Giske, Osvold, Brandhaug, Loken, Sorloth, Sundby (Berg) (Jakobsen), Fjortoft.
SCOTLAND: Leighton (Man U), Nicol (Liverpool), Malpas (Dun U), Gillespie (Liverpool), McLeish (Aberdeen), Miller (Aberdeen), Aitken (Celtic) (*sub* Durrant, Rangers), McStay (Celtic), Johnston (Nantes), McClair (Man U), Gallacher (Dun U).

SCOTLAND v YUGOSLAVIA
Wednesday, 19 October 1988   *Hampden – 42,771*

The record books show Yugoslavia to have won nothing. Their best World Cup standing was fourth in 1962. Since then they had trailed hopelessly in the qualifiers for 1966, '70, '78, '86. In the last European Championship, England had trounced them, home (2-0) and away (4-1). Scotland had never lost in six meetings (winning the most recent, 6-1 in 1984). Yugoslavian muggins, one might think. But no. Ask any connoisseur, and he will insist that Yugoslavia's are among the most technically advanced players on the continent.

Yugoslavia's leading clubs had long shone in European club competition. Red Star Belgrade would be crowned European champions in 1991. The under-achievement of the national side could, perhaps, be attributed to some extent to the ethnic tensions that by the early 1990s would tear the country apart. Asking Serbs to play happily alongside Croats and Bosnians was asking too much.

Very soon, the cream of Yugoslavia's crop would reap the rewards of expatriate football. In 1988, only Katanec was earning a foreign dollar, for Stuttgart. When Scotland journeyed to Belgrade, a year hence, much of the team would have migrated. Ivica Osim, a former Yugoslav international and now team manager, had to get on with the job.

This match held special significance for Aberdeen stalwart Willie Miller, for it marked his sixty-second cap, one more than the previous record for a defender, held by Danny McGrain.

Jim Leighton would look back on the game less fondly. He was racked by a back spasm as he kicked a ball in training and had to stand down, permitting a rare cap to Hibernian's Andy Goram. Another absentee would not return so quickly. Iain Durrant had been subject to a vicious over-the-top tackle at Pittodrie that threatened to wheelchair him. It would keep him out of the international side for years. Gillespie was also out, replaced by Gough, who following a spell at Tottenham was back in Scotland with Rangers.

Yugoslavia's cynical brilliance made them almost South American in their footballing philosophy. Nicol's diagonal drive was parried, and at the other end Gough's lackadaisical header nearly set up Cvetkovic, before Scotland went ahead on the quarter-hour. It was an untidy goal, but merited on the pressure Scotland had exerted. Malpas sprinted down the left, exchanged passes with Jim Bett, and shot fiercely at Ivkovic. The ball flew back at Johnston, whose stab at goal was deflected over the line.

Yugoslavia's equaliser was no less convincing. Gough's header might have doubled Scotland's advantage when the same player felled Vujovic in full flight. Stojkovic's free kick thundered against a post and Goram conceded a corner. The ball wasn't cleared and Katanec looped it into the net. Highlights of the second half included two close-range Vujovic headers, and two deplorable fouls, by one Speedie (on Spasic), the other by Jozic (on McStay).

Roxburgh said to the post-match press conference: 'Most people would accept that both teams gained a point.' True, but Yugoslavia were the happier.

SCOTLAND (1) 1   YUGOSLAVIA (1) 1
Johnston 17   Katanec 36

SCOTLAND: Goram, Gough, Malpas, Nicol, McLeish, Miller, Aitken (Speedie), McStay, Johnson, McClair, Bett (McCoist).
YUGOSLAVIA: Ivkovic, Stanojkovic, Spasic (Sabanadzovic), Jozic, Hadzibejic, Radanovic, Stojkovic, Katanec, Cvetkovic (M Jankovic), Bazdarevic, Vujovic.

CYPRUS v SCOTLAND
Wednesday, 8 February 1989   *Limassol – 25,000*

Cyprus 0 Scotland 5. That was the score when Scotland last descended on the sun-drenched Mediterranean island in search of World Cup points. But that was twenty years back. Cypriot national teams were no longer so obliging. They no longer lost by that kind of margin, and from time to time pulled off mighty shocks. Their most recent upset had seen them draw 1-1 with France with the aid of a late penalty. When, a month later, France lost 2-3 in Belgrade after being 2-1 up, it was clear that France would have to pull their socks up.

It was a sign of how poorly the Cypriot threat was regarded when Saturday's Scottish Premier League programme went ahead as planned, rather than be postponed as for other qualifiers. In England, Jim Leighton played despite his back problems, but his international place was in doubt to the last. Roxburgh was hoping to blood Bryan Gunn sooner or later, though on this occasion the luckless Norwich keeper had had his gloves and boots stolen from his car. The injured Miller was replaced by Narey, and David Speedie, now with Coventry, returned to the front line. Aitken and Gough had recently completed domestic suspensions and were straining at the leash.

Cypriot manager Panicos Iacovou tried to play down the chances of David 'doing' Goliath. 'We are a poor country, a little country, and the World Cup is unfair to us,' he bleated. He was kidding nobody. His players were adept at wasting seconds here, minutes there. They liked to belt the ball into the moat surrounding the pitch, dispensing with the need for ball boys to fetch it. Players had to get it themselves, as if in a park game. The pitch in Limassol's Tsirion Stadium was reckoned even worse than that in Nicosia, where France had been held, and where Scotland had won in 1968.

Having taken his team to Italy for a friendly in Perugia, losing 0-2, Roxburgh knew his players needed to show patience in Limassol's Tsirion Stadium. In fact, patience wasn't needed. Scotland were in front after eight minutes. Savva, trying to clear, headed into the path of Johnston who, though hustled by Socratou, found the net. It was Mo Jo's third World Cup goal in three matches. It was also the third time Scotland had snatched an early lead, but now a tummy bug took Nicol from the field, Ian Ferguson deputising. Scotland had failed to protect early strikes against Norway and Yugoslavia, but Cyprus were another matter. It therefore came as a body blow when Koliandris cancelled out the lead, after an up-and-under had deceived Narey.

Worse was to follow. Barely had the teams kicked off for the second half when Koliandris took a free kick which Malpas knocked behind. The corner unleashed a frantic melee. Leighton failed to lay claim to the ball and Iannou smashed it in.

Defeat by Cyprus was unthinkable. It was sixteen years since Cyprus last won a World Cup eliminator, when they beat Northern Ireland 1-0. They had lost twenty-two on the trot since then, a run that ended only with the draw against France. Should Scotland now lose, it was hard to know which would be the more painful, the shame, or the shattering of World Cup dreams.

Fortunately, Scotland were soon back on terms. Speedie's chip set up Gough's deft leveller. But one point was hardly enough. That, however, seemed all Cyprus would begrudge Scotland. Aston Villa's high-scoring Alan McInally would have played from the start on any other pitch, but he liked to run with the ball, impossible on this patch. Now he pulled off his tracksuit.

East German referee Siegfried Kirschen was clearly irritated by Cypriot time-wasting, allowing the game to drag deeper and deeper into injury time. Ninety-six minutes had elapsed when Aitken's free kick from the left was headed joyously high into the net by Richard Gough. It was a super header that – after another whole minute's play – clinched a dubious victory and prompted riots in the stadium. Scotland's players were locked inside their dressing room for their own protection. The referee fared worse, being knocked to the ground by irate fans. The scheduled press conference was cancelled and as soon as the coast was clear the Scotland party was whisked away to the airport.

Next morning the Cypriot press castigated the 'disgraceful referee', citing 'Scottish intoxication with German whisky.' Complained manager Iacovou: 'We didn't lose one point. It was stolen from us.'

CYPRUS (1) 2   SCOTLAND (1) 3
Koliandris 14, Ioannu 47   Johnston 9, Gough 54, 90

CYPRUS: Pantzarias, Pittas, Miamiliotis, Christodolu, Socratou, Yiangudakis, Koliandris, Savva (Petsas), Savvides, Nikolau, Ioannu.
SCOTLAND: Leighton, Gough, Malpas, Aitken, McLeish, Narey, Nicol (I Ferguson), McStay, McClair, Speedie (McInally), Johnston.

SCOTLAND v FRANCE
Wednesday, 8 March 1989   *Hampden – 65,204*

Andy Roxburgh was the most cautious of managers, naming his teams at the last possible moment and seldom being rash enough to predict results. Against France, in a match that was clearly going to sort the men from the boys, Roxburgh went so far as to say Scotland would win.

French football was in turmoil. The team that finished fourth in the 1982 World Cup and third in 1986 were in grave danger of missing out in 1990. Their form outside France had collapsed, not having won in fourteen away internationals. They had already dropped three World Cup points, in Cyprus and Yugoslavia. Should they drop two more at Hampden they would need a footballing miracle to survive. Their predicament had already prompted the French to dispense with manager Henri Michel and – as the Germans had done with Franz Beckenbauer – turn to their greatest player. Michel Platini had three times been voted European Footballer of the Year. But he, like Beckenbauer, like Roxburgh at the time of his appointment, knew nothing of management. In Platini's case, the name was enough.

France had crossed Scotland's path in the World Cup in the 1958 finals, when Scotland had been sunk by goals from Raymond Kopa and Just Fontaine. The countries had met once since, in Marseille in 1984, France winning 2-0.

Knowing the importance of this match, and needing to expose his players beforehand to 'British' football, Platini arranged a friendly in Dublin with Jack Charlton's Irish Republic. Platini played five in midfield and the game ended goalless. He would settle for the same score in Glasgow.

He would have to do without the injured Luc Sonor and Jean Tigana, the latter so vital to the side that won the 1984 European Championship. First caps were awarded in midfield to Laurey and Durand. Monaco's Patrick Battiston and Marcel Amoros were veterans of the 1982 World Cup. Marseille's Jean-Pierre Papin would lead the attack. The team was home based.

For Scotland, Ian Ferguson won his third cap, in place of McClair. As the match brought Alex McLeish's sixtieth cap, McLeish would captain the side.

This would be a match of contrasting assessment. Conscious that France had so much at stake, many Scots were surprised at how easily they folded on a wet and windy evening. Scotland scored twice without reply. Hot-shot Maurice Johnston broke the deadlock. Gough headed Gillespie's free kick into the path of McCoist. His shot appeared to strike Johnston, who might have been offside but for Amoros playing him on. Johnston seized his chance to score. Within seconds Johnston might have scored again, but this time he drove Nicol's cross way off target. McCoist also had the ball in the net, but Johnston was offside.

A second, killer goal was not long delayed. Nicol powered past Amoros and Johnston headed his cross beyond Bats. The keeper almost saved, but couldn't prevent the ball rolling over the line. Mo Jo had now scored five goals in four matches in the current campaign. In any language, that was a rich vein of form.

But had France taken their chances, they must surely have won. Leighton had to make good early saves from Laurey and Blanc, and when the keeper couldn't hold Frank Sauzée's free kick, he redeemed himself by blocking Papin's point-blank follow-up.

Afterwards Platini lamented his strikers' failings: 'I have never known a French team create so many away chances and not score.' Yet Scotland now had seven points, four more than France in third place. Yugoslavia's watching Ivica Osim was equally pleased by the result. France had a mountain to climb.

SCOTLAND (1) 2   FRANCE (0) 0
    Johnston 28, 52

SCOTLAND: Leighton, Gough, Malpas, Aitken, McLeish, Gillespie, Nicol, McStay, McCoist (McClair), Ferguson (Strachan), Johnston.
FRANCE: Bats, Amoros, Silvestre, Sonor, Battiston, Sauzée, Durand (Paille), Laurey, Papin, Blanc, Xuereb (Perez).

SCOTLAND v CYPRUS
Wednesday, 26 April 1989   *Hampden – 50,081*

Scotland had almost slipped up in Cyprus, and France had. It was matches like these that at the end of the day might determine who qualified and who did not. Premier League matches were allowed to take their course, and Roxburgh had to keep his fingers crossed that his phone stayed quiet on Saturday night. As always, he dreaded news of injuries. As it was, he was already plagued with psychological injuries. In the week after the Hillsborough tragedy, Liverpool's footballers were in no mood to play. John Aldridge withdrew from Ireland's team, John Barnes from England's, and Gary Gillespie and Steve Nicol sought compassionate leave from Scotland's.

Roxburgh drafted into the team Hearts' uncapped Dave McPherson. Pat Nevin of Everton and Chelsea's Gordon Durie won rare caps, buttressing the attacking duo of Johnston and McCoist. Johnston, who cost £1 million when signing for Nantes in 1987, was said to be set on leaving. He hadn't scored for Nantes since his two goals against France, and had been scathingly dismissed by Michel Platini. When Roxburgh suggested that Johnston's value to Scotland was 'immeasurable', Platini laughed it off. 'All four French strikers are better than Johnston,' he retorted.

Roy 'Feed the Bear' Aitken reclaimed the captaincy from McLeish. This was Aitken's forty-fifth international. He had been capped at Under-15, -18, and -21 level, and was now captaining his country for the sixteenth time. For a player accused in some quarters of playing with his heart rather than his head, Aitken had done mighty well for himself.

It took Roxburgh's irregulars twenty-six minutes to break down the Cypriot barricades. Nevin's cross was headed down by Gough to Johnston who, back to goal, bicycle-kicked past Haritou. It was Johnston's eighth World Cup goal, in total, a Scottish record. One wonders what Platini might have said.

The floodgates should have opened. McCoist and Gough collided when both might have scored. But, as in Limassol, Cyprus had the nerve to draw level. It was shortly after the break when Nicolau ran on to Pittas's free kick, stuck out a foot and flicked the ball over Leighton. It was Cyprus's first, and last, shot.

Who knows what might have happened had Scotland had time to dwell on that setback. In fact, Scotland scowled for just fifty seconds. That was the time it took for McStay to brush past two challenges and square for McCoist to sidefoot Scotland's winner. Charlie Nicholas, now with Aberdeen, appeared for the final quarter of an hour. It was his twentieth and last cap. By the close, Scotland might have had six.

Scotland's season was over. At the weekend France and Yugoslavia drew 0-0 in Paris. In June, Yugoslavia won 2-1 in Oslo. Yugoslavia and Scotland were almost home and dry.

Qualifying Group 5 on 15 June 1989

	P	W	D	L	F	A	Pts
Scotland	5	4	1	0	10	5	9
Yugoslavia	5	3	2	0	10	4	8
Norway	5	2	0	3	8	6	4
France	5	1	2	2	4	6	4
Cyprus	6	0	1	5	5	16	1

SCOTLAND (1) 2   CYPRUS (0) 1
  Johnston 26, McCoist 63   Nicolau 62

SCOTLAND: Leighton, Gough, Malpas, Aitken, McLeish, McPherson, Nevin (Nicholas), McStay, Johnston, McCoist, Durie (Speedie).
CYPRUS: Charitou, Castanas, Pittas (Elia), Christodolou, Michael, Yiangudakis, Petsas, Nicolau, Savvides, Y Ioannou, Koliandris.

YUGOSLAVIA v SCOTLAND
Wednesday, 6 September 1989   *Zagreb – 35,000*

The new season couldn't come quickly enough for Andy Roxburgh. The day before Scotland turned out in Zagreb, Norway and France drew 1-1 in Oslo. France were suckers for late goals, Rune Bratseth heading a last gasp equaliser to frustrate them yet again. That result meant Scotland needed just one more point from their three final fixtures. Better they snatched it sooner rather than later, and not invite much gnawing of finger nails. News of Cyprus's punishment for the crowd disturbances following Scotland's injury-time win in Limassol brought howls of protest from the SFA. Cyprus were ordered to play their home match with Yugoslavia in neutral Athens. That 'punishment' rewarded Yugoslavia, who would escape the handicaps of dreadful pitch and maniacal fans imposed on Scotland and France.

Once again, Roxburgh's plans were plagued by injuries. To the surprise of everyone, since he was a Catholic, Maurice Johnston had been snapped up by Graeme Souness at Rangers. But Johnston was unfit, missing his first match of the campaign. His goal supply would be missed. Two others from Ibrox – Richard Gough and Ian Ferguson – likewise cried off. A fourth Ranger, Ally McCoist played, though he was in bad nick and was on the bench more often than not. Rangers were bottom of the league. Gary Gillespie filled Gough's shirt, despite being unable to command a place in Liverpool's first team.

Deep down, Roxburgh must have been concerned about his goalkeeper. After a distinguished career with Aberdeen and Manchester United, Jim Leighton was looking edgy. Errors were creeping into his game. Publicly,

Roxburgh stood by his man. Leighton, the manager reminded reporters, had kept twenty-five clean-sheets in fifty games, and had never let Scotland down.

Roxburgh was more concerned by the opposition, now flung to all corners of Europe. France had proved particularly hospitable to the Yugoslavs. Brnovic, Vujovic and the splendid Susic had been snapped up by Paris St Germain, Hadzibegic and Bazdarevic by Sochaux. The best of the lot, Dragan Stojkovic, was still with Red Star Belgrade. Just twenty-four years old, and approaching fifty caps, Stojkovic was another of those Slavic players high on talent but low on application. Roxburgh felt he was prone to 'show off' on the pitch. But the quality of the Yugoslavs was not in question: 'If we try to mark them man-for-man they will murder us,' confessed Roxburgh.

Roxburgh was not ill-judged in his admiration. Scotland were penned back inside their half. Leighton fisted out Balpic's shot and Stojkovic left the crossbar twanging after a snap twenty-five yarder. That Scotland should break out and score was hardly in the script, but that is what happened. McCoist had already had a 'goal' chalked off for a foul by Gillespie. Now the Liverpool defender knocked on McCoist's cross for Durie to head into a gaping goal.

A sensational victory was on the cards. Indeed, a sensation was what we got, but not in the way that Roxburgh must have hoped as he urged his players to play it tight in the second half. Within twenty minutes Scotland were trailing 1-3, trailing to three of the duffest goals Roxburgh could have conceived. First, Leighton fluffed Balpic's cross and Katenec headed into an untended goal. Second, Stojkovic's free kick from the right was turned into his own net by Steve Nicol, under pressure from Katanec. Third, Jakovljevic burst down the left, crossed under the bar and Gillespie, trying to hoof it clear, crashed it into his own net. One wondered the last occasion Scotland, or any other team, had conceded two own goals in one match.

Scotland had hoped to become the first nation to qualify. Instead, that honour fell to Yugoslavia. Following this, their first ever win over the Scots, Ivica Osim could afford to be magnanimous. 'Scotland will surely join us in Italy,' he said. When asked to explain the dramatic turnaround, Osim replied: 'We changed out tactics after half-time to copy the Scottish style.' Read what you like into that.

YUGOSLAVIA   (0) 3   SCOTLAND   (1) 1
    Katenec 54, Nicol 60 (o.g.),   Durie 37
    Gillespie 64 (o.g.)

YUGOSLAVIA: Ivkovic, Spasic, Balpic, Katanec, Hadzibegic, Brnovic, Susic, Bazdarevic, Jakovljevic (Savicevic), Stojkovic, Vujovic.
SCOTLAND: Leighton, Gillespie, Malpas, Aitken, McLeish, Miller, Nicol, McStay, McCoist, McLeod, Durie (McInally).

FRANCE v SCOTLAND
Wednesday, 11 October 1989   *Paris – 30,000*

If France were to be resurrected from the ashes they needed to beat Scotland and Cyprus in Paris and hope that Norway would spring a surprise at Hampden.

Of Scotland's three lives, one had been gobbled up in Zagreb; they didn't want to lose their second in Paris. Earlier in the day Norway had lost 0-1 in Yugoslavia. This was good news, for Norway were now out of contention and would lack incentive at Hampden – if it came to that.

The only newish face to line up for Scotland belonged to industrious Murdo MacLeod of Borussia Dortmund. Otherwise it was a team of battle-hardened regulars that Roxburgh sent out on their mission. Gordon Strachan had surprised many by moving into the English second division with Leeds, when he was still on top of his game. Maurice Johnston, of course, was in tandem with Ally McCoist at Ibrox. Roxburgh hoped their enhanced understanding could be put to good purpose. Johnston's knowledge of French football was also much in demand. He was, besides, the only player to have played at the Parc des Princes. His insight into French team selection makes interesting reading. Johnston dismissed Michel Platini as 'crazy' for proposing to play Montpellier's Eric Cantona in attack, when his club played him in midfield. Cantona had scored twice against Sweden the previous month. France would have to do without Papin and their captain, Amoros. The loss of Papin was good news to Roxburgh, who confessed that had he been fit he would have played a sweeper.

Scotland started brightly. Gough's firm header was clutched by Bats at the second attempt. Gough was doubtless aware that Scotland had scored first in all their matches to date, but he now pushed his luck trying to clear on the touchline. In a trice Ferreri slipped the ball to Deschamps, lurking in space. Leighton, scuttling across his line, was unable to keep out the shot.

Once play had settled, Scotland resumed the offensive. But the chances were falling to McCoist rather than Johnston, and McCoist was not in the mood to take them. He shot into the side-netting rather than square to his better placed colleague; his six-yard volley came back off the bar; and his free header at the far post went nowhere.

Scotland continued to dictate the second half, assisted by di Meco's wild lunge at Johnston that earned the Frenchman a red card. But then it all went wrong. Ferreri and Cantona interchanged beautifully, leaving Cantona clean through to round Leighton at his leisure. Two goals down was more than Scotland deserved, but by the end it was three. Scottish own-goals were all the rage, it seemed, Nicol's heel deflecting Durand's harmless shot past Leighton.

If France failed to qualify, they couldn't blame their home form. They would drop just one point and concede no goals.

FRANCE   (1) 3   SCOTLAND   (0) 0
  Deschamps 25, Cantona 61,
  Nicol 89 (o.g.)

FRANCE: Bats, Silvestre, Le Roux (Casoni), Sauzée, di Meco, Durand, Pardo, Deschamps, Ferreri, Cantona, Perez (Bravo).
SCOTLAND: Leighton, Gough, Malpas, Nicol, McLeish, Aitken, Strachan (McInally), McStay, McCoist, McLeod (Bett), Johnston.

SCOTLAND v NORWAY
Wednesday, 15 November 1989   *Hampden – 63,987*

Scotland had reached the nine-point mark back in April. Seven months later they were still stuck on nine points, and this time there were no more chances. If they shipped goals to Norway as they had to Yugoslavia and France, Scotland would have burned their last bridge and would be watching the World Cup on TV. Scotland had only to draw against opponents with nothing to play for. Lest Scots needed reminding, that was the situation, in reverse, when Scotland journeyed to Sofia in 1987, snatching a late winner to break Bulgaria's hearts. Would Norway do a Scotland?

The tension in the Scottish camp must have been unbearable. There was the rare sight of past and present Scotland managers squabbling in public. Alex Ferguson suggested that Roxburgh calm the increasingly jittery Leighton by reassuring him that his place was not in doubt. Roxburgh retorted that if he did that, and Leighton got injured, his replacement – Andy Goram or Bryan Gunn – would be deflated by knowing they were not in the side on merit. Besides, Roxburgh had other worries. Gillespie, Gough, Nicol, Durie and Durrant were already out of the reckoning. Roxburgh tried to retain the team's basic shape, recalling Jim Bett in midfield and Davie Cooper, now with Motherwell, on the flank. Leighton played, equalling Alan Rough's record fifty-five goalkeeping caps.

Scotland set off like an express train, buffeting the Norwegian defence. Twice McCoist drove hard against Thorstvedt's legs. But as the coveted early goal refused to come, play fragmented. In one heart-stopping moment Sorloth's shot was blocked on the line by McPherson, who took a knock.

The first half whistle was overdue when Malpas cleared upfield. The ball fell to McCoist who, to the delirium of his countrymen, lobbed Thorstvedt from twenty-five yards. Hampden exploded.

Now it was a case of counting down the minutes. Norway created chances. Gulbrandsen missed two, and Fjortoft's twenty-yard curler beat Leighton, only to strike the inside of a post. At the other end McPherson headed against the bar when by scoring he might have calmed everyone's nerves. With ten minutes to play Hampden was already a wall of noise. Scotland started to play keepball, too early, but the ninety minutes were up when Bayern Münich's Erland Johnsen let fly from almost on the halfway line. The ball skidded past Leighton and into the corner. The celebrations on the terraces were hardly interrupted, and seconds later the final whistle blew. Scotland were through, but had they needed to win Leighton would have been inconsolable.

SCOTLAND   (1) 1   NORWAY   (0) 1
    McCoist 45   Johnsen 90

SCOTLAND: Leighton, McPherson, Malpas, Aitken, McLeish, Miller (MacLeod), Johnston, McStay, McCoist, Bett, Cooper (McClair).
NORWAY: Thorstvedt, Hansen, Bratseth, Kojedal (Halworsen), Bjornebye, E Johnsen, Gulbrandsen, Ahlsen, Skammelsrud (Bohinen), Sorloth, Fjortoft.

Qualifying Group 5

		Home				Away					
	P	W	D	L	F	A	W	D	L	F	A	Pts
YUGOSLAVIA	8	4	0	0	11	3	2	2	0	5	3	14
SCOTLAND	8	2	2	0	6	3	2	0	2	6	9	10
France	8	3	1	0	6	0	0	2	2	4	7	9
Norway	8	1	2	1	6	6	1	1	2	4	3	7
Cyprus	8	0	1	3	4	9	0	0	4	2	11	1

Other group results

France v Norway	1-0	Norway v Cyprus	3-1
Cyprus v France	1-1	Norway v Yugoslavia	1-2
Cyprus v Norway	0-3	Norway v France	1-1
Yugoslavia v France	3-2	Yugoslavia v Norway	1-0
Yugoslavia v Cyprus	4-0	Cyprus v Yugoslavia	1-2
France v Yugoslavia	0-0	France v Cyprus	2-0

World Cup finals – ITALY   **June-July 1990**

Scotland's immediate objective in Italy, of course, was to do what they had never done before, and survive the first round of matches. In 1974, '78 and '82 they had finished third. In 1986, in Mexico, their task had been rendered easier by FIFA offering carrots to teams finishing third. Scotland duly finished fourth. One began to suspect that should FIFA invite all four teams to go through, Scotland would somehow finish fifth.

In Italy, the format would be identical to that in Mexico. Four of the nations finishing third would live to fight another day. Only eight of the twenty-four finalists would be sent packing after the first round. Scotland had been one of the eight in Mexico and would not relish the same fate again.

The draw for the finals in 1990 was gentler than it had been in 1986, but then it could hardly be otherwise. Scotland came out of the hat with Brazil, which was bad news, Costa Rica, which was good, and Sweden, who – on first impressions – seemed likely to be contesting second place with Scotland.

This group – Group C – would be based in the north-west of Italy, closest to home. Scotland would face Costa Rica and Sweden in the Stadio Luigi Ferraris, Genoa, home of Sampdoria and Genoa. Their third match, with Brazil, would take place at Turin's Stadio Delle Alpi, the base for Juventus and Torino.

Season 1989-90 had not been encouraging to Roxburgh and his players. In three World Cup games they had taken just one point and conceded seven goals, three of them self-inflicted. Worse was to come in the friendlies prior to the finals. The one high spot was a 1-0 victory over defending champions, Argentina, at Hampden in March. But what should have been a mighty fillip was obliterated by other results. Losing at home to East Germany (0-1) was bad enough, but not nearly as bad as being duffed 1-3 by Egypt at Pittodrie. The squad flew out to Malta to acclimatise with just one win in seven and with the own-goal tally now risen to four. Scotland were rated 66-1 to lift the trophy. Of their immediate opponents, Brazil were quoted at 4-1, Sweden at 50-1, and Costa Rica at 1,000-1. England received odds of 10-1, while the Irish Republic were considered a better bet than Scotland, at 40-1.

Roxburgh's squad compilation was aggravated by injuries to Steve Nicol (English Football Writers' 'Player of the Year' 1989) and Davie Cooper, which kept them out. Forwards Brian McClair and John Robertson failed to make the short-list, though either of them might have been called up had Maurice Johnston – whose goal-tally made him indispensable to the Scottish effort – not shrugged off a torn stomach muscle that made him doubtful to the very last. Fellow striker Ally McCoist was pained by a hamstring, but told nobody until the last moment. Alan McInally had been wandering around with his arm in a sling for some weeks and Murdo MacLeod was afflicted by a groin strain that eventually saw him return to his German club, Borussia Dortmund, in an effort to get fit. Stewart McKimmie had been hurt on his home ground against Egypt, but had won his race against time. Likewise, Alex McLeish (Scottish 'Player of the Year'), who broke his nose in the same match and hadn't played since. Worst of all, veteran defender Willie Miller had finally succumbed to age and injury and would not play for Aberdeen or Scotland again. Gary Gillespie had been troubled by a hamstring all season, and would make only a fleeting appearance in the finals. After a lifetime with Celtic, skipper Roy Aitken had been transferred to Newcastle United in the English second division. It was a big step up from playing Bournemouth to playing Brazil. Alan Hansen was bypassed yet again.

Roxburgh's goalkeeping dilemma had escalated into a crisis. Jim Leighton's slump had precipitated the ultimate indignity, dropped by Manchester United for the FA Cup Final replay after conceding three goals to Crystal Palace. With hindsight, that humiliation might have ended Leighton's top-flight career (it is a credit to the man that it did not). For Roxburgh, the penny dropped later than it did for Alex Ferguson, and to that extent Roxburgh must shoulder part of the blame for the goalkeeping lapses in Italy. Roxburgh would argue that Leighton had not let Scotland down, which wasn't strictly true, and that Andy Goram was not yet ready for a World Cup, which was a moot point.

Seldom does a player arrive on-stage at the World Cup finals having played little or no part in the preliminaries. One such player was Everton's Stuart McCall, a red-haired, busy player who tempted Goodison to part with close on £1 million to Bradford City for his services. McCall would be ever-present in Italy, and emerge from the competition with reputation far higher then when he entered it.

As they say, it never rains but it pours. Inspecting his squad, it is apparent that Roxburgh awarded numbers 1-11 for his preferred eleven, and numbers 12-22 for the back-up boys. Just to glance through the names was to confront Scotland's major weakness, the lack of almost anyone who could hold a candle to Souness, Dalglish, Strachan, Miller – players who had anchored the World Cup squads of 1982 and 1986. Even the most diehard supporter accepted that this was the weakest of any recent Scottish squad. Little wonder that Alex Ferguson, considering the modest talent at Roxburgh's disposal, feared the worst. One wonders, for example, how many of the twenty-two would have forced a place in a British eleven, or even, come to that, in Bobby Robson's semi-final bound England team.

No	Name	Position	Club	Age	Caps	Goals
1	Jim Leighton	Goalkeeper	Manchester U	31	55	–
2	Alex McLeish	Central defence	Aberdeen	31	70	–
3	Roy Aitken (c)	Defence/Midfield	Newcastle	31	53	1
4	Richard Gough	Defence	Rangers	28	49	5
5	Paul McStay	Midfield	Celtic	25	46	6
6	Maurice Malpas	Full-back	Dundee United	27	34	–
7	Maurice Johnston	Forward	Rangers	27	33	13
8	Jim Bett	Midfield	Aberdeen	30	25	1
9	Ally McCoist	Forward	Rangers	27	23	8
10	Murdo MacLeod	Midfield	Bor' Dortmund	31	16	1
11	Gary Gillespie	Central defence	Liverpool	29	11	–
12	Andy Goram	Goalkeeper	Hibernian	25	9	–
13	Gordon Durie	Forward	Chelsea	24	6	2

14	Alan McInally	Forward	Bayern Münich	27	7	3
15	Craig Levein	Central defence	Hearts	25	5	–
16	Stuart McCall	Midfield	Everton	26	5	–
17	Stewart McKimmie	Full-back	Aberdeen	27	4	1
18	John Collins	Midfield	Hibernian	22	3	2
19	David McPherson	Central defence	Hearts	26	4	–
20	Gary McAllister	Midfield	Leicester	25	3	–
21	Robert Fleck	Forward	Norwich	24	1	–
22	Bryan Gunn	Goalkeeper	Norwich	26	1	–
			Averages	**27.0**	**21.0**	

In terms of age and experience, the squad was similar to that of other recent World Cups, averaging twenty caps per man.

World Cup	Ave Age	Ave Caps
1954	27.7	4.8
1958	27.1	9.9
1974	25.9	13.9
1978	27.3	19.1
1982	26.8	23.1
1986	27.1	21.9
1990	27.0	21.0

COSTA RICA v SCOTLAND
Monday, 11 June 1990   *Genoa – 30,867*

Costa Rica were strangers to World Cup finals. That they were present at all in Italia '90 was due less to unearthing eleven heroes than to the fact that Mexico had flouted the rules (playing over-age players in a youth competition) and found themselves banned. Mexico's domination of the Central and North American group (CONCACAF) was such that she had missed just a couple of finals since World War II. CONCACAF's relative strength could be measured in the fact that Mexico have suffered more defeats in World Cup finals, seventeen, than any other nation.

Costa Rica and the United States were CONCACAF's virginal candidates in 1990. Costa Rica had even lost to Guatemala and to the United States in qualifying. All of this suggests they should have been lambs for the slaughter. The most peaceful Central American country, with no army of its own, Costa Rica was surely going to fare even worse than Mexico customarily did. For all their limitations, Costa Rica were no less impatient for success. They had gone through four different managers in qualifying. The new president of the Costa

Rican FA had demanded the sacking of Marvin Rodrigues in February, who had taken them through, following defeat by a Mexican second division club in the warm-ups. To guide them through the finals they had hoped to recruit Cesar Menotti, architect of Argentina's success in 1978. When he declined, they turned successfully to Yugoslavian Bora Milutinovic who, assisted by home advantage, steered Mexico to the quarter-finals in 1986. Milutinovic would enjoy just two months' familiarisation with his players before the gloves came off. The two players expected to hold their own were the captain, Roger Flores, even at thirty-three a dependable central defender, and the dark-skinned Juan Cayasso, addicted to Alfred Hitchcock movies off the pitch, adept in midfield on it. None of the squad played abroad. Seeking exposure to Scottish-type football, Costa Rica played Wales in Cardiff and lost 0-1.

Returning from Malta, where Scotland recorded a 2-1 victory over the Maltese national side, the squad flew back for final preparations at Kilmarnock before flying out to Italy. Genoa's airport was as quiet as death when they landed. No flags, no fanfares, no welcome. Scotland were evidently expected to slip out of the tournament as anonymously as they had slipped in.

Group C opened with Brazil playing Sweden in Turin. Roxburgh was on record as hoping for a draw or a Swedish victory, though there was a counter-argument which favoured a Brazil win, which would still leave Sweden and Scotland in contention.

Behind closed doors at the resort of Rapallo, on the Ligurian riviera, Roxburgh wrestled with the task of fielding eleven fit players. His urgent worry was Maurice Johnston. Having strained a stomach muscle in training in Malta, he could not be rushed into action without the risk of incurring a hernia. For some days Johnston couldn't even stand upright, let alone run. As a precaution, FIFA were asked if Scotland might replace him. FIFA, not surprisingly, said no. Mercifully, Johnston made a rapid recovery and staked his place in the side.

Though there was no colour clash between Scotland's navy and Costa Rica's red, the black and white TVs still common in the Third World couldn't pick up the contrast. As Scotland were theoretically the away team, it was they who changed, parading their second strip of white, yellow and blue hoops. It was a strip unlikely to win prizes for design or colour coordination.

'Flower of Scotland' echoed round the stadium and Scotland were off. Zaïre and New Zealand had taught them painful lessons in past World Cups. Why couldn't Scotland play the underdogs last instead of first, when they had all their tricks up their sleeves? Roxburgh did nobody any favours by dismissing the match as Costa Rica's cup final. How wrong he was to be.

Scotland stuck to their basic 4-4-2. Big Alan McInally partnered Johnston in attack, supposedly to unsettle goalkeeper Gabelo Coneja. Costa Rica fell back on their defensive Plan A. Not having the physique to challenge the Scots one-to-one, they were adept at quickly off-loading the ball to a team-mate. Indeed,

Spot the ball! It is heading for the net as Cayasso shoots over Leighton. (v Costa Rica)

after six minutes Cayasso ran hard at McLeish, who dithered, permitting a wicked shot that flew wide.

Costa Rica seemed little interested in trying their luck again, for Cayasso's shot was the first-half sum of their enterprise. Most of the time they had been driven back by Aitken's promptings behind the midfield, though Conejo looked not the slightest bothered by the intimidatory presence of McInally. Both Johnston and McCall came close to unthreading the defence. Play broke down repeatedly on the edge of the Costa Rican penalty box, though Johnston's shot was turned away by the athletic Conejo.

The tartan faithful, packed into both ends of the ground, would have been content with the first-half showing, confident that the Costa Rican wall would soon be breached. When the teams reappeared, Richard Gough stayed behind, having aggravated a long-standing foot injury. His World Cup was over and he would fly home for treatment. It was a bad blow to Roxburgh's plans. Gough's presence would be sorely missed. For the moment, his place was taken by Stewart McKimmie. Within four minutes of the change of ends Scotland sprung a leak. Ramirez's pass split their defence. Jara's backheel perplexed McKimmie and McPherson and set up Cayasso, who had ghosted free on the left. Leighton flung himself to block the expected ground shot; the ball clipped the top of his body and flew up into the net. The 'Hitchcock man' had scored.

One need hardly ask what it felt like to be losing to Costa Rica. Scotland had forty-one minutes to equalise, but they couldn't. Bett and McStay wasted much useful possession. By the end, Scotland would have forced nineteen goal attempts to their opponents' four. McInally headed over. When Johnston swivelled and let fly from eight yards, Conejo thrillingly turned the ball away. Scotland might have saved the game when McCall's pull-back was impeded by Marchena's hand, though Argentine referee Loustau saw nothing illegal.

So Scotland, hoping to top Group C, found themselves bottom instead. There were no contingencies for losing to Costa Rica: the result was without question Scotland's most damaging in their World Cup history. 'It was like a bad dream,' said Roxburgh, as ten thousand tartan fans demanded heads roll. 'The pits,' was how Denis Law described the performance. One commentator was moved to write: 'it was not a question of win or lose, but who they [Scotland] would lose to.'

Coming on top of the dismal, desperate draw between England and Ireland, British football was the laughing stock.

COSTA RICA   (0) 1   SCOTLAND   (0) 0
    Cayasso 49

COSTA RICA: Conejo, Flores, Gonzales, Montero, Chávez, Chavarria, Ramirez, Gómez, Cayasso, Marchena, C Jara (Medford).
SCOTLAND: Leighton, Gough (McKimmie), McLeish, McPherson, Malpas, Aitken, McStay, Bett (McCoist), McCall, Johnston, McInally.

SWEDEN v SCOTLAND
Saturday 16 June 1990   *Genoa – 31,823*

Scotland had plotted to reach the second round by taking two points off Costa Rica and one off Sweden. Nothing could be vouchsafed in their final match against Brazil. Costa Rica's victory threw these calculations out of the window. To repair the damage, Scotland must endeavour to beat Sweden.

The Swedes had topped England's qualifying group, drawing 0-0 twice with Bobby Robson's outfit. Like Norway, Sweden was exporting her best players to England and the continent, though so far not to Scotland. Sweden's silver-haired captain, Glenn Hysén, had been imported into Liverpool's defence, Roland Nilsson into Sheffield Wednesday's. Other expatriates to face Scotland included Peter Larsson and Stefan Pettersson of Ajax, Anders Limpár of Cremonese, Jonas Thern of Benfica, and Johnny Ekström of Cannes. Gothenburg and Malmö provided the bulk of Sweden's home based players.

Like Scotland, Sweden occupied a mid-ranking place in Europe's football hierarchy, though her achievements were far greater. Four times Sweden had

Stuart McCall, hidden from view, pops Scotland in front. (v Sweden)

been placed in the top five – according to FIFA's rankings. Scotland had never been higher than ninth (in 1974). Mind you, Sweden tended to yo-yo, failing to qualify in 1982 (thanks to Scotland and Northern Ireland) and again in 1986. By 1988 they were beating all and sundry, and Hysén and Larsson graced a Rest of the World XI that played an English Football League XI. But by 1990 Sweden appeared in the doldrums again. Generally, they liked playing British teams. On top of two draws with England, they had beaten Wales three times in two years, scoring ten goals. Scotland, though, had beaten Sweden twice in the 1982 qualifiers. History suggested this would be a tough one for Sweden, though they had looked better losing to Brazil than Scotland had to Costa Rica.

Sweden is one of those countries where all clubs play a certain style (4-4-2, with emphasis on British-type harassment) and all players are schooled in set ways. This made it easier for home based players and mercenaries to meld into an international unit. Manager Olle Nordin was four years into the job and was confident that Sweden would do well, notwithstanding the defeat by Brazil, which he felt was harsh. Neither Sweden nor Scotland could lose this one.

Roxburgh juggled with his formation yet again. Roy Aitken dropped back to sweeper and Craig Levein came into the back four. Paul McStay and Jim Bett – the latter having enjoyed a productive season with Aberdeen – had looked out of touch and were dropped. So was McInally. In came Murdo MacLeod, who packed a shot, while the attack was bolstered by the inclusion of Gordon Durie and Robert Fleck. For Sweden, Hysén returned, having missed the match with Brazil. This threw up an intriguing confrontation; Hysén had been sent off for Liverpool for belting Norwich's Fleck at Carrow Road.

With both teams needing to win, the match was like a cup-tie. With Scottish fans urging them on, Scotland soared into a tenth-minute lead. McPherson back-headed MacLeod's corner into the goalmouth where McCall pounced for his first international goal.

To their credit, Scotland did not attempt to sit on their lead. But the Swedes lacked flexibility and seemed unable to switch their tactics. McLeish kept a tight rein on the young prodigy, Tomas Brolin. Chances were squandered at both ends before the match entered its final, dramatic climax. Paul McStay replaced Durie. Within minutes, the outstanding Aitken raced on to Fleck's pass, speared deep into the Swedish penalty area and fired in a shot that Ravelli parried. Aitken was first to the rebound, only to be upended by Roland Nilsson. Johnston's penalty was hard and true, and his ninth World Cup goal seemed to have sealed Sweden's fate.

Scottish sides like to keep their fans on their toes. The bearded Glenn Strömberg of Atalanta, a late substitute for Peter Larsson, latched on to a through ball and, unchallenged, pulled a goal back. Scotland hung on, their supporters greeting the final whistle with the *Guantanamara* refrain of: 'do it the hard way, we always do it the hard way.'

Scotland's fourth win in the finals of the World Cup looked merited on play, though was disputed by various lies, damned lies and statistics. Sweden had recorded five shots on target to Scotland's four, won four corners to two, and fouled fifteen times compared with Scotland's twenty-seven. It was undeniably a famous win, but it still left Roxburgh one point behind schedule. That point would have to be garnered from Brazil.

SWEDEN (0) 1	SCOTLAND (1) 2
Strömberg 85	McCall 10, Johnston 83 pen

SWEDEN: Ravelli, R Nilsson, Hysén, Larsson (Strömberg), Schwarz, Limpár, Thern, Ingesson, Brolin, J Nilsson, Pettersson (Ekström).
SCOTLAND: Leighton, McLeish, Malpas, McPherson, Levein, Aitken, McLeod, Durie (McStay), McCall, Johnston, Fleck (McCoist).

BRAZIL v SCOTLAND
Wednesday, 20 June 1990   *Turin – 65,502*

Brazil are always fancied for the World Cup, simply because they are Brazil. This particular Brazilian team was less well fancied than most, if only because the great names of the recent past – Socrates, Zico, Pelé – appeared incomparably superior to the current crew. Brazil's win over Sweden was scarcely merited on the run of play, and though – unlike Scotland – Brazil had overcome Costa Rica, their winning goal had needed a deflection. Manager Sebastiao Lazaroni had begun coaching at the tender age of twenty, and took up his position with the national side early in 1989. He was said to be pledged to modify Brazil's devil-take-the-hindmost attacking style, strengthening the defence and introducing a sweeper for the first time. Brazil's cherished 4-4-2 was discarded. Success in the 1989 Copa America, for the first time since 1949, silenced Lazaroni's critics – for the time being.

Brazilian qualification for the World Cup finals was assured in bewildering circumstances. Needing a point from their final home match, against Chile, the opponents indulged in the ultimate gamesmanship, faking an injury to goalkeeper Roberto Rojas that led to the Chileans walking off. The deception was discovered, Rojas banned for life and Chile from the next World Cup. Brazil were awarded the match 2-0.

One of Brazil's problems was that half the squad played in Europe, which ruled out useful get-togethers in qualifiers and warm-ups. The natural port of call was Portugal, with her common language, and the natural club, Benfica. National captain Ricardo Gomez, Valdo, Silas, and Aldair all played for the Portuguese giants; Dunga, Alemão, Muller and Careca played in Italy. Careca had not long returned to action with Napoli after breaking a bone in his foot.

Two wins out of two was enough to see Brazil through to the knock-out stages. This prompted the inevitable chit-chat about how they might approach this, their third, meaningless match. Noises from the Brazilian camp in Asti suggested Brazil didn't fancy landing up in the same half of the programme as the hosts, Italy, and might contrive a result that avoided it. But Brazil's team was well settled. Romario of PSV Eindhoven and Ricardo Rocha were the only introductions to an otherwise unchanged side that needed just a draw to top Group C and entertain in the knock-outs the third-placed team from Group A. Brazil had no way of knowing that team would be Argentina.

Now that Scotland were chasing a draw, rather than a win, Roxburgh made three further changes. Levein failed a fitness test and Fleck and Durie were discarded as quickly as they had been installed. McKimmie, McCoist and McStay were given the nod. Gary Gillespie would come on as a sub, leaving only John Collins, Gary McAllister and the two standby goalkeepers unused in the tournament. Scotland were done with Genoa, site of mixed fortunes, and decamped to St Vincent in the Italian Alps. There they prepared for the crunch match with Brazil to be played in Turin's Stadio Delle Alpi, which replaced the venerable Stadio Comunale as home of Juventus and Torino.

The fact that both teams required a draw almost turned this rain-sodden yawn into a non-event. As one commentator noted, if the match had been a

McLeish stares in horror as Muller puts Scotland out of the World Cup. (v Brazil)

horse race, Brazil's lethargy would have demanded a stewards' enquiry. The only venom came from Dunga's free kick, struck with such ferocity that it nearly separated MacLeod's head from his body and took him, concussed, from the field. One might have expected the Brazilian newcomers, Romario especially, to be fighting for their places, but he appeared as dulled as the rest, and he was eventually pulled off in favour of Muller.

By half-time Scotland had not created a whiff of a half-chance and both sides trooped off to jeers from the neutrals ringing in their ears. It is a moot point whether the second half was any better, before the sting in the tail. The best Scotland could offer beforehand was an Aitken header which Branco hooked away. Robert Fleck swapped places with McCoist. Fleck had no sooner shaken the cobwebs from his limbs than he witnessed a calamitous goal. McStay squandered possession in midfield. Alemão meandered goalwards, saw nothing better to do than to shoot, and half-hit his shot along the ground. Leighton was down in good time, but couldn't cling on to the ball, which became the focus of a triple lunge, from Leighton, Gillespie and Careca. The ball broke from the melee across the goal. It might have run out of play, but McLeish froze and Muller was on hand to tap it over the line from a sharp angle. Leighton looked a picture of misery. His Manchester United career was over, and now, he presumed, his international career too.

So near. Taffarel somehow blocks Johnston's point-blank shot. (v Brazil)

With Scotland forced to attack, the remaining eight minutes saw more action than the preceding eighty-two. Scotland created little until the egg-timer was empty. Then Gillespie headed across goal to Johnston, whose swivelling shot from close range was somehow turned over by Taffarel at point-blank range. Johnston couldn't believe it and beat the grass with his hands in despair.

BRAZIL (0) 1   SCOTLAND (0) 0
  Muller 82

BRAZIL: Taffarel, Jorginho, Ricardo Gomes, Branco, Rocha, Galvão, Dunga, Alemão, Valdo, Careca, Romario (Muller).
SCOTLAND: Leighton, McKimmie, McLeish, McPherson, Aitken, Malpas, McStay, McCall, MacLeod (Gillespie), Johnston, McCoist (Fleck).

So the form book stayed true. Brazil had never failed to reach the latter stages; Scotland had never reached them. Mathematically Scotland stayed alive, on a life-support machine, as it were, another twenty-four hours. Costa Rica's 2-1 victory over Sweden sent the Central Americans through in second place. Scotland finished third, with an identical record to Austria in Group A. One or t'other would have stayed on, provided South Korea prevented Uruguay winning in Group E. Uruguay scored the winning goal in injury time. Having sunk Scotland in 1986, Uruguay repeated the act in 1990. So, for the umpteenth time, Scotland failed by a whisker.

Costa Rica and Brazil both fell at the next hurdle. England ploughed on, riding their luck to the semi-final, where it finally ran out. West Germany took the title, beating Argentina in the worst Final the competition had ever seen.

Final positions – Group C

	P	W	D	L	F	A	Pts
BRAZIL	3	3	0	0	4	1	6
COSTA RICA	3	2	0	1	3	2	4
Scotland	3	1	0	2	2	3	2
Sweden	3	0	0	3	3	6	0

Scotland appearances and goalscorers (substitute appearances in brackets)
World Cup qualifying rounds and final competition 1990

	Apps	Goals		Apps	Goals
Aitken R *	11	–	McCall S	3	1
McLeish A *†	11	–	McInally A	1 (3)	–
Malpas M *	11	–	Speedie D *	1 (2)	–
McStay P *	10 (1)	1	Ferguson I	1 (1)	–
Johnston M *	10	7	Fleck R	1 (1)	–
Leighton J *	10	–	McKimmie S	1 (1)	–
McCoist A	6 (3)	2	Strachan G *†	1 (1)	–
Gough R *	6	2	Cooper D *	1	–
Nicol S *	6	–	Gallacher K	1	–
McPherson D	5	–	Goram A	1	–
MacLeod M	4 (1)	–	Levein C	1	–
Miller W *†	4	–	Narey D *†	1	–
McClair B	3 (2)	–	Nevin P	1	–
Bett J *	3 (1)	–	Durrant I	– (1)	–
Gillespie G	3 (1)	–	Nicholas C *	– (1)	–
Durie G	3	1			

* Appeared in 1986 World Cup.
† Appeared in 1982 World Cup.
‡ Appeared in 1978 World Cup.

141 apps   14 goals
85 Scottish League
43 English League
8 German League
5 French League
31 players used

12

THE 1994 WORLD CUP

Four years on, here we go again. If those Scots game for a flutter had put money on their team's chances in Group C in Italy, the shrewdest would have backed them to fail, preferably on goal difference. For that was how it always seemed to be. It was sad, but prospects for 1994, in the United States of all places, seemed no brighter. The talent wasn't coming through.

There was no question of firing Andy Roxburgh over the defeat by Costa Rica, or for Leighton's mishap, either of which if avoided would have put a smile on Scotland's face. The second round would have beckoned. Roxburgh was given a clean bill of health to steer Scotland to yet another place in the sun.

Though the prize was smaller, the finals of the European Championship were harder to reach than the finals of the World Cup. Only eight places were at stake compared with a dozen or more in the global competition. Scotland had never before surmounted that obstacle, but no sooner was Italia '90 laid to rest than they set about slaying powerful opponents – Switzerland, Romania, Bulgaria (plus San Marino) – and took their place in Sweden along with England and the mighty. Defeats by Holland and Germany brought Scotland down to earth, but a fine victory over the Commonwealth of Independent States (the former Soviet Union) made for a grand finale.

It was this tournament that bore the brunt of Europe's political upheavals. The Soviet Union no longer existed. Nor did Yugoslavia. Her demise paved the way for Denmark's late call-up and triumph against the odds. The country that began the competition as 'West Germany' ended it as 'Germany'.

The tournament thrust Richard Gough into the limelight as a player on the brink of world class. Gough had looked good in Mexico, missed through injury all but forty-five minutes in Italy, but was now ready to lead the assault on America. Unfortunately, Gough's relationship with Roxburgh was fractious. Before the new campaign was out, Gough would turn his back on him.

Eyeing the rest of the squad in Sweden, one is struck by the retention of players who had failed in Italy. Roxburgh had not wielded a new broom; he didn't have one. Jim Leighton had inevitably stepped down, giving a chance to the patient Goram. Goram had signed for Rangers, UEFA's foreign quotas in

European club competition having precipitated their English keeper, Chris Woods' reluctant departure from Ibrox. Indeed, the one player absent in Italy but called up in Sweden was full-back Tommy Boyd, an itinerant footballer, hopping from Motherwell to Chelsea and back to roost at Celtic.

It was, then, hard to pinpoint reasons for Scotland's progress in the European Championship – other than Roxburgh's sagacity – for his was by no means a powerful squad. As for the coming World Cup, the disintegration of eastern Europe inflated the list of eligible nations and the size of the qualifying zones. All zones now contained six nations (apart from that with the two Irelands, which had seven). That meant a qualifying campaign of ten matches, a quarter of a league season. This was both good news – the rub of the green would even out over such a long course; and bad – teams left behind at the start would face a year stacked with meaningless fixtures.

Group 1 comprised Scotland, Italy, Portugal, Switzerland, Estonia, Malta. Leaving aside the last two, who would surely fight for the scraps, that left four realistic contenders for two places. Italy's record in the World Cup set them apart. It would prove a setback of drastic proportions should they fail. Scotland, Switzerland and Portugal would probably scramble for the second slot. Scotland had headed Portugal in the '82 qualifiers and Switzerland in the recent European qualifiers. Scotland's chances, in other words, were better than even. Curiously, Scotland were the only ones of the five to make the European finals. Though this lent them added weight, it added to the others' resolve.

On the club scene, Rangers continued to clear up everything in their path. Progress in Europe, however, had stalled. Not since 1986, when Aberdeen reached the European Cup quarter-finals, had a Scottish club reached the later stages of a European competition. Nowadays, they were tumbling at the first or second hurdle, though Rangers were about to change all that.

Qualifying Group 1

SWITZERLAND v SCOTLAND
Wednesday, 9 September 1992   *Berne – 10,000*

Opening with a testing away tie was Scotland's well-worn path to qualification. Four times out of five they had begun with an away match, winning three. The exception, defeat in Prague in the 1978 campaign, was overcome only by beating Wales at Anfield instead. In other words, history suggested Scotland must not leave Berne empty-handed.

Switzerland were one of those nations whose ups were never high and whose downs were never low. They hadn't graced the finals of a World Cup since 1966, when they had lost three out of three. Scotland had beaten them twice in reaching the 1958 World Cup, and taken three points in reaching the

1992 European finals. Scotland's overall record in Switzerland was modest, so a second successive 2-2 draw in Berne's Wankdorf Stadium would suit them nicely.

Switzerland were all topsy-turvy. They had switched managers and styles. The German Uli Stielike had given way to the Englishman Roy Hodgson, who had seen his players off to a flying start with a 6-0 demolition in Estonia. Hodgson had been in charge of Neuchatel Xamax when they annihilated Liam Brady's Celtic 5-1. He had imported a flat back four to the Swiss side, and stirred up a few hornets – according to the media – by disparaging Ally McCoist. Hodgson could call upon the services of veterans Geiger and Egli (sent off at Hampden). The team was home based, with the exception of Adrian Knup of Stuttgart and the exciting Stephane Chapuisat of Borussia Dortmund.

Scotland were captained by the resourceful Gough, bolstered at the back by Dave McPherson – whom Rangers had brought back to Ibrox from Tynecastle – and driven forward in midfield by Gary McAllister from English champions Leeds. Andy Goram played despite having mislaid his passport, which required special clearance to be hastily agreed. The one notable omission was that of Maurice Johnston. He should have been in his prime, but had been shown the door at Ibrox in a £1.5 million deal that took him to Everton. It was money ill spent, for Johnston never again climbed the heights. Net-bulging was entrusted to Gordon Durie and Ally McCoist, who had scored in this very stadium.

One year on from Scotland's last visit, the atmosphere was very different. Then, it had been electric; now, at the conception of a new competition, flat. Even the joy of a home goal after just seventy seconds failed to ignite the sparse crowd. It was a goal British teams do not expect to lose, Knup climbing higher than Gough and McPherson to connect with Alain Sutter's corner.

Scotland didn't panic: last time, they had recovered from two goals down. Novice full-back Ivan Quentin had been earmarked to bear the brunt of their assaults. When McCall sent Durie free, the full-back was nowhere as Durie cut the ball back to McCoist, who connected a split second before Egli. It was the thirteenth minute, and it was McCoist's thirteenth goal for Scotland.

With Quentin increasingly exposed, Scotland threatened for long spells. McCoist miscued badly. Durrant substituted for McClair, but the decisive goal came at the other end. Boyd lost his footing attempting to clear Sutter's cross, which was headed in by Knup. Worse was to follow. A free kick from thirty yards was powered past Goram by dead-ball specialist Georges Bregy.

Scotland fell apart. Richard Gough plucked the ball out of the air like a balloon and was sent off, the first player under Roxburgh and the first Scottish captain to be dismissed for 120 years. Gough later complained that the ball had reared up off a sprinkler.

Roxburgh offered no excuses for the defeat. 'We have lost a battle but not the war.'

SWITZERLAND (1) 3	SCOTLAND (1) 1
Knup 2, 71, Bregy 81	McCoist 13

SWITZERLAND: Pascolo, Hottiger, Quentin, Egli, Geiger, Bregy (Piffaretti), A Sutter, Ohrel, Knup (B Sutter), Sforza, Chapuisat.
SCOTLAND: Goram (Rangers), Gough (Rangers), Malpas (Dun U), McCall (Rangers), Boyd (Celtic) (*sub* Gallacher, Coventry), McPherson (Rangers), Durie (Spurs), McAllister (Leeds), McCoist (Rangers), McStay (Celtic), McClair (Man U) (*sub* Durrant, Rangers).

SCOTLAND v PORTUGAL
Wednesday, 14 October 1992   *Ibrox – 22,583*

Defeat in Berne had to be quickly rectified by victory at home. Refurbishment of the national stadium necessitated alternative venues. Several possibilities were mooted, pre-eminent among them Murrayfield and Ibrox. Murrayfield had the advantage of size and neutrality, but belonged to the wrong sport and was in the wrong city. Ibrox was in the right city but belonged to the wrong club. Friction between Glasgow Rangers and the SFA went back through the mists of time. But, strapped for choice, the SFA settled on Ibrox for Scotland's first three World Cup-ties.

Scotland's home record against Portugal read P6 W4 D1 L1. Portugal's last visit was in the 1980 qualifiers, when they had packed their defence and escaped with a 0-0 draw. Like Switzerland, Portugal had had a barren time in the World Cup, their appearance in the 1986 finals being their first for twenty years. In 1990 Portugal and Switzerland had shared the same qualifying zone, finishing third and fourth behind Belgium and Czechoslovakia. Having failed in the European qualifiers, Portugal looked to be building afresh.

At club level, Portugal were among the best. Porto had won the European Cup in 1987, Benfica reached the Final in 1990, and were just one win from the final again, in 1991.

The present match was special for Paul McStay, promoted to captain in the absence of the suspended Gough. It was the sixty-second cap for the Celtic skipper, equalling Danny McGrain's record for the most capped Celtic player. The team was depleted through the absence of the injured Dave McPherson and Stewart McKimmie, necessitating an untried central defensive partnership of Craig Levein and Derek Whyte. Though UEFA placed a ceiling of 40,000 on the Ibrox capacity, the stadium was barely half-full. Maybe those who stayed away knew something, though the match was overshadowed by the portentous clash between Rangers and Leeds in the European Cup.

Ex-England manager Bobby Robson, now with Sporting Lisbon, advised Roxburgh to hit Portugal with everything he had, and to stick a marker on danger-man Paulo Futre. Then with Atletico Madrid, Futre had shattered Manchester United's dreams in the Cup-Winners' Cup. Roxburgh, it appeared, discarded the advice, not liking to man-mark and preferring patience to power.

Roxburgh got it wrong. Portugal, by no means as negative as he predicted, secured a point without over-exerting themselves. The match was low-key, the atmosphere missing. Of Scotland's few chances, one came when McCoist killed a pass from McStay but couldn't direct his shot-on-the-turn on target. Otherwise, all Scotland had to show was a tame Levein header and long range pot-shots by McCall and McStay. When Kevin Gallacher beat Vitor Baia to Levein's long ball, it bounced unkindly for the Scotland forward. Scotland improved only marginally when Iain Durrant came on as a substitute. Though Portugal rarely penetrated the Scottish half, Futre missed the game's two best chances, one of which, near the end, saw the ball drift agonisingly close to Goram's post, the other being blocked by the keeper's legs.

The result opened a fresh inquest into the lacklustre performance of Ally McCoist, so prolific for Rangers. But McCoist was a player who thrived when his team steamrollered opponents, which Rangers did but Scotland did not.

Roxburgh put a brave face on a colourless display and a bad result. The one ray of hope came from Italy, who had been held at home, 2-2, by the Swiss.

SCOTLAND   (0) 0   PORTUGAL   (0) 0

SCOTLAND: Goram, Malpas, Boyd, McCall, Whyte, Levein, Gallacher (McClair), McStay, McCoist, McAllister, Collins (Durrant).
PORTUGAL: Vitor Baia, Jaoa Pinto, Helder, Veloso, Fernando Couto, Oceano, Vitor Paneira, Semedo (Figo), Domingos, Futre, Andre.

SCOTLAND v ITALY
Wednesday, 18 November 1992   *Ibrox – 33,029*

Scotland v Italy in the World Cup evoked memories of John Greig's last-gasp winner in 1965, during Italy's only previous visit to Scotland. That glorious win had not been enough. Scotland were blown away in the return. Indeed, Greig's stood as the only goal Scotland had ever scored against Italy.

Italy's record in the World Cup was daunting, thrice winners, most recently in 1982. They had failed to reach the finals only once, in 1958, when kept out by Northern Ireland. They had finished third in 1990, on home soil, but the pain of losing a semi-final to Argentina on penalties had sent the national side into a trough of despond. This manifested itself when failing to reach the 1992 European finals, dropping three points to unsung Norway. Italy were rebuilding, but were novices at the art of qualifying. As holders and hosts in 1986 and 1990, they hadn't been asked to qualify for twelve years.

Glancing through the Italian eleven, only three players remained from the side that beat England 2-1 to claim third place in 1990 – Maldini, the veteran Milan sweeper, Franco Baresi, and Juventus wonder-boy Roberto Baggio. The rest were comparatively unknown. Following the draw against Switzerland, manager Arrigo Sacchi dropped his captain, Gianluca Vialli, a £12 million Juventus buy, and goalkeeper Marchegiani. Vialli was the world's second most expensive footballer. The most expensive, Milan's Gianluigi Lentini, played. Sampdoria's Gianluca Pagliuca kept goal. With Italy having little need to export her star players, the entire team was home based.

The cautious Roxburgh usually delayed naming his side until the last moment. So wrecked by injury was his squad that he now did so two days early. Gordon Durie was included, despite being accused of feigning an injury for Tottenham (Durie would be cleared). The boldest inclusion was that of Hearts' promising Alan McLaren, just twenty-one, who was given the daunting task of marking Baggio. Scotland looked to the lively Durrant, restored to fitness, to prise open the Italian defence.

Typically, optimism boiled to the surface. Italy would be whipped and Scotland would march on. Realistically, this was Scotland's last chance. In World Cup terms, a draw would be a disaster.

Typically, too, Scotland gave their all, knowing that no shame would attend being beaten by Italy. The passion was there from the start, though Scotland had to survive an uncertain opening. Baggio, well marshalled by McLaren, shot tamely at Goram. Scotland's best chances fell to Gordon Durie. When Maldini's errant header fell to him, he drove the ball inches too high. Durie scuffed another chance, screwing the ball out towards the corner flag.

Italy had to reshuffle when Alberto di Chiara was stretchered off, following a lunge by Maurice Malpas. Costacurta, the sub, brought Milan's representation up to six. McAllister almost connected when fastening on to Goram's clearance, and substitute Eoin Jess was thwarted by a desperate tackle from Baresi. For Italy, Lentini had two chances to prove his worth, but twice he dallied in front of goal. Eranio almost snatched a late winner when he sprung the offside trap, but that would have been cruel to Scotland.

Ideally, Roxburgh desired Scotland to win at home and draw away. By such standards, Scotland were now three points behind schedule, and that chasm looked unbridgeable.

SCOTLAND   (0) 0   ITALY   (0) 0

SCOTLAND: Goram, McPherson, Malpas, McStay, McLaren, Whyte, Durie (Jess), McAllister, McCoist, Durrant (J Robertson), Boyd.
ITALY: Pagliuca, Mannini, di Chiara (Costacurta), Maldini, Baresi, Lentini, Albertini, Eranio, Bianchi, Signori (Donadoni), R Baggio.

SCOTLAND v MALTA
Wednesday, 17 February 1993   *Ibrox – 35,490*

Malta's manager, Philip Psaila, didn't take kindly to his players being dubbed 'rabbits'. Not that Scotland could feel confident about 'killing' anybody. They had faced Malta twice without distinction prior to the 1990 finals, drawing 1-1 and scraping home by the odd goal in three.

Switzerland had already accounted for Malta, 3-0. Victory would do little for Scotland's chances, for all their rivals would surely beat Malta too. In twenty years Malta had never beaten anybody in the World Cup, but they had just picked up a rare point, 0-0 at home to Estonia. Malta had lost only six goals in four matches, and showed signs of being tight at the back if lamentable up front. Malta's one mercenary, Carmel Busuttil, played for Genk in Belgium. He was credited with fifty-six caps and sixteen international goals.

With Durie injured for Spurs at the weekend, Roxburgh announced a first cap for Eoin Jess, the young Aberdeen striker who had been making a name for himself. Pat Nevin won an unexpected recall. He had dropped out of the English Premier League to sign for Tranmere Rovers and, at twenty-nine, presumed his international days had gone. But, as Roxburgh pointed out, Nevin was the best orthodox winger available. It was mid-February, but Ally McCoist had already bagged over forty goals for Rangers. He shrugged off a thigh strain to play. McPherson (groin) and McLaren (calf) were less fortunate. A virus running through the squad as they prepared at St Johnstone's MacDiarmid Park threatened to deplete the squad still more. Alex McLeish's first, and last, outing of the campaign was his twenty-seventh in the World Cup, a Scottish record.

The improbably high attendance was down to seventeen thousand tickets being distributed to schoolchildren, whose shrill squeals – reminiscent of an audience at a schoolboy international – invited hands to be clamped over ears.

Scotland's Under-21s defeated Malta's 3-0, and that was also the result of the seniors. Scotland looked useful, but only when no account was taken of the opposition. McStay and Jess had fine matches, the only pity being that Jess failed to score. McCoist scored twice, taking his international tally to fifteen, the most Scottish goals of any Rangers player. McCoist's first followed Nevin's reverse pass to Jess; his second converted Jess's low shot at the far post. In between, McAllister had squandered a penalty after McCoist had been fouled by Buhagiar. The spot-kick came back off the bar. Scotland's third goal came in the dying minutes. Jess won a corner, which McCoist headed down to Nevin. At the final whistle all the talk was of Eoin Jess, a star in the making.

A month later Italy put the score into perspective, blitzing Malta 6-1.

SCOTLAND (1) 3   MALTA   (0) 0
McCoist 15, 68, Nevin 84

SCOTLAND: Goram, McPherson (J Robertson), Boyd, McStay, McLeish, McLaren, Nevin, McAllister (Ferguson), McCoist, Collins, Jess.
MALTA: Cluett, S Vella, Buhagiar (E Camilleri), Galea, Brincat, Buttigieg, Busuttil, Saliba, J Camilleri, Laferla, Sultana (R Vella).

PORTUGAL v SCOTLAND
Wednesday, 28 April 1993   *Lisbon – 28,000*

This was Scotland's last chance. A win in Lisbon might, just might, rekindle hopes of stealing a place in USA. At the very least, a victory would put the skids under Portugal, whose own chances had been slashed by losing 1-3 at home to Italy. Portugal and Scotland each had four points from four games, but were now six points adrift of the top two. But no Scotland team had ever won in Portugal; indeed, even to score seemed beyond them. Scotland had managed one goal in four straight defeats since 1959.

Roxburgh's main selection problems were in midfield, where countless aspirants were jostling for pole position – McStay, Collins, McClair, Durrant, McCall, Ian Ferguson. Eoin Jess had broken his ankle. Kevin Gallacher was back, looking sharp after his £1.5 million transfer to Kenny Dalglish's Blackburn Rovers. Roxburgh looked to his Rangers contingent – veterans of ten undefeated games in the European Cup – to provide the backbone. He dubbed Goram the 'base' of his 'Rangers spine'.

Roxburgh's homework told him that Portugal were dangerous at set pieces, that they seldom scored from open play, and that Benfica's Paulo Futre and Sporting Lisbon's Jorge Cadete – twenty-eight caps, fifteen goals – would be a handful for McPherson and Levein. Other than Oceano, of Spanish club Real Sociedad, and Barros, of Monaco, the Portuguese team was home based.

Lisbon's Stadium of Light, in journalese, turned the lights out on Scotland, who by the end were totally eclipsed. Five minutes into the game McCoist's casual lay-off to McStay was snapped up by Rui Costa, who speared the ball into the path of Rui Barros, who thrashed it past Goram. Portugal had not, after all, needed a set piece to score. Thereafter, one Scottish move after another broke down in its infancy. When Gallacher did beat Vitor Baia, a linesman's flag was raised. At the other end, Fernando Couto saw two efforts beaten out.

Roxburgh must have been impatient for half-time, but before his players could seek sanctuary Portugal scored again. A dazzling left-side move saw Futre lure Goram off his line. Futre's pass (or shot?) fell neatly for Cadete.

It would be worth a dime for Roxburgh's half-time comments. It would be worth considerably more for his thoughts forty-five minutes later, by which time his team had been flayed alive. Levein had done a manful job policing Futre, but when a thigh-strain forced Levein to depart from the fray Scotland fell apart. Portugal smashed three goals in five minutes. Futre poached the first, after Paulo Sousa hit a post; and Futre himself made two goals for others.

Scotland's night of misery was completed when McCoist – who, in the midst of the goal-glut had forced a fine save from Baia – was carried off with what was later diagnosed as a fractured leg.

Not since 1973 had Scotland lost 0-5 (to England), and not since 1961 had that margin of defeat been exceeded (3-9 v England). Not since losing 0-7 to Uruguay in 1954 had Scotland been so humiliated by a 'foreign' team.

PORTUGAL (2) 5	SCOTLAND (0) 0
Rui Barros 5, 70,	
Cadete 45, 72, Futre 67	

PORTUGAL: Vitor Baia, Abel Xavier, Jorge Costa, Rui Costa (Veloso), Fernando Couto, Oceano, Rui Barros, Sousa, Semedo, Futre, Cadete (Domingos).
SCOTLAND: Goram, Gough, McInally, McPherson, McKimmie, Levein (Nevin), McStay, McCall, McCoist, Collins (Durrant), Gallacher.

ESTONIA v SCOTLAND
Wednesday, 19 May 1993   *Tallinn – 5,100*

The domestic season was over. It ended in despair for Rangers, so near yet so far in the European Cup. It ended in despair for Andy Roxburgh. Results indicated he was presiding over the worst Scottish team for a generation. Scots in their mid-twenties had never known their national team to miss the World Cup finals. They had grown up to expect. Players like Eoin Jess were not even born when Scotland last failed to reach a World Cup. At long last fans were reacquainted with failure. Worse, they were reacquainted with humiliation, something they could only have read about in the past.

There was no more putting on brave faces. Scotland's World Cup hopes were dead, though eternal optimists kept the candle burning. To have even a fighting chance of qualification, teams clearly had to take eight points off Malta and Estonia, plus a minimum of six from the six games against the front runners. That required a total of fourteen, just to be in with a shout. Scotland could still reach fourteen, if they won their last five, including Switzerland at home and Italy away. Even that might not be enough.

Rangers knew the score. Their seven Scottish internationals had withstood the strain of forty-four league games, ten domestic cup-ties, and ten European Cup-ties, in addition to the demands of the national team. They were in no fit shape and pulled out of the trip to Estonia.

Estonia sounds like a Hans Christian Andersen sort of place, and the capital, Tallinn, indeed, has a charm of its own. One of the three Baltic republics to have broken away from the Soviet Union, Estonia were setting out on the big bad road of international football with its dreams and broken hearts. Most of the national side played for a team called 'Flora'. Estonia had set the tone with their first match, crushed 0-6 at home to Switzerland. They had even rewritten the records, losing 0-1 to Malta, providing the visitors with their first World Cup win. That result reduced Estonia to the category not of minnows, but tadpoles. Estonia were still searching for their first goal in Group 1.

With Scotland tired and dispirited after a long season and thankless results, the back-to-back fixtures with Estonia were an unwelcome bother. Roxburgh fended off speculation that he might, or should resign. After all, Scotland were still mathematically alive. Shorn of Rangers players and building for the future, it was a new look Scotland eleven that he sent out in the almost tropical heat of Tallinn's Kadriorg Stadium. Gunn, Hendry, Bowman, Wright, Irvine, Booth and John Robertson would surely not have played had Scotland been in the hunt. Also in the squad, though not picked, was Dundee United's Christian Dailly, at nineteen the youngest player ever selected by Roxburgh. The talented Duncan Ferguson, also of Dundee United, might have played had he been fit.

Scotland were on a hiding to nothing, with everything to lose, nothing to gain. They might have scored inside a minute. Kaljend's weak back-pass set up Robertson, who shot equally weakly at Poom. In this match Scotland forsook guile in favour of the big welly, tactics which almost rebounded against them. From Estonia's first corner, Kallaste shot against Bryan Gunn's bar. The ball bounced down, up, and out. The linesman was not Russian and shook his head.

Half-time was approaching when Robertson's cross to the far post heralded Gallacher's first international goal. Not till the hour did Scotland put the game beyond Estonia, when Gallacher set up John Collins. Aberdeen's Scott Booth, on for Hearts' John Robertson, seized on a deflected cross by Pittodrie team-mate Wright to open his account for Scotland.

ESTONIA (0) 0   SCOTLAND (1) 3
                        Gallacher 43, Collins 59,
                        Booth 73

ESTONIA: Poom, R Kallaste, Lensalu, Prins, Kaljend, T Kallaste, Borisov, Kristal (Hepner), Reim, Veensalu (Putsov), Bragin.
SCOTLAND: Gunn, Wright (McLaren), Boyd, McStay, Hendry, Irvine, Gallacher, Bowman, J Robertson (Booth), McClair, Collins.

SCOTLAND v ESTONIA
Wednesday, 2 June 1993   *Aberdeen – 14,307*

June is no time for World Cup qualifiers, when players' minds are elsewhere. It was now that behind-the-scenes tensions between Roxburgh and Richard

Gough were publicly aired. Although Roxburgh had granted the player most of his sixty-one caps, and installed him as captain, Gough now refused to play under him. What's more, Gough told the world. Roxburgh found it hard enough motivating his players without that kind of distraction.

The SFA selected Aberdeen's Pittodrie Stadium for this less than heady encounter. The first scare was Scotland's. The diminutive Reim darted between Irvine and Hendry to force a sharp save from Gunn, back on the ground where he undertook his apprenticeship. When Olumets' corner was turned in the net by Rajala, an intoxicated Estonian fan dashed on the pitch to celebrate. His joy was cut short by a linesman's raised flag.

The bemused spectators were soon clapping wildly. An incisive attack down the left took Nevin behind the Estonian defence. Brian McClair was on hand to score his second goal in thirty internationals.

Goal number two was even more impressive. Pat Nevin had been needed for Tranmere's (unsuccessful) promotion play-offs and missed the trip to Estonia. He celebrated his recall by meeting John Collins' pass with an exquisite chip.

Victory might have been beyond Estonia, but a goal was not. Sergei Bragin, a half-time substitute, gathered the ball in midfield and drove a pile-driver past Gunn. The strike uncorked the kind of celebrations normally reserved for world champions. Scotland were knocked out of their stride and might have suffered yet greater damage had Marco Kristal not knocked Nevin off his feet. The Bulgarian referee gave the penalty, and Nevin performed the honours.

Scotland trooped off, doubtless in dread of a future *Trivial Pursuit* question: 'Against whom did Estonia score their only goal in ten World Cup matches?'

SCOTLAND (2) 3   ESTONIA (0) 1
McClair 16, Nevin 27, 72 pen   Bragin 57

SCOTLAND: Gunn, McLaren (J Robertson), Boyd, McStay, Hendry, Irvine, Gallacher, Ferguson (Booth), McClair, Collins, Nevin.
ESTONIA: Poom, R Kallaste, Lensalu (Bragin), Prins, Kaljend, T Kallaste, Borisov, Kristal, Reim, Olumets (Veensalu), Rajala.

SCOTLAND v SWITZERLAND
Wednesday, 8 September 1993   *Aberdeen – 24,000*

The Group 1 table showed Scotland to be just two points off second place. It was a mirage, of course, true only from a distance. All other contenders would beat Estonia home and away as well, so, relatively, Scotland had not advanced one jot. Scotland's candle would stay flickering only if they beat Switzerland at Pittodrie, in what would be Roxburgh's sixty-first game in charge, equalling Jock Stein's total as full-time manager between 1978 and 1985.

Though history was with Scotland – the Swiss managing one draw in five visits – current form favoured Switzerland. Under Roy Hodgson they were still unbeaten in Group 1, amassing twelve points out of fourteen. Besides, any team that could take three points off the Italians were no mugs.

Injuries permitting, Roxburgh plumped for an inexperienced if adventurous side, captained by Gary McAllister in the absence of the injured Paul McStay. Alan McLaren was still unemployed after keyhole surgery on his knee, while Duncan Ferguson, Rangers' £4 million signing from Dundee United, feared a prison sentence after being convicted for his part in a pub brawl. Rangers' ex-Aberdeen full-back David Robertson turned out in the stadium where he made his name. Gordon Durie and Scott Booth were paired up front.

Scotland set off with an intricate move involving McAllister and Booth, whose cross was volleyed wide by Durie. The Swiss spurned ideas of playing for a draw, encouraging a fast open game. Bowman and Robertson cleared from Adrian Knup, while at the other end Herr headed out from under his crossbar. Ten minutes from the interval Booth laid off Durie's cross for McAllister, but with the goal gaping his shot struck Pascolo's legs.

Scotland scored soon after the change of ends. Robertson caught the Swiss defence square, slipped the ball to Collins who shot through the advancing keeper's legs. When Nevin skirted three defenders he might have set up a second, but opted to pass to Booth rather than the better placed Durie. Instead of being two down, Switzerland were soon level. Gunn suffered a rush of blood in sprinting from goal to topple Sforza, who was headed nowhere and whom Robertson was covering. French referee Quiniou pointed to the spot to hand Switzerland their lifeline. Bregy scored, sending 3,000 Swiss fans delirious.

SCOTLAND (0) 1   SWITZERLAND (0) 1
  Collins 50   Bregy 69 pen

SCOTLAND: Gunn, McKimmie, D Robertson, Levein, Irvine, Nevin, Bowman (O'Donnell), McAllister, Collins, Booth (Jess), Durie.
SWITZERLAND: Pascolo, Quentin, Rothenbuhler (Grassi), Herr, Geiger, Bregy (Sylvestre), Sutter, Ohrel, Sforza, Knup, Chapuisat.

ITALY v SCOTLAND
Wednesday, 13 October 1993   *Rome – 61,178*

So Switzerland, having slammed the door on Scotland in Berne, a year later finally turned out the lights. The Scottish public was remarkably sanguine, accepting their team's demise with good grace, sparing Andy Roxburgh the kind of tabloid filth that would await Graham Taylor. Roxburgh had done the best he could with the players at his disposal. SFA chief executive Jim Farry

John Collins gives Scotland hope at Pittodrie. (v Switzerland)

announced that the manager's position was secure, but after pondering his position Roxburgh stepped down. His assistant, Craig Brown, was asked to carry the team through their final two matches.

The Scottish club scene was likewise in the throes of revolution. Liam Brady quit as manager of Celtic, cursed with living in Rangers' shadow, and the Scottish League was refashioned, shrinking the Premier League, but creating an extra division and inviting two Highland League clubs out of the cold.

Brown's first act was to relieve Paul McStay of the captaincy and entrust it to Gary McAllister. McStay, troubled by events on and off the park at Celtic, and in poor form, would not even play. To boost morale Brown suggested Scotland had better midfield players than Italy. But then pigs can fly.

Three Aberdeen players lined up – Stewart McKimmie and Brian Irvine in defence, and Eoin Jess, happily recovered from his broken ankle. Gunn held his place in goal. Alan McLaren had kept a grip on Roberto Baggio at Hampden, and was now asked to do so again. Stuart McCall enjoyed a return to international duty. Iain Durrant's fitful Scotland career resumed from the substitutes' bench.

The match may have been meaningless to Scotland, but it was life or death to Italy, who had to beat Scotland and Portugal to qualify. The Italians speculated on how Scotland might approach the match, half-hearted or defiant.

By picking no players from Roma, Arrigo Sacchi ensured that many irate Romans thronging the Olympic Stadium would be rooting for Scotland! Italian football, heavily regionalised, was like that.

The game started with an explosion for Italy, a snigger for the Scots. Just three minutes had passed when Roberto Baggio shielded the ball and laid it into the path of Donadoni, whose low shot ought not to have beaten an international goalkeeper, but which beat Bryan Gunn at his near post.

That was all Italy needed to turn on the style. On the quarter hour they scored a splendid second. Baggio's deft pass cleaved open the Scottish defence and Lazio's Casiraghi showed perfect timing to beat Irvine and Gunn with one touch. A sublime goal, but again, Gunn might have saved.

That goal of genius promptly sparked a comical one. When Pagliuca failed to hold Jess's stinging drive, Kevin Gallacher made such a hash of poking back the rebound that he almost missed.

They all count, as they say, and for an hour Scotland stretched the Italians to the limit. Pagliuca scooped away one Durie effort, while another cannoned into substitute Durrant when it may have been net-bound. Jess had been withdrawn, with Craig Brown stating publicly, 'he was out of his depth.' At the other end, Baggio was flattened by Boyd, and might have won a penalty.

The match was not settled till ten minutes from time when Roberto Baggio set up his third goal of the night. Eranio's thunderous strike exonerated Gunn.

The reason for Scotland's demise in Group 1 was now apparent. They had failed to beat any of the three teams above them, and lost to all three away.

ITALY (2) 3	SCOTLAND (1) 1
Donadoni 3, Casiraghi 16,	Gallacher 17
Eranio 80	

ITALY: Pagliuca, Mussi, Costacurta, Baresi, Benarrivo, Eranio, D Baggio, Donadoni, Stroppa, Casiraghi, R Baggio.
SCOTLAND: Gunn, McKimmie, Irvine, McLaren, Boyd, Bowman, McAllister, McCall, Durie, Gallacher, Jess (Durrant).

MALTA v SCOTLAND
Wednesday, 17 November 1993   *Valletta – 7,000*

A trip to Malta would have been welcome had qualification depended upon it. Jack Charlton's Republic of Ireland had secured their place in Italia '90 by winning in Valletta. For Scotland, now, it was the biggest of non-events. On a night when the World Cup fates of England, Wales, Ireland and all of Europe would be settled, Malta v Scotland would be relegated to the odd centimetre in the world's football press. Somewhere in some tiny paragraph or two it was observed that Craig Brown had been confirmed as the new Scotland manager. The SFA were sticking to their policy of continuity.

Jim Leighton had been performing capably since signing for Hibernian, but surely even he could not have anticipated an international call-up, four years after his error against Brazil. He would now be the *ninth* goalkeeper called into the Scottish squad over the past year or so, the others being Goram, Gunn, Main, Marshall, Maxwell, Smith, Walker and Geddes. Though Craig Brown introduced just one fresh face – Dundee United's Billy McKinlay – the tally of players called upon in ten qualifiers now stood at thirty-five. Of these, none was ever-present: in fact, none had started more than seven matches. In this transitional era it was hard to know who was in and who was out.

Whether Valletta's Ta'Qali Stadium witnessed the death of an old Scottish team or the birth of a new one remains to be seen. Craig Brown's reign got off to a predictable win. McAllister contributed to Scotland's first goal – touching the ball into the path of Billy McKinlay, who flashed a shot into the net from twenty-five yards – and the second, placing a free kick sweetly on to Hendry's head.

The evening would end in darkness, not only for England and Wales, but for France, knocked out in the last minute by Bulgaria, and for Portugal, beaten in Italy. For the first time since the war, no British nation would challenge for the World Cup.

MALTA   (0) 0   SCOTLAND   (1) 2
                            McKinlay 16, Hendry 74

MALTA: Cluett, S Vella, Buhagiar (Saliba), Galea, Brincat, Buttigieg, Busuttil, Spiteri, Suda (Scerri), Laferla, Gregory.
SCOTLAND: Leighton, McLaren, McKinnon, Durrant (Boyd), Hendry, Irvine, Ferguson, McKinlay (Booth), Nevin, McAllister, Gallacher.

Qualifying Group 1

			Home				Away				
	P	W	D	L	F	A	W	D	L	F	A	Pts
ITALY	10	4	1	0	14	4	3	1	1	8	3	16
SWITZERLAND	10	4	1	0	12	2	2	2	1	11	4	15
Portugal	10	4	0	1	14	3	2	2	1	4	2	14
Scotland	10	2	3	0	7	2	2	0	3	7	11	11
Malta	10	0	1	4	1	7	1	0	4	2	16	3
Estonia	10	0	0	5	0	15	0	1	4	1	12	1

Other group results

Estonia v Switzerland	0-6		Malta v Switzerland	0-2
Italy v Switzerland	2-2		Switzerland v Italy	1-0
Malta v Estonia	0-0		Estonia v Malta	0-1
Switzerland v Malta	3-0		Portugal v Malta	4-0
Malta v Italy	1-2		Estonia v Portugal	0-2
Malta v Portugal	0-1		Estonia v Italy	0-3
Portugal v Italy	1-3		Portugal v Switzerland	1-0
Italy v Malta	6-1		Portugal v Estonia	3-0
Switzerland v Portugal	1-1		Italy v Portugal	1-0
Italy v Estonia	2-0		Switzerland v Estonia	4-0

Scotland appearances and goalscorers (substitute appearances in brackets)
World Cup qualifying rounds 1994

	Apps	Goals		Apps	Goals
Boyd T	7 (1)	–	Levein C *	3	–
McAllister G	7	–	McKimmie S *	3	–
McStay P *†	7	–	Malpas M *†	3	–
Gallacher K	6 (1)	2	Durrant I *	2 (4)	–
Collins J	6	2	Ferguson I *	2 (1)	–
Goram A *	5	–	Gough R *†	2	–
Irvine B	5	–	Whyte D	2	–
McCoist A *	5	3	Booth S	1 (3)	1
McLaren A	4 (1)	–	Robertson J	1 (3)	–
Nevin P *	4 (1)	3	Leighton J *†	1	–
Durie G *	4	–	McInally J	1	–
Gunn B	4	–	McKinlay W	1	1
McCall S *	4	–	McKinnon R	1	–
McPherson D *	4	–	McLeish A *†‡	1	–
Jess E	3 (2)	–	Robertson D	1	–
McClair B *	3 (1)	1	Wright S	1	–
Bowman D	3	–	O'Donnell P	– (1)	–
Hendry C	3	1			

* Appeared in 1990 World Cup.   *129 apps   14 goals*
† Appeared in 1986 World Cup.   *93 Scottish League*
‡ Appeared in 1982 World Cup.   *36 English League*
                                                  35 players used

Appendix 1
Clubs supplying players in World Cups 1950-94 (includes qualifying rounds and final stages)

	Club	Caps	Players	Caps	Other clubs
1	**Rangers**	167	McCoist A	14	
			Caldow E	12	
			Greig J	12	
			Cooper D	9	+1 Motherwell
			Gough R	8	+7 Dundee U
			Jardine S	8	
			Durrant I	7	
			McKinnon R	7	
			Young G	7	
			Baxter J	6	+1 Sunderland
			Cox S	6	
			Forsyth T	6	
			Ferguson I	5	
			Goram A	5	+1 Hibs
			Henderson W	5	
			Johnston M	5	+4 Celtic, +5 Nantes
			Wilson D	5	
			Baird S	4	
			Brand R	4	
			McCall S	4	+3 Everton
			McPherson D	4	+5 Hearts
			Stein C	4	
			McColl I	3	
			Shearer R	3	
			Waddell W	3	
			Woodburn W	3	
			Provan D	2	
			Scott A	2	+1 Everton
			Forrest J	1	
			Johnston W	1	+3 WBA
			McMillan I	1	
			Robertson D	1	
			32 players		
2	**Celtic**	158	McStay P	24	
			McGrain D	16	
			Aitken R	15	+3 Newcastle
			Evans R	10	
			McNeill W	10	
			Dalglish K	9	+17 Liverpool
			Boyd T	8	
			Collins R	7	+1 Leeds
			Collins J	6	

		Crerand P	5	+3 Man U
		Hay D	5	
		Murdoch R	5	
		Fernie W	4	
		Gemmell T	4	
		Hughes J	4	
		Johnston M	4	+5 Nantes, +5 Rangers
		Johnstone J	4	
		Lennox R	3	
		Provan D	3	
		McPhail J	2	
		Mochan N	2	
		Chalmers S	1	
		Connelly G	1	
		Haughney M	1	
		Hunter A	1	
		Kennedy J	1	
		Macari L	1	+3 Man U
		McKay D	1	
		Simpson R	1	
		29 players		
3	**Aberdeen** 107	McLeish A	27	
		Miller W	23	
		Leighton J	11	+10 Man U, +1 Hibs
		Strachan G	7	+8 Man U, +1 Leeds
		Bett J	6	+5 Lokeren
		Irvine B	5	
		Jess E	5	
		McKimmie S	5	
		Booth S	4	
		Harper J	3	
		Kennedy S	3	
		Leggat G	2	
		Martin F	2	
		Clark R	1	
		McGarr E	1	
		Nicholas C	1	+5 Arsenal
		Wright S	1	
		17 players		
4	**Manchester Utd** 68	Leighton J	10	+11 Aberdeen, +1 Hibs
		Buchan M	9	
		McClair B	9	
		Strachan G	8	+7 Aberdeen, +1 Leeds
		Law D	6	+2 Torino, +3 Man C
		Morgan W	6	

			Albiston A	5	
			Holton J	4	
			Jordan J	4	+9 Leeds, +2 Milan
			Crerand P	3	+5 Celtic
			Macari L	3	+1 Celtic
			Burns F	1	
			12 players		
5	**Liverpool**	67	Dalglish K	17	+9 Celtic
			Nicol S	14	
			Hansen A	10	
			Souness G	9	+9 Sampdoria
			Younger T	6	
			Gillespie G	4	
			Liddell W	3	
			St John I	2	
			Lawrence T	1	
			Yeats R	1	
			10 players		
6	**Leeds**	58	Bremner W	15	
			Jordan J	9	+4 Man U, +2 Milan
			McAllister G	7	
			Gray F	6	+5 Nott'm F
			Lorimer P	6	
			Harvey D	5	
			Gray E	4	
			McQueen G	4	
			Collins R	1	+7 Celtic
			Strachan G	1	+7 Aberdeen, +8 Man U
			10 players		
7	**Dundee United**	44	Malpas M	20	
			Gough R	7	+8 Rangers
			Narey D	6	
			Bowman D	3	
			Sturrock P	3	
			Bannon E	2	
			Gallacher K	1	+2 Coventry, +5 Blackburn
			McInally J	1	
			McKinlay W	1	
			9 players		
8	**Hibernian**	30	Blackley J	3	
			McLeod J	3	
			Ormond W	3	
			Reilly L	3	

			Smith G	3	
			Turnbull E	3	
			Brownlie J	2	
			Johnstone R	2	
			Martin N	2	+1 Sunderland
			Cormack P	1	
			Goram A	1	+5 Rangers
			Hamilton W	1	
			Leighton J	1	+11 Aberdeen, +10 Man U
			Rough A	1	+17 Partick
			Stanton P	1	
			15 players		
9	**Tottenham**	28	Archibald S	9	+3 Barcelona
			Gilzean A	8	
			Brown W	5	+1 Dundee
			Durie G	4	+3 Chelsea
			White J	2	
			5 players		
10	**Nott'm Forest**	25	Robertson J	11	
			Gray F	5	+6 Leeds
			Burns K	4	+2 Birmingham
			Gemmill A	3	+2 Derby, +4 Birmingham
			Imlach S	2	
			5 players		
11	**Hearts**	24	McLaren A	5	
			McPherson D	5	+4 Rangers
			Levein C	4	
			Robertson J	4	
			Mackay D	2	
			Murray J	2	
			Bauld W	1	
			Ford D	1	
			8 players		
11	**Partick Thistle**	24	Rough A	17	+1 Hibs
			McKenzie J	4	
			Davidson J	2	
			Forsyth A	1	
			4 players		
13	**Manchester City**	19	Hartford A	10	+3 Everton
			Donachie W	6	
			Law D	3	+2 Torino, +6 Man U
			3 players		

14	Chelsea	18	McCreadie E	8	
			Cooke C	5	+1 Dundee
			Durie G	3	+4 Spurs
			Speedie D	2	+3 Coventry
			4 players		

15	Everton	17	Sharp G	5	
			Hartford A	3	+10 Man C
			McCall S	3	+4 Rangers
			Gray A	1	+6 Wolves, +1 Villa
			Nevin P	1	+5 Tranmere
			Parker A	1	+1 Falkirk
			Rioch B	1	+4 Derby
			Scott A	1	+2 Rangers
			Young A	1	
			9 players		

16	Dundee	15	Cowie D	6	
			Hamilton A	5	
			Brown W	1	+5 Spurs
			Cooke C	1	+5 Chelsea
			Robertson H	1	
			Ure I	1	
			6 players		

17	Blackpool	14	Mudie J	7	
			Brown A	4	
			Farm G	3	
			3 players		

18	Arsenal	10	Nicholas C	5	+1 Aberdeen
			Graham G	2	
			Herd D	2	
			Forbes A	1	
			4 players		

18	Coventry	10	Hutchison T	4	
			Speedie D	3	+2 Chelsea
			Gallacher K	2	+1 Dun U, +5 Blackburn
			Carr W	1	
			4 players		

18	Derby County	10	Rioch B	4	+1 Everton
			Steel W	3	
			Gemmill A	2	+3 Forest, +4 Birmingham

			Masson D	1	+3 QPR
			4 players		
21	**Birmingham**	9	Gemmill A	4	+2 Derby, +3 Forest
			Herriot J	3	
			Burns K	2	+4 Forest
			3 players		
21	**Sampdoria**	9	Souness G	9	+9 Liverpool
			1 player		
23	**Blackburn**	8	Gallacher K	5	+1 Dundee U, +2 Coventry
			Hendry C	3	
			2 players		
23	**Ipswich**	8	Wark J	6	
			Brazil A	2	
			2 players		
23	**Preston**	8	Docherty T	6	
			Cunningham W	2	
			2 players		
26	**Clyde**	7	Ring T	4	
			Robertson A	2	
			Linwood A	1	
			3 players		
26	**Norwich**	7	Gunn B	4	
			Fleck R	2	
			Bone J	1	
			3 players		
26	**Wolverhampton**	7	Gray A	6	+1 Villa, +1 Everton
			Curran H	1	
			2 players		
29	**Motherwell**	6	Quinn P	2	
			Cooper D	1	+9 Rangers
			McKinnon R	1	
			O'Donnell P	1	
			Pettigrew W	1	
			5 players		
29	**West Ham**	6	McAvennie F	4	
			Stewart R	2	
			2 players		

31	**Charlton**	5	Hewie J	5	
			1 player		
31	**Bor' Dortmund**	5	MacLeod M	5	
			1 player		
31	**Lokeren**	5	Bett J	5	+6 Aberdeen
			1 player		
31	**Nantes**	5	Johnston M	5	+4 Celtic, +5 Rangers
			1 player		
31	**Newcastle**	5	Aitken R	3	+15 Celtic
			Brennan F	2	
			2 players		
31	**Tranmere**	5	Nevin P	5	+1 Everton
			1 player		
37	**East Fife**	4	Aitken G	2	+1 Sunderland
			Fleming C	1	
			Morris H	1	
			3 players		
37	**WBA**	4	Johnston W	3	+1 Rangers
			Fraser D	1	
			2 players		
39	**Airdrie**	3	Leslie L	3	
			1 player		
39	**Aston Villa**	3	Evans A	1	
			Gray A	1	+6 Wolves, +1 Everton
			McInally A	1	+3 Bayern
			3 players		
39	**Barcelona**	3	Archibald S	3	+9 Spurs
			1 player		
39	**Bayern Münich**	3	McInally A	3	+1 Villa
			1 player		
39	**Burnley**	3	Aird J	2	
			Blacklaw A	1	
			2 players		

39	**Kilmarnock**	3	Forsyth C	1	
			McGrory J	1	
			McLean T	1	
			3 players		
39	**Morton**	3	Cowan J	3	
			1 player		
39	**QPR**	3	Masson D	3	+1 Derby
			1 player		
39	**St Mirren**	3	Thomson W	2	
			Telfer W	1	
			2 players		
39	**Sunderland**	3	Aitken G	1	+2 East Fife
			Baxter J	1	+6 Rangers
			Martin N	1	+2 Hibs
			3 players		
49	**Middlesbrough**	2	Whyte D	2	
49	**AC Milan**	2	Jordan J	2	+9 Leeds, +4 Man U
49	**Portsmouth**	2	Henderson J	2	
49	**Sheffield United**	2	Colquhoun E	2	
49	**Torino**	2	Law D	2	+3 Man C, +6 Man U
54	**Bolton**	1	Moir W	1	
54	**Dunfermline**	1	Connachan E	1	
54	**Falkirk**	1	Parker A	1	+1 Everton
54	**Huddersfield**	1	Watson J	1	
54	**Leicester**	1	Gibson D	1	
54	**Third Lanark**	1	Mason J	1	

59 teams   *1072*

Appendix 2
Scotland World Cup goalscorers 1950-94 (includes qualifying rounds and final stages)

Name	Goals	Apps	Name	Goals	Apps
Johnston, Maurice	9	14	McKinlay, Billy	1	1
Jordan, Joe	7	15	Henderson, Jackie	1	2
Dalglish, Kenny	7	26	Johnstone, Bobby	1	2
Stein, Colin	6	4	McPhail, John	1	2
Mudie, Jackie	6	7	Murray, Jimmy	1	2
Law, Denis	5	11	Robertson, Archie	1	2
McCoist, Ally	5	14	Harper, Joe	1	3
Robertson, John	4	11	Hendry, Colin	1	3
Morris, Henry	3	1	Ormond, Willie	1	3
St John, Ian	3	2	Provan, Davie	1	3
Brand, Ralph	3	4	Scott, Alec	1	3
Nevin, Pat	3	6	Smith, Gordon	1	3
Wark, John	3	6	Steel, Billy	1	3
Gilzean, Alan	3	8	Sturrock, Paul	1	3
McStay, Paul	3	24	Baird, Sam	1	4
Fleming, Charlie	2	1	Booth, Scott	1	4
Young, Alex	2	1	Gemmell, Tommy	1	4
Herd, David	2	2	Gray, Eddie	1	4
Reilly, Lawrie	2	3	Holton, Jim	1	4
Waddell, Willie	2	3	Johnstone, Jimmy	1	4
Brown, Allan	2	4	Macari, Lou	1	4
Murdoch, Bobby	2	5	McAvennie, Frank	1	4
Collins, John	2	6	Masson, Don	1	4
Lorimer, Peter	2	6	Henderson, Willie	1	5
Collins, Bobby	2	8	Hewie, John	1	5
Gallacher, Kevin	2	8	Wilson, Davie	1	5
Gemmill, Archie	2	9	Morgan, Willie	1	6
Cooper, Davie	2	10	Narey, David	1	6
McNeill, Billy	2	10	Nicholas, Charlie	1	6
Greig, John	2	12	Durie, Gordon	1	7
Gough, Richard	2	15	McCall, Stuart	1	7
Strachan, Gordon	2	16	McClair, Brian	1	9
Bone, Jimmy	1	1	Bett, Jim	1	11
Chalmers, Steve	1	1	Archibald, Steve	1	12
Gibson, Davie	1	1	Hartford, Asa	1	13
Linwood, Alec	1	1	Bremner, Billy	1	15
Mason, Jimmy	1	1	Souness, Graeme	1	18
			(own goals)	2	
			Total	148	

Appendix 3
Scotland World Cup goalkeepers 1950-94 (includes qualifying rounds and final stages)

Name	World Cups	Apps	Goals	Ave per match
Harvey, David	1974	5	2	0.40
Leighton, Jim	1986, '90, '94	21.5	21	0.98
Cowan, Jimmy	1950	3	3	1.00
Herriot, Jim	1970	3	3	1.00
Clark, Bobby	1974	1	1	1.00
Forsyth, Campbell	1966	1	1	1.00
Hunter, Ally	1974	1	1	1.00
Lawrence, Tommy	1970	1	1	1.00
Simpson, Ronnie	1970	1	1	1.00
Rough, Alan	1978, '82, '86	17.5	19	1.09
Gunn, Bryan	1994	4	5	1.20
Brown, Bill	1958, '62, '66	6	8	1.33
Goram, Andy	1990, '94	6	9	1.50
Leslie, Lawrie	1962	3	5	1.67
McGarr, Ernie	1970	1	2	2.00
Thomson, Billy †	1982	1	2	2.00
Younger, Tommy	1958	6	13	2.17
Farm, George	1954	3	8	2.67
Blacklaw, Adam	1966	1	3	3.00
Martin, Fred	1954	2	8	4.00
Connachan, Eddie *	1962	1	4	4.00
* Extra time matches	Totals	89	120	

† Billy Thomson's other appearance, as a brief substitute, is overlooked for present purposes.

Scotland have called upon 21 World Cup goalkeepers, far more than England (13), Wales, or Northern Ireland.
In 26 World Cup fixtures between 1950 and 1966, Scotland kept a clean sheet just 3 times.

Appendix 4
Scotland World Cup captains 1950-94 (includes qualifying rounds and final stages)

Captain	World Cups	Captain	W	D	L
Billy Bremner	1970, '74	12	7	3	2
Graeme Souness	1982, '86	11	4	2	5
Roy Aitken	1990	10	4	2	4
George Young	1950, '54	7	5	1	1
Archie Gemmill	1978, '82	7	3	3	1
Paul McStay	1994	6	3	2	1
Eric Caldow	1962	5	3	0	2

Captain	World Cups		W	D	L
Bruce Rioch	1978 (Czech H, Peru, Holland)	3	2	0	1
Gary McAllister	1994 (Switz H, Italy A, Malta A)	3	1	1	1
Billy McNeill	1966 (Pol A, Fin A, Pol H)	3	1	1	1
Danny McGrain	1982 (Isr H, Swe H, N Zealand)	3	3	0	0
Willie Cunningham	1954 (Austria, Uruguay)	2	0	0	2
Tommy Docherty	1958 (Spain A, Switz H)	2	1	0	1
Tommy Younger	1958 (Yugo, Paraguay)	2	0	1	1
Asa Hartford	1982 (N Ire A, Port A)	2	0	1	1
Willie Miller	1986 (Wales A, Uruguay)	2	0	2	0
Sammy Cox	1954 (Eng H)	1	0	0	1
Bobby Evans	1958 (France)	1	0	0	1
Denis Law	1966 (Fin H)	1	1	0	0
Jim Baxter	1966 (Italy H)	1	1	0	0
Richard Gough	1994 (Switz A)	1	0	0	1
John Greig	1966 (Italy A)	1	0	0	1
Davie Hay	1974 (Czech A)	1	0	0	1
Alex McLeish	1990 (France H)	1	1	0	0
Don Masson	1978 (Wales A)	1	1	0	0

Appendix 5

Scottish World Cup appearances from Scottish, English and overseas leagues 1950-94 (includes qualifying rounds and final stages)

World Cup	Caps	Scottish League	English League	Italian League	German League	Belgian League	French League	Spanish League	% Scottish League
1950	33	26	7						82%
1954	55	35	20						64%
1958	77	52	25						68%
1962	55	45	8	2					82%
1966	66	39	27						59%
1970	72	38	34						53%
1974	84	35	49						42%
1978	86	25	61						29%
1982	136	49	85	2					36%
1986	138	79	42	9		5		3	57%
1990	141	85	43		8		5		60%
1994	129	93	36	–					72%
Totals	1072	601	437	13	8	5	5	3	56%

The percentage of players drawn from the Scottish League fell steeply, from 82% for the 1962 World Cup down to 29% under Ally MacLeod in the 1978 World Cup. Jock Stein, Alex Ferguson, Andy Roxburgh and Craig Brown have dramatically swung the pendulum back in favour of Scottish League players.

Appendix 6

Scotland's full World Cup record 1950-94 (includes qualifying rounds and final stages)

	P	W	D	L	F	A	Pts
Cyprus	4	4	0	0	18	3	8
Wales	6	3	2	1	9	5	8
Sweden	3	3	0	0	5	1	6
Northern Ireland	4	2	2	0	12	4	6
Czechoslovakia	7	3	0	4	10	15	6
Switzerland	4	2	1	1	7	7	5
Republic of Ireland	2	2	0	0	7	1	4
Estonia	2	2	0	0	6	1	4
Malta	2	2	0	0	5	0	4
Iceland	2	2	0	0	4	0	4
Finland	2	2	0	0	5	2	4
Israel	2	2	0	0	4	1	4
Denmark	3	2	0	1	6	2	4
Spain	4	2	0	2	8	8	4
Australia	2	1	1	0	2	0	3
Norway	2	1	1	0	3	2	3
Yugoslavia	4	0	3	1	4	6	3
Italy	4	1	1	2	2	6	3
New Zealand	1	1	0	0	5	2	2
Zaïre	1	1	0	0	2	0	2
Holland	1	1	0	0	3	2	2
Austria	2	1	0	1	2	3	2
France	3	1	0	2	3	5	2
Portugal	4	0	2	2	1	7	2
Soviet Union	1	0	1	0	2	2	1
Iran	1	0	1	0	1	1	1
Poland	2	0	1	1	2	3	1
Uruguay	2	0	1	1	0	7	1
West Germany	3	0	1	2	4	6	1
Brazil	3	0	1	2	1	5	1
Paraguay	1	0	0	1	2	3	0
Austria	1	0	0	1	0	1	0
Costa Rica	1	0	0	1	0	1	0
Peru	1	0	0	1	1	3	0
England	2	0	0	2	2	5	0
35 nations	*89*	*41*	*19*	*29*	*148*	*120*	*101*
World Cup finals	20	4	6	10	23	35	14
World Cup qualifiers	69	37	13	19	125	85	87
Home record in qualifiers	35	22	9	4	72	31	53
Away record in qualifiers	33	15	4	14	51	50	34
Qualifiers on neutral ground	1	0	0	1	2	4	0

Appendix 7

Scotland appearances and goalscorers in the World Cup 1950-94
(includes qualifying rounds and final stages)

Apps		1950		1954		1958		1962		1966		1970		1974		1978		1982		1986		1990		1994	
		A	G	A	G	A	G	A	G	A	G	A	G	A	G	A	G	A	G	A	G	A	G	A	G
27	McLeish, Alex																	6		9		11		1	
26	Dalglish, Kenny													7	1	7	3	8	2	4	1				
24	McStay, Paul																			6	2	11	1	7	
23	Miller, Willie																	8		11		4			
22	Leighton, Jim																			11		10		1	
20	Malpas, Maurice																			6		11		3	
18	Aitken, Roy																			7		11			
18	Rough, Alan													7		10		1							
18	Souness, Graeme													1		8	1	9							
16	McGrain, Danny													5		3		8							
16	Strachan, Gordon																	7	1	7	1	2			
15	Bremner, Billy							3		6	1	6													
15	Gough, Richard																			7		6	2	2	
15	Jordan, Joe													5	3	7	2	3	2						
14	Johnston, Maurice																			4	2	10	7		
14	McCoist, Ally																					9	2	5	3
14	Nicol, Steve																			8		6			
13	Hartford, Asa													7	1	6									
12	Archibald, Steve																	9	1	3					
12	Caldow, Eric					7		5																	
12	Greig, John									6	2	6													
11	Bett, Jim																			7	1	4			
11	Gray, Frank																	11							
11	Law, Denis					2	2	4	2	2	1			3											
11	Robertson, John (Forest)															1		10	4						
10	Cooper, Davie																			9	2	1			
10	Evans, Bobby	2		3		5																			
10	Hansen, Alan																	9		1					
10	McNeill, Billy							4		3	1	3	1												
9	Buchan, Martin													4		5									
9	Gemmill, Archie													5	2	4									
9	McClair, Brian																					5		4	1
9	McPherson, Dave																					5		4	
8	Boyd, Tommy																							8	
8	Collins, Bobby					7	2	1																	
8	Crerand, Paddy							5		3															
8	Gallacher, Kevin																					1		7	2
8	Gilzean, Alan							2		6	3														
8	Gray, Andy															1		6		1					
8	Jardine, Sandy													5		3									
8	McCreadie, Eddie									4		4													

		1950		1954		1958		1962		1966		1970		1974		1978		1982		1986		1990		1994	
		A	G	A	G	A	G	A	G	A	G	A	G	A	G	A	G	A	G	A	G	A	G	A	G
7	Baxter, Jim							5		2															
7	Durie, Gordon																					3	1	4	
7	Durrant, Iain																					1		6	
7	McAllister, Gary																							7	
7	McCall, Stuart																					3	1	4	
7	McKinnon, Ron									2		5													
7	Mudie, Jackie					7	6																		
7	Young, George	3		2		2																			
6	Brown, Bill							1		1		4													
6	Burns, Kenny															4		2							
6	Collins, John																					6	2		
6	Cooke, Charlie									1		5													
6	Cowie, Doug			4		2																			
6	Cox, Sammy	3		3																					
6	Docherty, Tommy			2		4																			
6	Donachie, Willie													1		5									
6	Forsyth, Tom													1		5									
6	Goram, Andy																					1		5	
6	Lorimer, Peter											1		5	2										
6	Morgan, Willie													6	1										
6	Narey, David																	3	1	2		1			
6	Nevin, Pat																					1		5	3
6	Nicholas, Charlie																			5	1	1			
6	Wark, John																	6	3						
6	Younger, Tommy					6																			
5	Albiston, Arthur																			5					
5	Ferguson, Ian																					2		3	
5	Hamilton, Alec							1		4															
5	Harvey, David													5											
5	Hay, Davie													5											
5	Henderson, Willie									4		1	1												
5	Hewie, John					5	1																		
5	Irvine, Brian																							5	
5	Jess, Eoin																							5	
5	McKimmie, Stewart																					2		3	
5	McLaren, Alan																							5	
5	MacLeod, Murdo																					5			
5	Murdoch, Bobby									2		3	2												
5	Rioch, Bruce															5									
5	Sharp, Graeme																			5					
5	Speedie, David																			2		3			
5	Wilson, Davie							4		1	1														
4	Baird, Sam					4	1																		
4	Booth, Scott																							4	1
4	Brand, Ralph							4	3																

	Player	1950 A	1950 G	1954 A	1954 G	1958 A	1958 G	1962 A	1962 G	1966 A	1966 G	1970 A	1970 G	1974 A	1974 G	1978 A	1978 G	1982 A	1982 G	1986 A	1986 G	1990 A	1990 G	1994 A	1994 G
4	Brown, Allan	4	2																						
4	Fernie, Willie			2		2																			
4	Gemmell, Tommy											4	1												
4	Gillespie, Gary																					4			
4	Gray, Eddie											3	1	1											
4	Gunn, Bryan																							4	
4	Holton, Jim													4	1										
4	Hughes, John									3	1														
4	Hutchison, Tommy													4											
4	Johnston, Willie									1						3									
4	Johnstone, Jimmy									1		3	1												
4	Levein, Craig																					1		3	
4	Macari, Lou													1	1	3									
4	McAvennie, Frank																			4	1				
4	McInally, Alan																					4			
4	McKenzie, John			4																					
4	McQueen, Gordon													4											
4	Masson, Don															4	1								
4	Ring, Tommy					4																			
4	Robertson, John (Hearts)																							4	
4	Stein, Colin											4	6												
3	Aitken, George	2		1																					
3	Blackley, John													2		1									
3	Bowman, Davie																					3			
3	Cowan, Jimmy	3																							
3	Farm, George			3																					
3	Harper, Joe													2	1	1									
3	Hendry, Colin																							3	1
3	Herriot, Jim											3													
3	Kennedy, Stuart															2		1							
3	Lennox, Bobby											3													
3	Leslie, Lawrie							3																	
3	Liddell, Billy	2		1																					
3	McColl, Ian	1				2																			
3	McLeod, John							3																	
3	Martin, Neil									3															
3	Ormond, Willie					3	1																		
3	Provan, Davie (Celtic)																	3	1						
3	Reilly, Lawrie	2	1	1	1																				
3	Scott, Alec							1	1	1		1													
3	Shearer, Bobby							3																	
3	Smith, Gordon					3	1																		
3	Steel, Billy	3	1																						
3	Sturrock, Paul																	1	1	2					
3	Turnbull, Eddie					3																			
3	Waddell, Willie	2	2	1																					
3	Woodburn, Willie	3																							

		1950 A	1950 G	1954 A	1954 G	1958 A	1958 G	1962 A	1962 G	1966 A	1966 G	1970 A	1970 G	1974 A	1974 G	1978 A	1978 G	1982 A	1982 G	1986 A	1986 G	1990 A	1990 G	1994 A	1994 G
2	Aird, John			2																					
2	Bannon, Eamonn																			2					
2	Brazil, Alan																	2							
2	Brennan, Frank			2																					
2	Brownlie, John													2											
2	Colquhoun, Eddie													2											
2	Cunningham, Willie			2																					
2	Davidson, Jimmy			2																					
2	Fleck, Robert																					2			
2	Graham, George													2											
2	Henderson, Jackie					2	1																		
2	Herd, David							2	2																
2	Imlach, Stuart					2																			
2	Johnstone, Bobby					2	1																		
2	Leggat, Graham					2																			
2	Mackay, Dave					2																			
2	McPhail, John	1	1	1																					
2	Martin, Fred			2																					
2	Mochan, Neil			2																					
2	Murray, Jimmy					2	1																		
2	Parker, Alec					2																			
2	Provan, Dave (Rangers)									2															
2	Quinn, Pat							2																	
2	Robertson, Archie					2	1																		
2	Stewart, Ray																	2							
2	St John, Ian									2	3														
2	Thomson, Billy																	2							
2	White, John							2																	
2	Whyte, Derek																							2	
1	Bauld, Willie	1																							
1	Blacklaw, Adam									1															
1	Bone, Jimmy													1	1										
1	Burns, Francis											1													
1	Carr, Willie													1											
1	Chalmers, Stevie									1	1														
1	Clark, Bobby													1											
1	Connachan, Eddie							1																	
1	Connelly, George													1											
1	Cormack, Peter											1													
1	Curran, Hugh											1													
1	Evans, Allan																	1							
1	Fleming, Charlie			1	2																				
1	Forbes, Alec	1																							
1	Ford, Donald													1											
1	Forrest, Jim									1															
1	Forsyth, Alec													1											
1	Forsyth, Campbell									1															

	Player	1950 A	1950 G	1954 A	1954 G	1958 A	1958 G	1962 A	1962 G	1966 A	1966 G	1970 A	1970 G	1974 A	1974 G	1978 A	1978 G	1982 A	1982 G	1986 A	1986 G	1990 A	1990 G	1994 A	1994 G
1	Gibson, Davie									1	**1**														
1	Hamilton, Willie									1															
1	Haughney, Mike			1																					
1	Hunter, Alistair													1											
1	Kennedy, Jim									1															
1	Lawrence, Tommy											1													
1	Linwood, Alec	1	1																						
1	McGarr, Ernie											1													
1	McGrory, Jackie									1															
1	McInally, Jim																							1	
1	McKay, Duncan							1																	
1	McKinlay, Billy																							1	1
1	McKinnon, Rob																							1	
1	McLean, Tommy											1													
1	McMillan, Ian							1																	
1	Mason, Jimmy	1	1																						
1	Moir, Willie	1																							
1	Morris, Henry	1	**3**																						
1	O'Donnell, Phil																							1	
1	Pettigrew, Willie															1									
1	Robertson, David																							1	
1	Robertson, Hugh							1																	
1	Simpson, Ronnie											1													
1	Stanton, Pat											1													
1	Telfer, Willie					1																			
1	Ure, Ian							1																	
1	Watson, Jimmy			1																					
1	Wright, Steven																							1	
1	Yeats, Ron									1															
1	Young, Alex							1	**2**																
	own goals																**2**								
	89 games	3		5		7		5		6		6		7		7		11		11		11		10	
	148 goals		10		8		14		12		8		18		11		11		17		11		14		14
	211 different players	18		27		23		23		31		27		28		24		25		26		31		35	
	1072 caps		33		55		77		55		66		72		84		86		136		138		141		129

Appendix 8
Results of World Cup finals 1930-1990

URUGUAY – 1930

Pool I			P	W	D	L	F	A	Pts
France v Mexico	4-1	ARGENTINA	3	3	0	0	10	4	6
Argentina v France	1-0	Chile	3	2	0	1	5	3	4
Chile v Mexico	3-0	France	3	1	0	2	4	3	2
Chile v France	1-0	Mexico	3	0	0	3	4	13	0
Argentina v Mexico	6-3								
Argentina v Chile	3-1								

Pool II									
Yugoslavia v Brazil	2-1	YUGOSLAVIA	2	2	0	0	6	1	4
Yugoslavia v Bolivia	4-0	Brazil	2	1	0	1	5	2	2
Brazil v Bolivia	4-0	Bolivia	2	0	0	2	0	8	0

Pool III									
Romania v Peru	3-1	URUGUAY	2	2	0	0	5	0	4
Uruguay v Peru	1-0	Romania	2	1	0	1	3	5	2
Uruguay v Romania	4-0	Peru	2	0	0	2	1	4	0

Pool IV									
United States v Belgium	3-0	UNITED STATES	2	2	0	0	6	0	4
United States v Paraguay	3-0	Paraguay	2	1	0	1	1	3	2
Paraguay v Belgium	1-0	Belgium	2	0	0	2	0	4	0

Semi-finals

Argentina v United States	6-1	Uruguay v Yugoslavia	6-1

Final

Uruguay v Argentina	4-2

ITALY – 1934

1st Round		*2nd Round*		
Italy v United States	7-1	Germany v Sweden	2-1	
Germany v Belgium	5-2	Italy v Spain	1-1	1-0 (replay)
Spain v Brazil	3-1	Austria v Hungary	2-1	
Sweden v Argentina	3-2	Czechoslovakia v Switz'land	3-2	
Czechoslovakia v Romania	2-1			
Austria v France	3-2 (aet)			
Switzerland v Holland	3-2			
Hungary v Egypt	4-2			

Semi-finals

Czechoslovakia v Germany	3-1	Italy v Austria	1-0

Third/Fourth play-off		*Final*	
Germany v Austria	3-2	Italy v Czechoslovakia	2-1 (aet)

FRANCE – 1938

1st Round		2nd Round	
Switzerland v Germany	1-1 4-2 (replay)	Sweden v Cuba	8-0
Cuba v Romania	3-3 2-1 (replay)	Italy v France	3-1
Hungary v Dutch E Indies	6-0	Hungary v Switzerland	2-0
France v Belgium	3-1	Brazil v Czechoslovakia	1-1 2-1 (replay)
Czechoslovakia v Holland	3-0 (aet)		
Brazil v Poland	6-5 (aet)		
Italy v Norway	2-1 (aet)		

Semi-finals			
Italy v Brazil	2-1	Hungary v Sweden	5-1

Third/Fourth play-off		Final	
Brazil v Sweden	4-2	Italy v Hungary	4-2

BRAZIL – 1950

Pool I

			P	W	D	L	F	A	Pts
Brazil v Mexico	4-0	BRAZIL	3	2	1	0	8	2	5
Yugoslavia v Switzerland	3-0	Yugoslavia	3	2	0	1	7	3	4
Yugoslavia v Mexico	4-1	Switzerland	3	1	1	1	4	6	3
Brazil v Switzerland	2-2	Mexico	3	0	0	3	2	10	0
Brazil v Yugoslavia	2-0								
Switzerland v Mexico	2-1								

Pool II

			P	W	D	L	F	A	Pts
Spain v United States	3-1	SPAIN	3	3	0	0	6	1	6
England v Chile	2-0	England	3	1	0	2	2	2	2
United States v England	1-0	Chile	3	1	0	2	5	6	2
Spain v Chile	2-0	United States	3	1	0	2	4	8	2
Spain v England	1-0								
Chile v United States	5-2								

Pool III

			P	W	D	L	F	A	Pts
Sweden v Italy	3-2	SWEDEN	2	1	1	0	5	4	3
Sweden v Paraguay	2-2	Italy	2	1	0	1	4	3	2
Italy v Paraguay	2-0	Paraguay	2	0	1	1	2	4	1

Pool IV

			P	W	D	L	F	A	Pts
Uruguay v Bolivia	8-0	URUGUAY	1	1	0	0	8	0	2
		Bolivia	1	0	0	1	0	8	0

Final Pool

		Final Positions								
Uruguay v Spain	2-2	1	URUGUAY	3	2	1	0	7	5	5
Brazil v Sweden	7-1	2	Brazil	3	2	0	1	14	4	4
Uruguay v Sweden	3-2	3	Sweden	3	1	0	2	6	11	2
Brazil v Spain	6-1	4	Spain	3	0	1	2	4	11	1
Sweden v Spain	3-1									
Uruguay v Brazil	2-1									

SWITZERLAND – 1954

Pool I				P	W	D	L	F	A	Pts
Yugoslavia v France	1-0	BRAZIL		2	1	1	0	6	1	3
Brazil v Mexico	5-0	YUGOSLAVIA		2	1	1	0	2	1	3
France v Mexico	3-2	France		2	1	0	1	3	3	2
Brazil v Yugoslavia	1-1 (aet)	Mexico		2	0	0	2	2	8	0

Pool II				P	W	D	L	F	A	Pts
Hungary v South Korea	9-0	HUNGARY		2	2	0	0	17	3	4
W Germany v Turkey	4-1	W GERMANY		2	1	0	1	7	9	2
Hungary v W Germany	8-3	Turkey		2	1	0	1	8	4	2
Turkey v South Korea	7-0	South Korea		2	0	0	2	0	16	0
W Germany v Turkey	7-2 (play-off)									

Pool III				P	W	D	L	F	A	Pts
Austria v Scotland	1-0	URUGUAY		2	2	0	0	9	0	4
Uruguay v Czechoslovakia	2-0	AUSTRIA		2	2	0	0	6	0	4
Austria v Czechoslovakia	5-0	Czechoslovakia		2	0	0	2	0	7	0
Uruguay v Scotland	7-0	Scotland		2	0	0	2	0	8	0

Pool IV				P	W	D	L	F	A	Pts
England v Belgium	4-4 (aet)	ENGLAND		2	1	1	0	6	4	3
Switzerland v Italy	2-1	SWITZERLAND		2	1	0	1	2	3	2
England v Switzerland	2-0	Italy		2	1	0	1	5	3	2
Italy v Belgium	4-1	Belgium		2	0	1	1	5	8	1
Switzerland v Italy	4-1 (play-off)									

Quarter-finals
W Germany v Yugoslavia	2-0	Austria v Switzerland	7-5
Uruguay v England	4-2	Hungary v Brazil	4-2

Semi-finals
W Germany v Austria	6-1	Hungary v Uruguay	4-2 (aet)

Third/Fourth play-off / Final
Third/Fourth play-off		Final	
Austria v Uruguay	3-1	W Germany v Hungary	3-2

SWEDEN – 1958

Pool I			P	W	D	L	F	A	Pts
W Germany v Argentina	3-1	W GERMANY	3	1	2	0	7	5	4
N Ireland v Czechoslovakia	1-0	N IRELAND	3	1	1	1	4	5	3
W Germany v Czecho'vakia	2-2	Czechoslovakia	3	1	1	1	8	4	3
Argentina v N Ireland	3-1	Argentina	3	1	0	2	5	10	2
W Germany v N Ireland	2-2								
Czechoslovakia v Argentina	6-1								
N Ireland v Czechoslovakia	2-1 (play-off, aet)								

Pool II

France v Paraguay	7-3	FRANCE	3	2	0	1	11 7	4
Yugoslavia v Scotland	1-1	YUGOSLAVIA	3	1	2	0	7 6	4
Yugoslavia v France	3-2	Paraguay	3	1	1	1	9 12	3
Paraguay v Scotland	3-2	Scotland	3	0	1	2	4 6	1
France v Scotland	2-1							
Yugoslavia v Paraguay	3-3							

Pool III

Sweden v Mexico	3-0	SWEDEN	3	2	1	0	5 1	5
Hungary v Wales	1-1	WALES	3	0	3	0	2 2	3
Wales v Mexico	1-1	Hungary	3	1	1	1	6 3	3
Sweden v Hungary	2-1	Mexico	3	0	1	2	1 8	1
Sweden v Wales	0-0							
Hungary v Mexico	4-0							
Wales v Hungary	2-1 (play-off)							

Pool IV

England v Soviet Union	2-2	BRAZIL	3	2	1	0	5 0	5
Brazil v Austria	3-0	SOVIET UNION	3	1	1	1	4 4	3
England v Brazil	0-0	England	3	0	3	0	4 4	3
Soviet Union v Austria	2-0	Austria	3	0	1	2	2 7	1
Brazil v Soviet Union	2-0							
England v Austria	2-2							
Soviet Union v England	1-0 (play-off)							

Quarter-finals

France v N Ireland	4-0	W Germany v Yugoslavia	1-0
Sweden v Soviet Union	2-0	Brazil v Wales	1-0

Semi-finals

Brazil v France	5-2	Sweden v W Germany	3-1

Third/Fourth play-off		*Final*	
France v W Germany	6-3	Brazil v Sweden	5-2

CHILE – 1962

Group 1

			P	W	D	L	F	A	Pts
Uruguay v Colombia	2-1	SOVIET UNION	3	2	1	0	8	5	5
Soviet Union v Yugoslavia	2-0	YUGOSLAVIA	3	2	0	1	8	3	4
Yugoslavia v Uruguay	3-1	Uruguay	3	1	0	2	4	6	2
Soviet Union v Colombia	4-4	Colombia	3	0	1	2	5	11	1
Soviet Union v Uruguay	2-1								
Yugoslavia v Colombia	5-0								

Group 2

Chile v Switzerland	3-1	W GERMANY	3	2	1	0	4	1	5
W Germany v Italy	0-0	CHILE	3	2	0	1	5	3	4
Chile v Italy	2-0	Italy	3	1	1	1	3	2	3
W Germany v Switzerland	2-1	Switzerland	3	0	0	3	2	8	0

W Germany v Chile   2-0
Italy v Switzerland   3-0

Group 3

Brazil v Mexico	2-0	BRAZIL	3	2	1	0	4	1	5
Czechoslovakia v Spain	1-0	CZECHOSLOVAKIA	3	1	1	1	2	3	3
Brazil v Czechoslovakia	0-0	Mexico	3	1	0	2	3	4	2
Spain v Mexico	1-0	Spain	3	1	0	2	2	3	2
Brazil v Spain	2-1								
Mexico v Czechoslovakia	3-1								

Group 4

Argentina v Bulgaria	1-0	HUNGARY	3	2	1	0	8	2	5
Hungary v England	2-1	ENGLAND	3	1	1	1	4	3	3
England v Argentina	3-1	Argentina	3	1	1	1	2	3	3
Hungary v Bulgaria	6-1	Bulgaria	3	0	1	2	1	7	1
Argentina v Hungary	0-0								
England v Bulgaria	0-0								

Quarter-finals

Yugoslavia v W Germany	1-0	Chile v Soviet Union	2-1
Brazil v England	3-1	Czechoslovakia v Hungary	1-0

Semi-finals

Brazil v Chile	4-2	Czecho'vakia v Yugoslavia	3-1

Third/Fourth play-off   *Final*

Chile v Yugoslavia	1-0	Brazil v Czechoslovakia	3-1

ENGLAND – 1966

Group 1

			P	W	D	L	F	A	Pts
England v Uruguay	0-0	ENGLAND	3	2	1	0	4	0	5
France v Mexico	1-1	URUGUAY	3	1	2	0	2	1	4
Uruguay v France	2-1	Mexico	3	0	2	1	1	3	2
England v Mexico	2-0	France	3	0	1	2	2	5	1
Uruguay v Mexico	0-0								
England v France	2-0								

Group 2

W Germany v Switzerland	5-0	W GERMANY	3	2	1	0	7	1	5
Argentina v Spain	2-1	ARGENTINA	3	2	1	0	4	1	5
Spain v Switzerland	2-1	Spain	3	1	0	2	4	5	2
Argentina v W Germany	0-0	Switzerland	3	0	0	3	1	9	0
Argentina v Switzerland	2-0								
W Germany v Spain	2-1								

Group 3

Brazil v Bulgaria	0-0	PORTUGAL	3	3	0	0	9 2	6
Portugal v Hungary	3-1	HUNGARY	3	2	0	1	7 5	4
Hungary v Brazil	3-1	Brazil	3	1	0	2	4 6	2
Portugal v Bulgaria	3-0	Bulgaria	3	0	0	3	1 8	0
Portugal v Brazil	3-1							
Hungary v Bulgaria	3-1							

Group 4

Soviet Union v North Korea	3-0	SOVIET UNION	3	3	0	0	6 1	6
Italy v Chile	2-0	NORTH KOREA	3	1	1	1	2 4	3
Chile v North Korea	1-1	Italy	3	1	0	2	2 2	2
Soviet Union v Italy	1-0	Chile	3	0	1	2	2 5	1
North Korea v Italy	1-0							
Soviet Union v Chile	2-1							

Quarter-finals

England v Argentina	1-0	Portugal v North Korea	5-3
W Germany v Uruguay	4-0	Soviet Union v Hungary	2-1

Semi-finals

W Germany v Soviet Union	2-1	England v Portugal	2-1

Third/Fourth play-off   *Final*

Portugal v Soviet Union	2-1	England v W Germany	4-2 (aet)

MEXICO – 1970

Group 1

			P	W	D	L	F	A	Pts
Mexico v Soviet Union	0-0	SOVIET UNION	3	2	1	0	6	1	5
Belgium v El Salvador	3-0	MEXICO	3	2	1	0	5	0	5
Soviet Union v Belgium	4-1	Belgium	3	1	0	2	4	5	2
Mexico v El Salvador	4-0	El Salvador	3	0	0	3	0	9	0
Soviet Union v El Salvador	2-0								
Mexico v Belgium	1-0								

Group 2

Uruguay v Israel	2-0	ITALY	3	1	2	0	1	0	4
Italy v Sweden	1-0	URUGUAY	3	1	1	1	2	1	3
Uruguay v Italy	0-0	Sweden	3	1	1	1	2	2	3
Israel v Sweden	1-1	Israel	3	0	2	1	1	3	2
Sweden v Uruguay	1-0								
Israel v Italy	0-0								

Group 3

England v Romania	1-0	BRAZIL	3	3	0	0	8	3	6
Brazil v Czechoslovakia	4-1	ENGLAND	3	2	0	1	2	1	4
Romania v Czechoslovakia	2-1	Romania	3	1	0	2	4	5	2
Brazil v England	1-0	Czechoslovakia	3	0	0	3	2	7	0
Brazil v Romania	3-2								
England v Czechoslovakia	1-0								

Group 4

			P	W	D	L	F	A	Pts
Peru v Bulgaria	3-2	W GERMANY	3	3	0	0	10	4	6
W Germany v Morocco	2-1	PERU	3	2	0	1	7	5	4
Peru v Morocco	3-0	Bulgaria	3	0	1	2	5	9	1
W Germany v Bulgaria	5-2	Morocco	3	0	1	2	2	6	1
W Germany v Peru	3-1								
Bulgaria v Morocco	1-1								

Quarter-finals

Uruguay v Soviet Union	1-0 (aet)	Brazil v Peru	4-2
Italy v Mexico	4-1	W Germany v England	3-2 (aet)

Semi-finals

Italy v W Germany	4-3 (aet)	Brazil v Uruguay	3-1

Third/Fourth play-off / *Final*

W Germany v Uruguay	1-0	Brazil v Italy	4-1

WEST GERMANY– 1974

Group 1

			P	W	D	L	F	A	Pts
W Germany v Chile	1-0	E GERMANY	3	2	1	0	4	1	5
E Germany v Australia	2-0	W GERMANY	3	2	0	1	4	1	4
W Germany v Australia	3-0	Chile	3	0	2	1	1	2	2
E Germany v Chile	1-1	Australia	3	0	1	2	0	5	1
E Germany v W Germany	1-0								
Chile v Australia	0-0								

Group 2

			P	W	D	L	F	A	Pts
Brazil v Yugoslavia	0-0	YUGOSLAVIA	3	1	2	0	10	1	4
Scotland v Zaire	2-0	BRAZIL	3	1	2	0	3	0	4
Brazil v Scotland	0-0	Scotland	3	1	2	0	3	1	4
Yugoslavia v Zaire	9-0	Zaire	3	0	0	3	0	14	0
Scotland v Yugoslavia	1-1								
Brazil v Zaire	3-0								

Group 3

			P	W	D	L	F	A	Pts
Holland v Uruguay	2-0	HOLLAND	3	2	1	0	6	1	5
Sweden v Bulgaria	0-0	SWEDEN	3	1	2	0	3	0	4
Holland v Sweden	0-0	Bulgaria	3	0	2	1	2	5	2
Bulgaria v Uruguay	1-1	Uruguay	3	0	1	2	1	6	1
Holland v Bulgaria	4-1								
Sweden v Uruguay	3-0								

Group 4

			P	W	D	L	F	A	Pts
Italy v Haiti	3-1	POLAND	3	3	0	0	12	3	6
Poland v Argentina	3-2	ARGENTINA	3	1	1	1	7	5	3
Argentina v Italy	1-1	Italy	3	1	1	1	5	4	3
Poland v Haiti	7-0	Haiti	3	0	0	3	2	14	0

Argentina v Haiti   4-1
Poland v Italy   2-1

Pool A

Brazil v E Germany	1-0	HOLLAND	3	3	0	0	8	0	6
Holland v Argentina	4-0	Brazil	3	2	0	1	3	3	4
Holland v E Germany	2-0	East Germany	3	0	1	2	1	4	1
Brazil v Argentina	2-1	Argentina	3	0	1	2	2	7	1
Holland v Brazil	2-0								
Argentina v E Germany	1-1								

Pool B

Poland v Sweden	1-0	W GERMANY	3	3	0	0	7	2	6
W Germany v Yugoslavia	2-0	Poland	3	2	0	1	3	2	4
Poland v Yugoslavia	2-1	Sweden	3	1	0	2	4	6	2
W Germany v Sweden	4-2	Yugoslavia	3	0	0	3	2	6	0
Sweden v Yugoslavia	2-1								
W Germany v Poland	1-0								

Third/Fourth play off   *Final*
Poland v Brazil   1-0   W Germany v Holland   2-1

ARGENTINA – 1978

Group 1

			P	W	D	L	F	A	Pts
Italy v France	2-1	ITALY	3	3	0	0	6	2	6
Argentina v Hungary	2-1	ARGENTINA	3	2	0	1	4	3	4
Italy v Hungary	3-1	France	3	1	0	2	5	5	2
Argentina v France	2-1	Hungary	3	0	0	3	3	8	0
France v Hungary	3-1								
Italy v Argentina	1-0								

Group 2

W Germany v Poland	0-0	POLAND	3	2	1	0	4	1	5
Tunisia v Mexico	3-1	W GERMANY	3	1	2	0	6	0	4
Poland v Tunisia	1-0	Tunisia	3	1	1	1	3	2	3
W Germany v Mexico	6-0	Mexico	3	0	0	3	2	12	0
Poland v Mexico	3-1								
W Germany v Tunisia	0-0								

Group 3

Austria v Spain	2-1	AUSTRIA	3	2	0	1	3	2	4
Brazil v Sweden	1-1	BRAZIL	3	1	2	0	2	1	4
Austria v Sweden	1-0	Spain	3	1	1	1	2	2	3
Brazil v Spain	0-0	Sweden	3	0	1	2	1	3	1
Spain v Sweden	1-0								
Brazil v Austria	1-0								

Group 4

Peru v Scotland	3-1	PERU	3	2 1 0	7	2	5
Holland v Iran	3-0	HOLLAND	3	1 1 1	5	3	3
Scotland v Iran	1-1	Scotland	3	1 1 1	5	6	3
Holland v Peru	0-0	Iran	3	0 1 2	2	8	1
Peru v Iran	4-1						
Scotland v Holland	3-2						

Group A

W Germany v Italy	0-0	HOLLAND	3	2 1 0	9	4	5
Holland v Austria	5-1	Italy	3	1 1 1	2	2	3
Italy v Austria	1-0	W Germany	3	0 2 1	4	5	2
Holland v W Germany	2-2	Austria	3	1 0 2	4	8	2
Holland v Italy	2-1						
Austria v W Germany	3-2						

Group B

Brazil v Peru	3-0	ARGENTINA	3	2 1 0	8	0	5
Argentina v Poland	2-0	Brazil	3	2 1 0	6	1	5
Poland v Peru	1-0	Poland	3	1 0 2	2	5	2
Argentina v Brazil	0-0	Peru	3	0 0 3	0	10	0
Brazil v Poland	3-1						
Argentina v Peru	6-0						

Third/Fourth play-off		*Final*	
Brazil v Italy	2-1	Argentina v Holland	3-1 (aet)

SPAIN – 1982

Group 1

			P	W D L	F	A	Pts
Italy v Poland	0-0	POLAND	3	1 2 0	5	1	4
Peru v Cameroon	0-0	ITALY	3	0 3 0	2	2	3
Italy v Peru	1-1	Cameroon	3	0 3 0	1	1	3
Poland v Cameroon	0-0	Peru	3	0 2 1	2	6	2
Poland v Peru	5-1						
Italy v Cameroon	1-1						

Group 2

Algeria v W Germany	2-1	W GERMANY	3	2 0 1	6	3	4
Austria v Chile	1-0	AUSTRIA	3	2 0 1	3	1	4
W Germany v Chile	4-1	Algeria	3	2 0 1	5	5	4
Austria v Algeria	2-0	Chile	3	0 0 3	3	8	0
Algeria v Chile	3-2						
W Germany v Austria	1-0						

Group 3

Belgium v Argentina	1-0	BELGIUM	3	2 1 0	3	1	5
Hungary v El Salvador	10-1	ARGENTINA	3	2 0 1	6	2	4
Argentina v Hungary	4-1	Hungary	3	1 1 1	12	6	3
Belgium v El Salvador	1-0	El Salvador	3	0 0 3	1	13	0

Belgium v Hungary   1-1
Argentina v El Salvador   2-0

Group 4

England v France	3-1	ENGLAND	3	3	0	0	6	1	6
Czechoslovakia v Kuwait	1-1	FRANCE	3	1	1	1	6	5	3
England v Czechoslovakia	2-0	Czechoslovakia	3	0	2	1	2	4	2
France v Kuwait	4-1	Kuwait	3	0	1	2	2	6	1
France v Czechoslovakia	1-1								
England v Kuwait	1-0								

Group 5

Spain v Honduras	1-1	N IRELAND	3	1	2	0	2	1	4
Yugoslavia v N Ireland	0-0	SPAIN	3	1	1	1	3	3	3
Spain v Yugoslavia	2-1	Yugoslavia	3	1	1	1	2	2	3
Honduras v N Ireland	1-1	Honduras	3	0	2	1	2	3	2
Yugoslavia v Honduras	1-0								
N Ireland v Spain	1-0								

Group 6

Brazil v Soviet Union	2-1	BRAZIL	3	3	0	0	10	2	6
Scotland v New Zealand	5-2	SOVIET UNION	3	1	1	1	6	4	3
Brazil v Scotland	4-1	Scotland	3	1	1	1	8	8	3
Soviet Union v New Zealand	3-0	New Zealand	3	0	0	3	2	12	0
Soviet Union v Scotland	2-2								
Brazil v New Zealand	4-0								

Group A

Poland v Belgium	3-0	POLAND	2	1	1	0	3	0	3
Soviet Union v Belgium	1-0	Soviet Union	2	1	1	0	1	0	3
Soviet Union v Poland	0-0	Belgium	2	0	0	2	0	4	0

Group B

W Germany v England	0-0	W GERMANY	2	1	1	0	2	1	3
W Germany v Spain	2-1	England	2	0	2	0	0	0	2
England v Spain	0-0	Spain	2	0	1	1	1	2	1

Group C

Italy v Argentina	2-1	ITALY	2	2	0	0	5	3	4
Brazil v Argentina	3-1	Brazil	2	1	0	1	5	4	2
Italy v Brazil	3-2	Argentina	2	0	0	2	2	5	0

Group D

France v Austria	1-0	FRANCE	2	2	0	0	5	1	4
Austria v N Ireland	2-2	Austria	2	0	1	1	2	3	1
France v N Ireland	4-1	N Ireland	2	0	1	1	3	6	1

Semi-finals

Italy v Poland	2-0	W Germany v France	3-3 (aet)
		(W Germany won on penalties)	

Third/Fourth play-off		*Final*	
Poland v France	3-2	Italy v W Germany	3-1

MEXICO – 1986

Group A

			P	W	D	L	F	A	Pts
Bulgaria v Italy	1-1	ARGENTINA	3	2	1	0	6	2	5
Argentina v South Korea	3-1	ITALY	3	1	2	0	5	4	4
Italy v Argentina	1-1	BULGARIA	3	0	2	1	2	4	2
South Korea v Bulgaria	1-1	South Korea	3	0	1	2	4	7	1
Argentina v Bulgaria	2-0								
Italy v South Korea	3-2								

Group B

			P	W	D	L	F	A	Pts
Mexico v Belgium	2-1	MEXICO	3	2	1	0	4	2	5
Paraguay v Iraq	1-0	PARAGUAY	3	1	2	0	4	3	4
Mexico v Paraguay	1-1	BELGIUM	3	1	1	1	5	5	3
Belgium v Iraq	2-1	Iraq	3	0	0	3	1	4	0
Paraguay v Belgium	2-2								
Mexico v Iraq	1-0								

Group C

			P	W	D	L	F	A	Pts
France v Canada	1-0	SOVIET UNION	3	2	1	0	9	1	5
Soviet Union v Hungary	6-0	FRANCE	3	2	1	0	5	1	5
Soviet Union v France	1-1	Hungary	3	1	0	2	2	9	2
Hungary v Canada	2-0	Canada	3	0	0	3	0	5	0
France v Hungary	3-0								
Soviet Union v Canada	2-0								

Group D

			P	W	D	L	F	A	Pts
Brazil v Spain	1-0	BRAZIL	3	3	0	0	5	0	6
Algeria v N Ireland	1-1	SPAIN	3	2	0	1	5	2	4
Spain v N Ireland	2-1	Northern Ireland	3	0	1	2	2	6	1
Brazil v Algeria	1-0	Algeria	3	0	1	2	1	5	1
Spain v Algeria	3-0								
Brazil v N Ireland	3-0								

Group E

			P	W	D	L	F	A	Pts
Uruguay v W Germany	1-1	DENMARK	3	3	0	0	9	1	6
Denmark v Scotland	1-0	W GERMANY	3	1	1	1	3	4	3
Denmark v Uruguay	6-1	URUGUAY	3	0	2	1	2	7	2
W Germany v Scotland	2-1	Scotland	3	0	1	2	1	3	1
Uruguay v Scotland	0-0								
Denmark v W Germany	2-0								

Group F

			P	W	D	L	F	A	Pts
Morocco v Poland	0-0	MOROCCO	3	1	2	0	3	1	4
Portugal v England	1-0	ENGLAND	3	1	1	1	3	1	3
England v Morocco	0-0	POLAND	3	1	1	1	1	3	3
Poland v Portugal	1-0	Portugal	3	1	0	2	2	4	2

England v Poland   3-0
Morocco v Portugal   3-1

Second Round

Mexico v Bulgaria	2-0	Brazil v Poland	4-0
W Germany Morocco	1-0	France v Italy	2-0
Belgium v Soviet Union	4-3 (aet)	Argentina v Uruguay	1-0
Spain v Denmark	5-1	England v Paraguay	3-0

Quarter-finals

W Germany v Mexico   0-0 (aet. W Germany won on penalties)
Belgium v Spain   1-1 (aet. Belgium won on penalties)
France v Brazil   1-1 (aet. France won on penalties)
Argentina v England   2-1

Semi-finals

W Germany v France   2-0   Argentina v Belgium   2-0

Third/Fourth play-off   *Final*
France v Belgium   4-2   Argentina v W Germany   3-2

ITALY – 1990

Group A

			P	W	D	L	F	A	Pts
Italy v Austria	1-0	ITALY	3	3	0	0	4	0	6
Czechoslovakia v USA	5-0	CZECHOSLOVAKIA	3	2	0	1	6	3	4
Italy v United States	1-0	Austria	3	1	0	2	2	3	2
Czechoslovakia v Austria	1-0	United States	3	0	0	3	2	8	0
Italy v Czechoslovakia	2-0								
Austria v United States	2-1								

Group B

Cameroon v Argentina	1-0	CAMEROON	3	2	0	1	3	5	4
Romania v Soviet Union	2-0	ROMANIA	3	1	1	1	4	3	3
Argentina v Soviet Union	2-0	ARGENTINA	3	1	1	1	3	2	3
Cameroon v Romania	2-1	Soviet Union	3	1	0	2	4	4	2
Argentina v Romania	1-1								
Soviet Union v Cameroon	4-0								

Group C

Brazil v Sweden	2-1	BRAZIL	3	3	0	0	4	1	6
Costa Rica v Scotland	1-0	COSTA RICA	3	2	0	1	3	2	4
Brazil v Costa Rica	1-0	Scotland	3	1	0	2	2	3	2
Scotland v Sweden	2-1	Sweden	3	0	0	3	3	6	0
Brazil v Scotland	1-0								
Costa Rica v Sweden	2-1								

Group D

Colombia v UAE	2-0	W GERMANY	3	2 1 0	10	3	5
W Germany v Yugoslavia	4-1	YUGOSLAVIA	3	2 0 1	6	5	4
Yugoslavia v Colombia	1-0	COLOMBIA	3	1 1 1	3	2	3
W Germany v UAE	5-1	United Arab Emirates	3	0 0 3	2	11	0
W Germany v Colombia	1-1						
Yugoslavia v UAE	4-1						

Group E

Belgium v South Korea	2-0	SPAIN	3	2 1 0	5	2	5
Spain v Uruguay	0-0	BELGIUM	3	2 0 1	6	3	4
Spain v South Korea	3-1	URUGUAY	3	1 1 1	2	3	3
Belgium v Uruguay	3-1	South Korea	3	0 0 3	1	6	0
Spain v Belgium	2-1						
Uruguay v South Korea	1-0						

Group F

England v Rep Ireland	1-1	ENGLAND	3	1 2 0	2	1	4
Egypt v Holland	1-1	REP IRELAND	3	0 3 0	2	2	3
England v Holland	0-0	HOLLAND	3	0 3 0	2	2	3
Egypt v Rep Ireland	0-0	Egypt	3	0 2 1	1	2	2
England v Egypt	1-0						
Rep Ireland v Holland	1-1						

Second Round

Cameroon v Colombia	2-1 (aet)	Argentina v Brazil	1-0
England v Belgium	1-0 (aet)	Yugoslavia v Spain	2-1 (aet)
Czechoslovakia v Costa Rica	4-1	Italy v Uruguay	2-0
W Germany v Holland	2-1	Rep Ireland v Romania	0-0 (aet)
		(Rep Ireland won on penalties)	

Quarter-finals

England v Cameroon	3-2 (aet)	Italy v Rep Ireland	1-0
W Germany v Czecho'vakia	1-0	Argentina v Yugoslavia	0-0 (aet)
		(Argentina won on penalties)	

Semi-finals

Argentina v Italy	1-1 (aet. Argentina won on penalties)
W Germany v England	1-1 (aet. W Germany won on penalties)

Third/Fourth play-off · *Final*

Italy v England	2-1	W Germany v Argentina	1-0